Durant's Right-Hand Man

The Life and Times of Dr. Edwin Campbell, Founder of the Chevrolet Motor Company and Durant's Assistant in the Creation of General Motors and General Motors of Canada.

By Paul Arculus

Copyright © 2011 by Paul Arculus
First Edition – September 2011

ISBN
978-1-77067-782-1 (Hardcover)
978-1-77067-783-8 (Paperback)
978-1-77067-784-5 (Ebook)

All rights reserved.

No part of this publication may be reproduced in any form, or by any means, electronic or mechanical, including photocopying, recording, or any information browsing, storage, or retrieval system, without permission in writing from the publisher.

Published by:

FriesenPress
Suite 300 – 852 Fort Street
Victoria, BC, Canada V8W 1H8

www.friesenpress.com

Distributed to the trade by The Ingram Book Company

The author is grateful to General Motors of Canada Limited for kind permission to use the 1913 Chevrolet logo and the 1933 General Motors logo on the cover of this book. These are registered trademarks of General Motors of Canada Limited. General Motors is not responsible for any of the contents of this book.

Table of Contents

Acknowledgements ... v

Introduction ... viii

Chapter One — *Unsettled Times* ... 1

Chapter Two — *1866* ... 23

Chapter Three — *University and Medical Practice* ... 55

Chapter Four — *1902 and the Consequences* ... 83

Chapter Five — *General Motors* ... 117

Chapter Six — *Problems* ... 143

Chapter Seven — *The Campbells Move to New York* ... 163

Chapter Eight — *Billy's Return* ... 179

Chapter Nine — *Divorce* ... 213

Chapter Ten — *Billy the Phoenix* ... 221

Chapter Eleven — *The Looming Crisis* ... 247

Chapter Twelve — *Edwin's Final Journey* ... 265

Chapter Thirteen — *Billy's Demise* ... 275

Chapter Fourteen — *Margery* ... 287

Chapter Fifteen — *Aftermath* ... 303

Conclusion ... 327

Sources ... 331

Index ... 335

Acknowledgements

A study such as this is inevitably dependent upon the input of many people and a number of key documents. It will become obvious to the reader that several books provided the much of the basic structure for this work. One of the key works was Lawrence Gustin's biography of Billy Durant: ***Billy Durant***. Among the many strengths of Gustin's work was that he was able to interview several of the principals of the story who were still alive at the time of his research. They included Billy's devoted wife Catherine and his faithful secretary Aristo Scrobogna. The other key books include Bernard Weisberger's extremely well documented biography of Durant: ***The Dreammaker***, Heather Robertson's history of the McLaughlin family: ***Driving Force***, George S. May's history of the automobile in Michigan: ***A Most Unique Machine***, Margery Durant's biography of her father: ***My Father***, William Durant's memoires published by Kettering University as ***William C. Durant. In His Own Words,*** and the Campbells' daughter Edwina's autobiography ***My First 90 Years***. There are numerous other works which have been used to provide insight into specific areas of Edwin, Margery and Billy's lives and a list of these is in the Biography at the conclusion of this work. Bill Minors of *Books Galore and More* in Port Perry was able to locate most of these publications for me.

David White and the staff at the Scharchburg Archives at the Kettering Institute in Flint were of invaluable help in locating relevant correspondence of Billy Durant and Edwin Campbell, as well as many of the photographs which appear in this work. I am also indebted to Susan Fowler of the 32nd Degree Masons, Valley of Detroit who provided me with information regarding Edwin's progress in the Masons. Samantha George, Curator of the Parkwood Estate Archives provided encouragement and some important documents and photographs. Geneva Wiskemann of Lansing, Michigan provided energetic assistance in researching the Michigan newspapers and various medical records for information on Edwin's professional life in Flint. Mark Bowden at the Burton Historical Collection at the Detroit Public Library provided much needed assistance in locating obscure material in Detroit newspapers. Susan Olsen at Woodlawn Cemetery in the Bronx, New York, where Edwin, Billy and Margery are buried, provided enthusiastic interest in this project and made available documentation related to their death and interment.

It should be made absolutely clear that this work would have been impossible without the direct help and guidance of Alex Sanger, Edwin's grandson. Although Alex never knew his grandfather, his respect and admiration for him is reflected in his own vast fund of knowledge and research on his grandfather's life and accomplishments. He shared with me an immense amount of documentation; press clippings, photographs, correspondence between Edwin and numerous individuals and all the complex legal documents surrounding Edwin's will and its execution. Some of these documents were not available to the earlier researchers. Alex also led me to find a copy of the limited edition autobiography *My First 90 Years* written by his mother Edwina, Edwin and Margery's daughter. This document gave a clear insight into the fascinating lives of Edwin and Margery. My sincere thanks to Margot Bogert, Edwin and Margery's granddaughter, who welcomed my wife and I in New York and introduced me to her cousin Alex Sanger and provided me with further material.

A number of people have offered their guidance and direction by editing the text at various stages of its completion; Bill Minors of *Books Galore and More* and Peter Hvidsten of *Observer Publishing*, both in Port Perry, Alex Sanger, Edwin's grandson, of New York, Mike McGill of Seagrave, Ontario, and of course, my ever patient wife Isabel (Liz) and our son Bruce Arculus of Scarborough, Ontario. My particular gratitude to Gail Chellew, a former teammate of mine on the staff at Port Perry High School, for her detailed proofreading and editing of the entire document. To all of them, my profound thanks.

Over the past five years or more, I have bored, amused and annoyed a number of people with my obsession with the story of Edwin and Margery. I appreciate their kindness, their patience their encouragement, and yes, their criticism in this project. Among those who have tolerated my obsession I must focus on my wife Isabel (Liz). She has patiently suffered through endless readings, "bouncing" of ideas and long journeys to New York, Flint and other Michigan locations in the search for details in Edwin and Margery's fascinating lives.

I am fully aware that my obsession with Edwin and Margery will continue for many years after the publication of this work. I must extend my gratitude to all who have endured my obsession. After reading this work, I sincerely hope that you will all understand my fascination and join with me in the appreciation and enjoyment of the immensely colourful and significant lives of Edwin Campbell, his wife Margery, her father Billy Durant and all those who surrounded them.

Port Perry, Ontario, Canada, 2011

Introduction

For every great individual, organization, or important event, there is usually someone behind the scenes, someone who plays a significant role but who is completely overlooked either by design, by desire, or by default. In the case of Dr. Edwin Ruthven Campbell there are convincing arguments for all three reasons, but the latter is by far the foremost.

William Crapo Durant's name is remembered by some automotive historians as his name adorned the cars which he manufactured briefly from 1921 to 1931. But by the knowledgeable he is remembered as one of the greatest of the giants of industry and as the creator of General Motors. Edwin Campbell was Durant's "man behind the scenes".

Edwin R. Campbell's parents and grandparents lived through the most turbulent period in North American history. After the British vacated the former Thirteen Colonies, various groups of Americans raided Canada in vain attempts to wrest British North America from the British. This happened in 1812, in 1838, in the year of Edwin's birth, 1866, and again in 1870. In all circumstances the Americans were repulsed, largely by local militia fired up by a fervent desire to defend their independence against what they believed was an inferior American system of government. In 1867 the provinces of Canada formed a single nation, and then began their struggle for unity and the problems of dealing with their own internal differences across this vast continent.

In the United States, in spite of the animosity and hatred which fed the Civil War, forward-looking men were born and nurtured, men who with their brilliance would help in the process of rescuing their nation from turmoil, and change the face of our planet forever. Their names ring loud and clear through the halls of time: Alexander Graham Bell, Thomas Edison, Henry Ford, Billy Durant, and others.

Campbell's name was not erased from history; it was simply overshadowed by the scope and achievements of those around him, and by his own quiet and unassuming manner. Henry Ford's name continues in legendary fashion, remembered through the nameplate on the cars which he began to build in 1901. There are others who continue to be remembered through their cars: Carl Benz, Henry Rolls, Ferdinand Porsche, Louis Chevrolet, David Buick, Charles Nash and Walter P. Chrysler. It is interesting to note that Buick, Chevrolet, Nash and Chrysler all worked for Durant and with Campbell.

Dr. Edwin R. Campbell became the physician to the family of Billy Durant, and was soon Durant's confidant and advisor. He married Durant's daughter Margery in 1906, and two years later he was a partner in Durant's ambitious enterprises. As a result of Durant's expansion of his automotive empire, he is usually regarded as a true czar, an absolute ruler in his control of the General Motors empire. However, upon closer examination it becomes quite clear that his control was not without advice and support from his son-in-law from 1906 until 1920. Edwin Campbell was not an engineering genius like Henry Ford or a great salesman and promoter like Durant; rather, his accomplishments lay in his organizational ability, his loyalty to his father-in-law, and his quiet enthusiasm for the automobile. As a result, he became the facilitator, supporter and strategist behind Durant in the creation of what became the world's largest corporation. Indicative of Campbell's personality and character, titles such as President and Chairman were not among his personal goals, but they were his clearly-stated objectives in his strategy for his father-in-law.

Campbell was part of the decision to create General Motors. It was Campbell who raised a significant amount of the finances necessary to create and sustain the corporation. It was Campbell's initiative, along with Louis Chevrolet and William Little, that led to the creation of the Chevrolet Motor Company and its later role in General Motors. Campbell arranged for his life-long friend Sam McLaughlin to produce Buicks in Canada, and used his influence with his father-in-law to create General Motors of Canada.

The time from World War I until the middle of the Depression was for many a tragic period in American history. It was a most unsettling time of booze, sex, drugs, failed relationships, crime, abysmal poverty, excessive wealth, greed, and corruption. It was the time of the flappers, the Jazz age, and Al Capone, and there, with his literary lens, F. Scott Fitzgerald. Ironically, Margery, Campbell's wife and Durant's daughter, was beset by the same tragic social and emotional problems that dominated the life of Fitzgerald's wife Zelda. Indeed, had their lives not been real, the story of Edwin and Margery in New York among the elite in American society could well have been a manuscript from F. Scott Fitzgerald. After their divorce, the account of Margery's numerous relationships, her marriages, her aviation exploits, and her problems with drugs, would stretch the imagination of the most creative novelist. But those aspects of her life became the reading material of the American public in the sensation-seeking press of the day.

The tapestry of Campbell's life and that of his wife Margery was vibrant and colourful. Campbell chatted with Edison, haggled with Henry Ford, and included among his friends and business associates the pioneers of the North American automotive industry: David Dunbar Buick, Walter P. Chrysler, Sam McLaughlin, Charles Nash, Ransom Olds and the Chevrolet brothers. His business partners and colleagues included Alfred Sloane, Percy Rockefeller, Albert Strauss, Pierre du Pont, J.P. Morgan and "Diamond Jim" Brady. Edwin and Margery moved among the high society of New York and became noted patrons of the arts. They socialized with leading lights of the entertainment industry: Charlie Chaplin, Irving Berlin and the Barrymores, as well as the newsmakers of the day: Admiral Richard Byrd, Charles Lindberg and Amelia Earhart.

Edwin and Margery's meeting and eventual marriage placed them clearly in recorded history. Their children William and Edwina added to the documented record of their relationship. This period had many aspects which were complete aberrations from the ideals of the Founding Fathers, and yet it was the time when the foundations of America's industrial and corporate might were set firmly in place. And it was the time when the Durant and Campbell families played out the most exuberant period of their lives.

The main difficulty in researching the adult life of Edwin Campbell is that only a small amount of documented evidence of his input in the critical events of this era remains. Some of the most momentous and far-reaching decisions in the history of the automobile industry — the decisions to take control of Buick, Olds and Cadillac, to create the Chevrolet Motor Company, to take over or create the supportive companies AC and DELCO, and to create General Motors in the United States and in Canada — these were not ideas developed in executive offices, duly recorded by diligent secretaries, and preserved for posterity in minutes of meetings. Rather, they were events which emanated from conversations between Campbell and Durant in the privacy of Campbell's home. Their daily conversations, which ranged from idle chatter to significant strategy sessions, were all informal and private in nature, and well beyond the purview of conscientious secretaries and their efficiently recorded minutes to be duplicated, submitted, approved and filed.

Durant and Campbell developed a relationship of infinite trust. No signed documents were needed. Their trust started as a casual meeting at a poker table. It developed into a doctor/patient relationship and then became a father-in-law/son-in-law kinship even though the two men were only five years apart in age. It then quickly evolved into a business association where the two were partners. Durant placed Edwin on the Board of Directors of the Durant Dort Carriage Company in 1908, shortly after Edwin's marriage to his daughter Margery. From this point, Edwin appeared on several boards with which Billy was involved. That spirit of closeness continued even after Edwin and Margery's divorce just over a decade later.

When Campbell moved into different ventures in California, with Durant still in the east, their trust was clearly reflected in the limited number of letters that exist. To base the interpretation of a relationship on a few letters would be naïve, presumptuous, and misleading. However, this correspondence between Campbell and Durant covers one of the most critical periods in the early history of General Motors. From the tone and content of the letters it is obvious that Edwin's role is not that of a follower, but clearly that of a guide and strategist, and the evidence points to that role beginning well before the correspondence started and continuing well beyond its close.

Many biographies paint Durant as somewhat impulsive in his business decisions. However, the correspondence between Campbell and Durant, particularly in 1916, points to a different image for this period in his life. In these letters Durant was clearly asking Campbell's advice, and Campbell responded, encouraging Durant to pursue specific lines of action, action which Durant duly took.

Edwin died on board the SS Majestic in 1929. The New York press gave little attention to his accomplishments and instead, given the tenor of the times, focused on his immense wealth. Edwin's death occurred at a dramatic period in the world of economics. Shortly after this date, Durant was forced into bankruptcy and never recovered. Whether Billy Durant's final business demise was in any way related to the absence of Edwin's advice is a matter for speculation. The fact is that Durant never regained his status as a business and industrial giant after Edwin's death.

Margery's role in these events is a little less difficult to determine, due to the press coverage of the major events of her life, her published biography of her father, and her daughter's autobiography. Unfortunately, the biography of her father was written well after her divorce from Edwin, and gives the impression that she was deliberately minimising the relationship. However, her admirable devotion to her father and her initial loyalty to Edwin appear clearly in several documents.

As every educator knows, success is not a natural consequence of brilliance. It is the result of a combination of many factors including attitude; stimulating family, friends and environment; good education; discipline; structure; motivation, all of these being particularly relevant in the formative years. In adulthood other factors are added to the mix, a key component being an ability to make strategic decisions and to develop an awareness of pending opportunities. All of this was to be found in the background, character and personality of Edwin Campbell.

This work is an attempt to bring his name and his contributions back into a more prominent view, a view which he truly deserves.

Durant's Right Hand Man

Chapter One

UNSETTLED TIMES

The Campbells are Coming

At the north east corner of the Pine Grove Cemetery in Prince Albert, near Port Perry, Ontario, Canada, a large, polished grey granite monument stands, commemorating the memory of the Campbell family. On any clear day the sunbeams drift gently down through the dark canopy of huge pines to embrace the monument with a mottled blanket of flickering sun and shadow. On the east side of that monument, in Roman, bold, the inscription reads:

In loving memory of
Donald Campbell
born October 1st 1840
died October 7th 1906
Christina McArthur
wife of the above
died June 17th 1928
aged 94 years
Edwin R Campbell M.D.
died July 11th 1929.

Simple, yet it begs the reader to look between, around and behind the lines here inscribed, for only then can we begin to sense the triumphs and tragedies of the lives of these members of the Campbell family. Donald and Christina, the parents, are now embraced by the cool earth beneath. Not so their son Edwin. He lies not here, but a thousand miles and many worlds away, alone in a pleasant dell not far from the dissonant cacophony and belching smog of the machines he so diligently nourished. Less than a hundred yards away, in that far away cemetery stands a monument to his former father-in-law who sleeps deep within a huge, portalled, granite edifice and he is accompanied by his mother and his daughter. Memory of him has been diminished by time and the grasping ambition of envious empire builders who sought to erase his name from the record of what was once the world's largest corporation. These sturdy and decaying monuments commemorate largely forgotten men, forgotten among the countless hundreds who dedicated their lives to the creation and development of the machine that so embodied the spirit of the twentieth century and still dominates the economies of the world's greatest nations and motivates the thoughts and dreams of young and old.

The nature and character of Edwin Campbell exuded quietness, self control and independence. He was extremely confident without being arrogant even though his daughter described him as somewhat shy. He was deliberate but never ruled by convention. The major decisions that he took in life — his decision to begin his career and then live the remainder of his life not in the country of his birth but in a land alien to his background and rearing, his choice of a wife, even the art that he chose to commission and support — all were far removed from convention. But for Edwin, these were not the results of a spirit of stubbornness or rebellion but of a powerful inner confidence.

His confidence was born of intelligence and careful deliberation, and an understanding of the issues and consequences. He was a man who was comfortable, poised, self assured and positive in his own individuality. Above all, his confidence was carried with an air of humility and grace, even though he showed moments of anger and impatience with his wife and children.

These qualities were rare in society, particularly in the lofty society of the elite of New York where he spent the last quarter century of his short but eventful life.

What were the factors that moulded his character, his personality and his abilities? We can only begin to understand the answers to this question by taking a detailed look at the environment in which he was raised, and particularly the characters who surrounded him during his formative years.

The backgrounds and lineage of Edwin's parents, Donald Campbell and his wife Christina, are not unusual; in fact they have much in common with the pioneers of this part of Canada.

Edwin's grandparents, Archibald Campbell and his wife Sarah Leach, joined the many lured across the Atlantic away from the sometimes tragic, sometimes tranquil, but always moist and sheep-stained hillsides of Caledonia. They came by their thousands, tens of thousands, more, all with hope of a better life. Instead they found an existence full of hardship. Yet, through sweat and pain they also found a new tranquility and the strength to sustain more tragedies in the intense heat and mind-numbing cold of the new country. But they stayed, for here they owned their roof and their land.

A massive migration from Scotland arrived in Canada in the second and third decade of the nineteenth century. In 1828, a number of families, primarily from Argylshire in Scotland, made their way to York, now Toronto. They included the Campbells along with members of the McAlpine, McIntyre, McCorqudale families from the mainland of Argylshire and the McFaydens from the Island of Mull. During the agonizing five or more weeks crossing the wild Atlantic, they survived the endless days of wild waves, vomit and stale water, restless and fear-filled nights. They finally placed their feet on the firm ground of Quebec and journeyed on to York. Here they waited a few days while James Cameron secured the rights to land in Eldon Township, Victoria County, north-east of Toronto. The settlers gave Cameron $1.00 an acre for their parcels of land.

After the arrangements were confirmed, the immigrants made their way north, up Yonge Street to Lake Simcoe and from there to Beaverton.

The families quickly established temporary and primitive shelters in Beaverton and then, leaving their families in those quickly built hovels, the men hiked eastward through the bush to their respective land claims. By the autumn the men, having cleared enough land on which to build, again, basic accommodation, were united with their families

Archibald Campbell had built his log shanty on a 100 acre parcel close to today's hamlet of Argyl. Even as late as the census of 1861, the log shanty was still listed as "being built." Under these primitive conditions, Sarah gave birth to Catherine in 1834, Mary in 1836 and, on the first day of October 1840, her third child, Donald Archibald. She produced eight more children, all without the benefits of a doctor or medicine.

As their sons Donald, John, Alexander and Peter grew to maturity, each continued farming by acquiring land in Eldon Township. Donald, on May 12 1860, married Christina McArthur. He was 20 years old and she, a mature 26. Following the patterns of his mother and father, he sweated on his land while Christina gave birth to their first child Florence, on April 7, 1862.

In 1863 Donald bought a 60 acre parcel of land in lot 10 in the 13th Concession of Reach Township. Here their second child Duncan Donald, was born on March 14, 1864.

Disheartened by the hardships of the farming life Donald and Christina began a restless search for contentment and sold their farm to Archibald McArthur, Christina's brother. Late in 1865 when Christina was heavy with their third child, Donald bought a tavern in Saintfield, a hamlet in Reach Township in the middle of Ontario County immediately to the south of Victoria County and about five miles northeast of the ambitious village of Port Perry, where they were later to settle, and a few more miles from Uxbridge. Here, in the tavern at Saintfield on February 12, 1866, Christina gave birth to their third child and second son Edwin Ruthven.

The colony into which he was born had survived turmoil and strife and was about to become a nation at a time when the economic impact of the Industrial Revolution was reaching into the remote communities of Reach Township. In addition, through the geographic proximity to the United States, events at Gettysburg and Washington were watched with anguish and, sometimes abject fear. The impact of the collision of the contrasting social and economic systems of North and South and the eventual disastrous results of those differences played out their consequences even in Ontario County. The eloquence of Lincoln at Gettysburg and the echoes of the pistol shot at Ford's theatre were still reverberating as Canada declared its nationhood in July 1867, a time when Edwin was approaching the middle of his second year.

As we grow from infancy to adulthood we all seek a sense of identity in space and time. We are all products of our reactions to our environment, accepting certain aspects, questioning some and rebelling against others. The world that greeted Edwin as a tiny infant was one of confusion and unprecedented change. Locally too, events and circumstances added to the blurred view of the individual's role in society. The confusion and pressures which surrounded Edwin during his youth may well have been the cause of him fleeing to an isolated community well away from Port Perry, to begin his medical practice immediately after graduation.

Temperance

The communities in which Christina and Donald chose to live and raise their children were fraught with the turbulence of extremism. Saintfield, where Edwin was born, was located one mile north of Greenbank, the hotbed of the Temperance movement for many miles around. In addition to the hyperactive Temperance Hall, the village of Greenbank boasted four churches.

The Order of the Sons of Temperance, more commonly known as the Temperance Society, was a group organized along the lines of a Masonic order. The Society was devoted to the promotion of total abstinence from alcohol and offered fraternal benefits to its members.

Meetings were held on a weekly basis and in many communities these meetings were the most important events outside the church.

In 1853, a law was passed which allowed each municipality to decide whether or not whiskey could be sold. Reach Township had twenty-four hotels and taverns, later to include Donald's, where one could buy liquor by the glass. In opposition, by 1858 there were numerous Temperance Societies in the surrounding communities. Prince Albert, Port Perry and Uxbridge each had active Temperance Societies but the most active was the group in Greenbank. The Temperance brethren of Greenbank made it their mandate to develop a strategy to close every tavern in the Township. In order to avoid that pressure the Campbells sold the tavern in 1869. Donald was still listed as a hotel keeper in the 1869 business directory.

The Campbells' next move was to a parcel of land in Brock Township immediately to the north of Reach Township. This property was 60 acres of Lot 20 in the 1st Concession. In the 1871 census, the property was listed as having a house, two barns and 44 acres of cleared land, but his occupation was listed not as "farmer" but as "merchant." Donald and Christina then sold the Brock Township property and returned to the Saintfield area where they bought 60 acres back from his brother-in-law Archibald McArthur. This sale was registered to Christina and remained under her name until sold in 1910 to Robert Hook. But Donald did not return to farming. He rented out the acreage and by 1877 had taken possession of the Queen's Hotel in Cannington, in Brock Township to the north, away from the reaches of the Greenbank Temperance folk.

The Greenbank Temperance Society eventually succeeded in closing Donald's former tavern and all but one of the remaining taverns one in their community, the Cottage Hotel at the south east of the four corners of Greenbank. Zealously they lobbied to get its liquor licence revoked. Finally in 1894, they bought the property and tore down this symbolic last outpost of iniquity. In its place they built a huge Methodist church with the foundation walls far surpassing those of the sinful hotel building. On this site on December 13, 1896, the new Greenbank Methodist Church was dedicated and opened, debt free. In neighbouring Port Perry however, the Temperance faithful occasionally met their match with those who supported the sale of alcohol "by the glass," in the taverns and hotels in town.

During their unsettled residencies, Donald and Christina produced four more children: Tryphena Alberta on May 22, 1868, Albert Archibald on February 23, 1870, Alexander on January 27, 1872 and finally, Donella Jane Edith was born on March 10, 1873.

Although Donald and Christina held on to their farm on the western side of Saintfield, they avoided the challenge of farming by renting it out to a succession of tenants, and eventually established their residence in Port Perry with their seven children and plunged them into the life of that young community — young, but steeped in tradition.

The thinking, the attitudes and the conversations which surrounded the Campbell family had a strong influence in the attitudes of all of their children and was further underpinned by the attitudes of their Scottish, English and Irish ancestors and a century of reaction to events which had happened in the United States to the south. In school, Edwin and his siblings would have had these attitudes reinforced on an ongoing basis as the stories of the town's namesake Peter Perry, and other pioneers were narrated with pride. The battles with the United States and the role of the local Militia in the repelling of the various attempts to capture Canada were at the core of the pride and patriotism which was instilled in the students. All lived in constant fear of further American attempts to wrest the colony from its British control. Throughout Victoria and Ontario Counties, no matter where one travelled, the conversations were the same in the taverns, the churches, the schools and at the stalls on market day. But slowly and inexorably a change in attitudes began to gain acceptance.

Orangemen

Just east of Port Perry was the village of Blackstock. It was originally called Tooley's Corners after one of its first settlers, but it soon changed its name to Williamsburg in honour of William of Orange, before it was renamed Blackstock in 1887. The Orange Orders, with pledges of loyalty and oaths of secrecy, became popular throughout Britain and later spread to North America. Irish immigration to British North America peaked during the period 1830 to 1845. The majority of these Irish immigrants arrived before the Great Famine of 1845 and were largely Protestant. The huge Irish migration to the United States arrived after the onset of the famine and they tended to be Roman Catholic.

Canadian Orangemen sprang to the support of the British cause during the 1812 war and by the 1820s Orange parades were among the more popular public events in York in Upper Canada. Cartwright Township in which Blackstock was situated played host to four separate and well attended chapters of the Orange Order. Many of the members made their way to those Orange Halls from Port Perry and neighbouring communities in Reach Township.

In 1866, the annual July 12 celebration of the anniversary of the battle of the Boyne was held in Saintfield. Members from seven Lodges were in attendance.

> *The brethren of the district clothed in their regalia, following their banners and preceded by the Uxbridge brass band, with almost any amount of fyfes and drums, presented a very fine appearance as they entered the village.*[1]

The residents of the village had erected banners and arches and "... *other arrangements indicative of their good will toward the Sons of William.*"

With his wife now nursing six month old Edwin, Donald Campbell entered into the spirit of the occasion and earned mention in the July 19 issue of the *Observer*:

> *Mr. Campbell too, of the Saintfield Hotel, deserves great credit for having spared neither expense nor trouble in preparing a most excellent dinner consisting of all the viands of the season.*[2]

After the meal, which was served outside in order to accommodate the huge crowd, those in attendance made their way to "the woods" where they were addressed by a number of speakers on such topics as Piety, Loyalty and Fidelity, Our Country and our Obligations, as well as the usual speeches on Orangism.

---

1   <u>Ontario Observer</u> *(Prince Albert) July 19, 1866.*

2   Ibid.

Williamsburg's Twelfth of July parade drew hundreds annually, in fact in 1871 it promised to be so big that the parade was moved to Port Perry to accommodate the thousands who came to witness the spectacle. The parade was immense. Numerous Orange orders and their members from surrounding communities, the animals and their keepers from the visiting circus and numerous bands in various stages of inebriation, all joined in the festivities. The day's events had something for everyone: a circus, a game of cricket, a competition for clog dancing and a tour of Lake Scugog on board the steamship *Anglo Saxon*. An estimated 10,000 arrived to cheer the parade led by "King Billy" on his white steed along Queen Street. The Campbell family may well have been in attendance.

Masons

Masonry has a long history in Canada. John Graves Simcoe was initiated into the Union Lodge in Exeter, England, before he took up his office as the first Governor of Upper Canada. The first Grand Lodge was organized here in 1792. Up to 1855 the various Provincial Grand Lodges operated under warrants granted by one or other of the Grand Lodges of England. In October 1855 the first independent Grand Lodge of Canada came into being with William Mercer Wilson as its first Grand Master. Donald Campbell became a member. Both Sam McLaughlin and Edwin Campbell followed their respective fathers by becoming members.

The Loyalists

By far the most profound influence on the broader sphere of thinking of the early settlers was the sense of loyalty to the British Parliamentary system and, to a large degree, the sense of loyalty to Britain itself. This stemmed not only from the loyalty of Canada's immigrants from Britain but, arguably more significantly, the experiences of the grandparents and great grandparents of the citizens of its land in their relationships with the United States.

At the close of the War of Independence, the departing British took with them the administrators and militia who formed the backbone for law and order and the administration of the former colonies. The vacuum gave way to a period of lawlessness and violence which continued for many years. This created an opportunity for the less scrupulous members of the new society to take law into their own hands. In the big cities, noticeably in New York, ruthless gangs took control of many precincts, gangs whose control lasted until well into the 20th century.[3]

In the towns and more rural areas of the former colonies, ruthless and devious opportunists as well as the cash strapped local governments, justified their Machiavellian ways by selecting scapegoats through whom they could acquire property, possessions and revenue. There were two main scapegoats: the Aboriginals whose land they wished to acquire in the Ohio and Mississippi valleys and westward, and secondly those who had indicated some support for the maintenance of British administration in the colonies.

Jefferson made it clear that before the War of Independence, the Thirteen Colonies were made up of three groups: one third who supported the Revolution, one third who opposed it and one third who were completely neutral in their opinion. Those who opposed the Revolution and many of those who wished to remain neutral became known as the "Loyalists." British citizens and their descendants made up a large segment of the Loyalists but they were joined by many Dutch and German settlers who believed in the British Parliamentary system, or for some reason did not trust the leaders of the Revolution. But by far the largest groups were the blacks, the slaves who formed a major part of the backbone to the economy of the colonies, particularly in the south.

Untold thousands of Loyalists fled south to the islands of the Caribbean. Many returned to Britain and more than fifty thousand fled north to the Canadas to join the increasing numbers of immigrants arriving from Britain. Forced to abandon all their land and possessions in the fledgling United States, the Loyalists escaped with only with what they

---

[3] Herbert Asbury, <u>Gangs of New York</u>. *(New York: Alfred A. Knopf, Inc., 1927) pp.38-348*

could carry. They settled in Nova Scotia, New Brunswick and in the region known as Upper Canada, now Ontario. In the latter region they settled in the Niagara Peninsula, the north eastern shores of Lake Ontario and the north shore of the Saint Lawrence River. They were joined by between fifty and one hundred thousand escaped slaves.

Robert Perry, the father of Port Perry's founder Peter Perry, was a Vermont farmer and a Loyalist who had fought against the Rebels and was wounded at the battle of Bennington. After the War of Independence, he and his family were brutalized and chased off their prosperous farm, forfeiting all their land and possessions. The Perry family and their compatriots reacted to these events by assuming a set of attitudes and points of view arising from their experiences. This outlook formed the basis of thinking for several generations of Canadians and was a firm part of the background to the environment in which the Campbell children were raised.

The Loyalist sentiment and thinking was reinforced by an ongoing series of events which continued after Edwin's birth. Diplomatic relations between the United States and British North America had steadily improved during the leadership of George Washington and John Adams. However when Jefferson assumed the presidency, the Federalist policies revived concerns among those who lived in the British territories in North America.

When Britain was preoccupied with its battles against Napoleon, war hawks in Washington urged on by President Madison and others, thought that these circumstances would provide an excellent opportunity to completely rid the North American continent of British influence. They decided to invade the British colonies in North America.

It should be noted that the population of the United States at that time was around 7.7 million whereas British North America had fewer than 500,000. The strategy was to carry out major thrusts into areas around Montreal and the Niagara Peninsula. When President Madison decided to pursue a road to war, the Canadian response was a rapid resurgence of old loyalty. The ill informed hawks in Washington had completely overlooked that issue and that the Niagara Peninsula was a major settlement location for those who had fled the former Thirteen Colonies. Although the United States forces had some initial military successes including the burning of York (now Toronto), they were eventually humiliated in their defeat by local militias formed in large part by Loyalists and their sons.

The attack on Canada in 1812 renewed the feelings of loyalty not only to the Crown but also to feelings of nationhood and the ability of Canada's people to oppose the potential imposition of a different system, a system which, to them, had little to be recommended.

For over a century, Loyalty and condemnation of the United States was passed on from parents to children like some religious relic.

Rebellion

By the 1820s, economic and political power in Upper and Lower Canada had become focused in a few families, largely affiliated with the Church of England in Upper Canada and the Roman Catholic Church in Lower Canada. These entrenched groups became known as, respectively, the Family Compact and the Chateau Clique. As their power and control grew, groups of citizens became intent on attempting to counterbalance their policies and reform the system.

Led by members of the Baldwin family, William Lyon Mackenzie, Peter Perry and his political partner, Marshall Spring Bidwell, the Reform Party emerged and slowly gained a political foothold in Upper Canada. A parallel movement led by Louis Papineau emerged in Lower Canada. Confrontation between the Family Compact and the Reformists soon became palpable. Perry had managed to push significant reform through the Legislature of Upper Canada. His efforts produced changes in laws regarding marriage and debt and the abolition of Debtors' Prisons. But William Lyon Mackenzie became impatient with the slow progress of reform and began to talk of overthrowing the system of government through militant means. As his advocacy of militancy increased, his support from fellow reformers Perry, Bidwell and the Baldwins diminished reciprocally.

Sir Francis Bond Head, the Lieutenant Governor of Upper Canada, incensed by the reformers and their success, dissolved the Legislature in 1836 and called an election. In the ensuing electoral campaign, contrary to all policies, Bond Head actively campaigned against Peter Perry and the Reformers. In the election the Reformers were ousted from power. This drove the increasingly militant Mackenzie into action. He organized a Rebellion. His supporters marched on York in December 1837. After a few skirmishes Mackenzie and his followers were ignominiously defeated. Some were taken prisoner others fled across the border to neighbouring states. Ultimately, two men, Peter Matthews and Samuel Lount, were executed and some prisoners were sent to Van Diemen's Land, now Tasmania.

The Patriot Hunters

There is a tendency to regard the 1837 Rebellions as being merely a reaction to the affairs of the Family Compact and the Chateau Clique, the establishment administrative bodies of Upper and Lower Canada. Although this was a major cause, the events of 1837 should be placed in a much larger context and the execution of Rebels Matthews and Lount, and the expulsion of William Lyon Mackenzie, did not bring the affair to a conclusion.

As early as 1835, many of those who later participated in the Rebellions, "Patriots" in Upper Canada and "Patriotes" in Lower Canada, had visited the United States where they had an eager audience for their anti-British rhetoric. Huge gatherings in support of the rebels were held in the towns and villages of the Border States. From Detroit, to Cleveland, Buffalo, Rochester, Albany and Burlington, vast crowds turned out to hear speeches advocating the overthrow of the British and their yoke of oppression on the people of Upper and Lower Canada. When the 1837 Rebellions collapsed, many participants in the Rebel cause fled to those communities in the United States to escape justice, and find refuge and support for their ideals.

The Rebels who fled to the United States in 1837 and 1838 found themselves confronted by a populace deep in an economic depression and high unemployment. In 1833 the rivalry of the New York City gangs, referred to earlier, produced mob warfare and resulted in a large part of the city being destroyed by fire. The action was repeated in December 1835 and the fire raged on for two days while looters roamed freely. Several insurance companies with clients in the devasted area of the city went bankrupt over the claims. The collapse of the insurance companies along with Jackson's domestic banking policy, and that of the London banks were major causes of the depression of 1837 and the long period of instability which followed.

One significant result of the depression and the London banks' role in that disaster was a renewed, even heightened, anti-British sentiment in the United States. Anglo-American relations were further strained by the dispute over the Maine-New Brunswick boundary. President Van Buren was faced with the possibility of war. Anxious to avoid conflict and its costs he succeeded in passing the Neutrality Act in March 1838. Under this legislation, American authorities could confiscate weapons and supplies destined for use against a neighbouring state.

Hunters' Lodges

During this period of tension an extensive organization of supporters for the Rebels' cause had arisen in the border regions of the United States in spite of Van Buren's legislation. The organization became known as the Hunters' Lodges, and its members, Patriot Hunters. In order to avoid reprisals, they evolved into secret societies. Grand Lodges of the hierarchical society were established in many centers including Detroit, Cleveland, Rochester, Buffalo and St Albans, as well as secret lodges in Montreal. In Lower Canada and in Vermont, they were known as the Frères Chasseurs or Brother Hunters. The secret society appears to have begun in Vermont under the leadership of Dr. Robert Nelson. He led a group of over five hundred members in a raid into Lower Canada (Quebec). His raid was aborted when they encountered a large Loyalist militia unit. By the fall of 1838, conventions were being held throughout the Border States and the secret society included members from Maine and Vermont all the way to Wisconsin, as well as Lower and Upper Canada

Membership in the organization at the height of its activities has been variously estimated between 40,000 and 90,000. The size of the membership was due to several factors including "promise of a cash bounty and a grant of new land in the new Canadian republic." The main aim of the Patriot Hunters was to succeed where the Mackenzie Rebellion had failed: to overthrow what they perceived as the tyranny of the British system of government and to free the settlers of Upper Canada from the yoke of oppression inflicted upon them by the British. Members swore an oath to defend and promote republican institutions around the world and:

> ...I promise, until death, that I will attack, combat and help to destroy... every power authority of Royal origin upon this continent; and especially, never to rest until all tyrants of Britain cease to have any dominion or footing whatever in North America. [4]

Those who had fled the rebellions in Upper Canada found ready support for their aims among the Hunters' Lodges in the northern states and convinced them that in spite of their defeat, that there was a significant support for their aims among the populace in the Canadas. In January 1838, a Hunter force occupied Bois Blanc Island near Amherstburg, south of Windsor. After a few days they were ignominiously driven off the island, back to the United States. A month later another force occupied Pelee Island in Lake Erie. They were also defeated but not before a bloody battle in which eleven Patriots were killed and eighteen wounded. In 1838 a total of ten recorded incidents of armed invasions of Canadian locations took place violating neutrality laws of the United States.

One of their major assaults became known as the "Battle of the Windmill," at Prescott, Upper Canada. Over four hundred Hunters sailed from Sacket's Harbour, New York, on 11 November. The invaders took possession of a number of buildings including the dominating windmill. A naval battle in the adjacent waters ensued. Somehow, the Hunters had

---

4   *Durham Papers, Section IV* , p 789

failed to realize that their attack was in the middle of devout Loyalist country. The Hunters had expected that they would receive overwhelming support from the "oppressed" citizens of the region. The reverse was the case. The dedicated militia was supported by British forces who brought in heavy cannons. After four days, the militia and the British forces gained the upper hand. At this battle alone, 136 Hunters were taken prisoner.

A few days after the "Battle of the Windmill," a further major attack was conducted against the village of Windsor by a large group of Hunters from Detroit and surrounding communities, supported by a contingent from Kentucky. After a bloody battle on 4 December in which more than twenty Hunters were killed, the attacking forces fled back across the river or were captured while escaping. The British captured a total of forty-four Hunters at Windsor. Colonel John Prince, a judge and elected member of the Legislative Assembly of Upper Canada, had five of the prisoners shot without trial and would have summarily executed more had his own men not discouraged his zeal.

Aftermath

The attacks of the Patriot Hunters into Upper and Lower Canada were abysmal failures. There were several reasons for these failures, one being the incompetent military leadership, but it was largely due to their grossly mistaken impression that most of the population of the provinces would be in support of their aims. Following their failure, the Patriot Hunters remained quiet, hoping to participate in an all out war as the Maine–New Brunswick border dispute reached a critical stage.

The trials of the 240 Hunter prisoners took place in Toronto and Kingston. A promising young lawyer named John A. Macdonald was retained as advisor for the defense of several of the prisoners at Kingston. Sixty-four of the prisoners were given conditional pardons and sent back to the United States. Ninety-two prisoners were sentenced to be transported to Van Diemen's Land, but only sixty were actually shipped to the penal colony. Eighteen of the Hunters were executed. The remaining prisoners were eventually released.

When Van Buren signed the neutrality treaty of 1838, the objectives of the Patriot Hunters were effectively outlawed. In addition, on 25 September 1840, President John Tyler issued a proclamation regarding:

> ...sundry secret lodges, clubs or associations exist on the northern frontier; that the members of these lodges are bound together by secret oaths, that they have collected arms and other military materials...
>
> Now, therefore, I, John Tyler, President of the United States, do issue this my proclamation, admonishing all such evil-minded persons...assuring them that the laws of the United States will be rigorously executed against their illegal acts and that if in any lawless incursion into Canada, they fall into British authorities, they will not be reclaimed as American citizens nor will any interference be made on their behalf...[5]

These decisions resulted in the United States alerting its military in order to prevent actions such as those committed by the Patriot Hunters in 1838. Nevertheless occasional skirmishes did take place. In 1840, at Queenston, the Brock monument was blown up and there was an attempt to set fire to Kingston and to blow up the locks on the Welland Canal. In December 1841, a number of houses, barns and other buildings belonging to Canadians who had opposed the efforts of the Patriot Hunters were torched. But these were the final desperate actions of members of an organization in its death throes.

When, in March 1838, Sir Francis Bond Head was recalled to London in disgrace, Canadians were given a joyous renewal of their faith in the British system of administration. This was further enhanced when the Constitution Act of 1841 presented Canadians with the basis of Responsible

---

5   James D. Richardson, <u>Messages and Papers of the Presidents</u>. (New York, Bureau of National Literature,1897) IV, pp 72-73

government and the re-organization of their country. These decisions in London eliminated much of the support that the Patriot Hunters might have had in Canada. The Hunters' lodges lost interest in the immediate cause and many turned their support to the Irish Repeal Association. Little more was heard of the Hunters after 1842. A reference to their continued existence was occasionally noted, indeed, Lord Elgin expressed his fear that the Hunters' Lodges were waiting for the Irish problem to explode. There is no doubt that the later Fenian ideals were a re-iteration of the Hunters' aims, but there is no indication that the 1866 Fenian raids or those who participated in them were more than vaguely connected with the Patriot Hunters and the events which they precipitated in 1838-1840.

The Watershed

The period from 1860 to 1870 was the most tumultuous and critical decade of the nineteenth century for those living in the United States and Canada. Many historians regard the decade as a social, political and economic watershed. In 1861 the Civil War exploded onto the lives of those living in the young republic and had resonance on their neighbours to the north. Accounts of the events of the conflict were recorded in great detail in the *Ontario Observer*, the weekly newspaper read by the Campbell family. Each issue of the newspaper, initially published in Prince Albert but in 1872 relocated in Port Perry, carried the main dispatches of the week from around the States. Coverage of the War began with a paragraph or two in each issue but by November 1861 commentary and dispatches filled two full columns.

British North America was faced with a dilemma: which side should it support? Because of their need for cotton to feed the burgeoning factories in the north of England, some reluctantly gave some support to the South. Others vehemently opposed its policies of slavery and the British press referred to the eleven breakaway Confederate states as "belligerent." In spite of Britain's tentative bias, many Canadians joined the Union army, ten thousand from Nova Scotia alone.

On October 17, 1861, the *Ontario Observer* carried Dr. Cheever's speech in Washington on the War and Slavery:

> *Which shall be destroyed? Slavery and Rebellion or the Nation? ...There is no salvation for this Union, no possibility of preserving it from destruction, no possibility of greatness or glory for our country, no possible protection of the country from ruin, except in abolishing slavery. ... The predictions of our enemies abroad will be realized, the Republic of the United States will have gone down in shame and blood; our freedom and greatness will remain but the record of a promise in history, broken by our own infatuation in clinging to the most wicked, licentious, cruel, barbarous and impious system of slavery on the face of the earth. Our country is lost except we abolish this wickedness, and this question is before us, whether slavery or the country will be destroyed.*"[6]

There is no doubt that the tumultuous events which surrounded the Campbell family and their neighbours, albeit at some distance, would continue to affect their lives. From the shots fired at Harper's Ferry and Fort Sumter, to the pistol shot of John Wilkes Booth at the Ford Theatre in Washington, a cacophony of sound rang out from the United States and echoed around the globe. Its reverberations resulted in dramatic change and it enabled the cause of Emancipation to be firmly entrenched in many halls of legislation. Although it would take yet another century before the insidious policies and attitudes engendered by slavery would begin to truly fade in the United States, the horrendous bloodshed of the 1860s defined a turning point.

Nevertheless, for Donald Campbell and thousands like him there was another cause for concern. Lincoln's inauguration in March 1861 was viewed with optimism but on December 26, 1861, the *Ontario Observer's* main editorial expressed in deep anguish the concern of the citizens of

---

6   *Ontario Observer* (Prince Albert) October 17, 1861.

Reach Township and indeed the whole country, as fears that the War would spill over into Canada gained momentum.

> It hangs over our heads. It gathers force and volume day by day and we may know not the hour it may discharge its red lightning upon our heads, if some wisdom does not ward it off. [7]

In the same issue, it was announced that:

> Our friend and townsman, P.A. Hurd Esq, Colonel of the 5th Battalion, Ontario Militia, has received orders from Headquarters to organize a company of 75 men for active service. …. Messrs Yarnold and Westby are also forming a company of cavalry in Reach and Whitby. Several parties have already joined and are drilling regularly twice a week. Certainly things look like war. May God, in his Providence, avert it, but if the Americans should put a foot on our soil, for the purpose of invading it, they will find that they have got into the wrong quarters, for the people of Canada love their Queen and Country and have too much respect for British laws and rule to be brought under American Republicanism, — but what we want is to leave them alone in their glory. We wish Col. Hurd success in forming his company, and have no doubt that, if war does come, the sturdy yeoman of North Ontario will do their duty, both to Queen and country.

In March 1863, the Reach Voluntary Infantry Company was formed. That Donald Campbell was not a passive bystander to these events was made clear when he took time to sign the Militia Ballot in January 1865. His name appears among the 240 others in Reach Township in support of the Militia. The complete list of signatories was printed on the front page of the *Ontario Observer* of February 2, 1865.

---

7   *Ontario Observer* (Prince Albert) December 26, 1861.

This fear was justified when in October 1864 a group of Confederate soldiers hiding in St John's in Canada East raided St. Albans, Vermont, burning buildings and robbing banks before fleeing back to hiding in Canada. Their objective, while secretly hiding in a remote part of Canada, was to steal money, arms and supplies in order to launch an attack on larger settlements in Canada. The event resulted in tense diplomatic exchanges.

Nevertheless, throughout the British Provinces this fervent mistrust of the "unscrupulous Yankees," was a major impetus to uniting the provinces into one nation. In Charlottetown, P.E.I on September 1864 a conference was held to discuss the Confederation of the provinces. At that Conference George Brown who owned the Toronto *Globe* newspaper, expressed the feelings of most Canadians when he said:

> *In these Colonies we have enjoyed great advantage under the protection of the mother Country (England) ... there never was a moment when the hearts of our people were so firmly attached to the parent state by ties of gratitude and affection.*

The *Ontario Observer* of February 2, 1865 editorialized:

> *Confederation is likely to carry in the House almost unopposed...We are satisfied to know that Confederation is so well received by the "wisdom" of the provinces as it already has by the people, — so often manifested by the unanimous meetings in its favor which have been held throughout the country.*[8]

One more incident of major concern in Canadian-American relations was yet to thrust itself on the stage and it happened the following year, 1866, the year of Edwin's birth.

---

8   <u>Ontario Observer</u> *(Prince Albert) February 2, 1865.*

Chapter Two

1866

Edwin Ruthven Campbell

The year 1866 was an important and happy year for the Campbell family but it was also a year of heightened apprehension for the citizens of the Canadas and the States on its borders.

For Christina Campbell, the year dawned as she entered the last stages of her pregnancy. On February 12 she gave birth to her third child and second son whom she and Donald named Edwin Ruthven Campbell. The origins of the baby's middle name are lost, but probably relate to his Scottish ancestry, as Ruthven occurs prominently as a family name in the Perth and Inverness areas of Scotland.

A month after Edwin's birth over 10,000 Canadian militiamen including those in Reach Township were placed on full alert after a huge group of Irishmen, supported by former Union and Confederate soldiers seeking a new cause, gathered for a mass rally in New York City and threatened to invade Canada intent on "rescuing Canada from British rule," and the emancipation of Ireland from the "tyranny of England." At the same time, Washington declared an end to reciprocity with Canada.

In Ireland during the 1850s, the Irish Republican Brotherhood, a secret society, came into being. The group soon became known as the "Fenians."

The society garnered immense support from the Irish and their descendants in the New England States. On April 10 a group of Fenians gathered at Eastport, Maine with plans to launch the attack on Canada. When news reached them of the large numbers of Militia at the ready supported by British warships off the coast of Nova Scotia they reconsidered their action and withdrew. Further, President Andrew Johnson issued statements declaring their actions illegal and improper.

Far from being deterred, a group of nearly a thousand Fenians under the leadership of John O'Neill crossed the Niagara River near Buffalo and launched a surprise attack on Fort Erie, cut off the vital communication links of telegraph and the Buffalo and Lake Huron Railway and proceeded inland. The next day over 20,000 Canadian militiamen took arms in response to the challenge. Fenians drove back the Canadians at Ridgeway and then retreated to Fort Erie to regroup. The Canadians retaliated by attacking Fort Erie and capturing it only to find that the Fenians had escaped back to Buffalo where they were treated to a heroes' welcome.

Meanwhile another group of Fenians launched an attack on Pigeon Hill in Quebec, where they plundered some villages on June 7. They quickly retreated when it was discovered that the U.S. government forces led by Major General George Mead of Gettysburg fame, seized their supplies at St. Alban's in Vermont. Meade's action forced a delay in the Fenian cause and it took some time for the Fenians to regroup, even though they were now in complete violation of the US neutrality laws. The *New York Herald* carried daily accounts of the events of the Fenian raids and kept its readers informed about the progress of events.

Fenianism in this city:

Reinforcements for the Irish Army-Fifteen Hundred Men Off to the Front Yesterday- Recruiting Going on Lively- Fiftteen Hundred Enrolled at Tammany Hall.[9]

---

9   *New York Herald*, Wednesday June 6, 1866

Eccles Hill, in Quebec, just south of Montreal was the scene of the Fenians' final attempt to achieve their goals. A Fenian force of several thousand was outflanked by local militia and sent scurrying back across the border into the U.S.

The Prince Albert Infantry Company

In Prince Albert, the Prince Albert Infantry Company under Captain T.C. Forman responded to the challenge to Canada's sovereignty. They reacted to the bugle call in early June and marched from Prince Albert to Whitby, a distance of some 17 miles where they boarded a train to Toronto. Once in Toronto the Company was given the duty of controlling the Toronto Jail where some 80 Fenians were being held.

In Port Perry, Henry Charles, the popular waterfront hotel owner was elected as captain of the Port Perry Home Guard. It was duly reported in the *Ontario Observer* on June 14:

> *The inhabitants of Port Perry seem determined that neither the "Finnegans" or any other set of marauders shall desecrate the sacred soil of Canada and have organized themselves into a Home Guard and elected Mr. H. Charles, captain. Mr. John Rolph of this place has kindly offered his services as drill instructor, free of charge, which they have availed themselves of.* [10]

In the same issue, the editor added:

> *To the world we have demonstrated that no man or association of men can put hostile foot upon our soil without finding a united and powerful people ready and willing to hurl a proud defiance at them, and with the help of God, able to defend their*

---

10   <u>Ontario Observer</u> *(Prince Albert) June 14, 1866.*

> homes, their altars and the brave old flag, the glorious Union
> Jack against all comers, come where or whence they will.

On Tuesday June 18, the Reach Volunteers returned home to accolades, and a hearty meal provided by the local merchants. The following Friday at the Town Hall, amidst bunting, paintings and banners for *"the boys"* a special supper of a *"bountiful supply of edibles"* was held for the militia and their families. Speeches and toasts began at eight o'clock.

> They have proved themselves good men and true and willing to
> battle for their Queen and Country and if necessary will again
> be found at their post in their country's hour of danger. [11]

Joshua Wright, the Reeve of Reach led the toasts requesting that the assembly *"fill their bumpers when necessary."* Toasts to *"The Queen,"* *"The Royal Family,"* *"The Governor General"* and *"The Army and Navy"* were followed by rousing songs. This was followed by more speeches and any excuse for a toast, even one for *"The Press."* The affair concluded at one o'clock in the morning with the singing of the National Anthem, *"Three cheers for the Queen,"* and *"Three cheers for the Prince Albert Volunteers."* One can only imagine the pain that would have greeted the celebrants in the morning!

All of these events gave a definite momentum to delegates from Canada, New Brunswick and Nova Scotia who met with the British Government in London on December 4 to push forward the finalization of the creation of the Dominion of Canada.

Change in Washington

Declarations of neutrality introduced by President Van Buren, enhanced by President Tyler and finally enforced by President Johnson, made the Fenians and their aims illegal. Johnson declared the Fenians to be *"certain evil disposed persons"* and their actions *"... a high misdemeanor forbidden by the*

---

[11] Ibid..

laws of the United States." [12] Johnson's actions made it clear to the Canadian people that there was a distinct change in the attitude of Washington. This opened the way for more trade between the two nations and paved the way for Canadians to feel free to travel to the United States. But the Fenian actions had also swung public opinion in Nova Scotia and New Brunswick toward support for Confederation.

Throughout the British Provinces there had been a fervent mistrust of the "unscrupulous Yankees," This mistrust was a major impetus to uniting the provinces into one nation. Various conferences were held for the representatives of the provinces to discuss Confederation. At Charlottetown, P.E.I on September 1864 a critical meeting led George Brown, who owned the Toronto *Globe* newspaper, to express the feelings of most Canadians when he said,

> *In these Colonies we have enjoyed great advantage under the protection of the mother Country (England) ... there never was a moment when the hearts of our people were so firmly attached to the parent state by ties of gratitude and affection.*

Peter Perry

The route that Archibald Campbell and his Scottish compatriots took to settle Eldon Township involved a northerly journey from York to Lake Simcoe and then eastward. Another group of settlers, those who occupied Reach Township, took a different route. This was from Whitby, north into the unoccupied township. The first white settlers in Reach Township were Reuben Crandell and his wife Catherine who cut their way through the virgin bush of north Whitby Township in 1821. They settled just a few metres east of the present day hamlet of Manchester, some eight kilometers south of Saintfield. Here they lived a solitary existence for well over

---

12   Proclamation of U.S. President Andrew Johnson, June 6, 1866.

two years having no contact with fellow settlers other than a rare visit to Whitby to buy food and supplies.

Crandell had not come directly from Britain. He and his wife had been born in Saratoga County in New York State and Reuben could trace his ancestry back to the early settlers of Rhode Island who had come from Monmouthshire shortly after the landing of the Pilgrim Fathers. But the Crandell family remained Loyalists and moved to Ontario in the early 1800s.

After the Crandells had settled in Reach Township in 1821, they were followed two years later by Abner Hurd who purchased 100 acres to the east of the Crandells. The Hurds began a settlement which later became known as Prince Albert. It was on Hurd's property that the Pine Grove Cemetery was established, the cemetery that now contains the monument to the Campbell family.

The first settler in what is now Port Perry was Elias Williams, another Loyalist who arrived at the Lake Scugog waterfront in 1831. In order to develop his plans for the lumber trade Peter Perry bought 80 acres of land including the waterfront from Williams twelve years later. It is interesting to note that Williams father was also a Vermont farmer who had fought against the Rebels and was subsequently forced to abandon his property and possessions to the Revolution.

Peter Perry became a leading reform politician during the period from 1826 to 1836. After leaving politics he became a real estate entrepreneur, buying the harbour at what is now Whitby and then the property at the southeastern corner of Lake Scugog as part of his vision to establish a complete communication and transportation system from Lake Ontario, north to Lake Huron.

His purchase of the Lake Scugog property was followed up by encouraging five Whitby businessmen to build steam powered lumber mills at the Lake Scugog waterfront. He also persuaded two Whitby businessmen to build a steamboat at the waterfront in 1851. The vessel, used to tow log booms down to the mills at the waterfont, was named the *Woodman*, the first steamboat in the entire Kawarthas. The lumber was transported overland to his harbour at Whitby. A considerable amount of that lumber was transported across Lake Ontario to be used in building houses in upper New York State, particularly at Oswego and vicinity.

Meanwhile, a kilometer or so to the south, Prince Albert had grown to become, by volume, the second largest grain handling centre in Canada. A profusion of stores, three churches and a number of industries supported a growing community of over 500 souls. One facet of Peter Perry's dream that did not die completely was his desire to have a railway linking his harbour on Lake Ontario with points north, beginning with his Scugog Village. His 1847 proposal for a railway line underwent a number of revisions over the years but it wasn't until 1868 that support for the project justified beginning work on the project. Almost immediately after the first shovel had been placed in the ground, Prince Albert's businesses and factories began to relocate in Port Perry. By 1873, Prince Albert had become a residential community with only one store. One of the last businesses to move was the *Ontario Observer*, a newspaper which had seen its first issue in Prince Albert in 1857.

Following the pattern of most railways built in Canada at that time, the railway was mired in controversy, incompetence and corruption. By the time the first train ran in 1871 the railway company was deep in debt. Nevertheless, in 1876 the railway was extended to Lindsay.

Unfortunately Perry died in 1851, the same year that the *Woodman* was launched and his dream of transportation was not developed any further.

Fortunately another astute businessman, Joseph Bigelow, arrived in Scugog Village just before the death of Perry. After Bigelow's arrival, Scugog Village was renamed Port Perry in honour of Peter Perry's accomplishments. Bigelow maintained the lumber trade and developed other businesses thus enabling Port Perry to become, to a large degree, a self-sustaining economic unit.

Samuel Stoutt

When Jefferson declared that "all are created free and equal," many described him as a Genius and point to the potentiality of the statement, while others shouted "Hypocrite" and point to Jefferson's insistence on keeping many slaves on his plantations and to Mary Hemmings, his black slave and mistress by whom he bore at least one child. In reality the slaves were not regarded as human beings, neither were the aboriginals. It took nearly two centuries for that aspect of democracy to evolve and achieve anything near its potentiality. The 200 or so blacks who ran Jefferson's plantations were held in slavery throughout his lifetime, albeit with some measure of benevolence. Only recently have some scholars begun to accept the premise that the delegates who framed the Constitution of the United States in Philadelphia in 1787 tended to look upon Blacks as mere property or chattels. Thus the phrase "that all men are Created Free and equal" applied to whites only.

The wave of humanitarian and legislative reform which swept through Britain in the early nineteenth century, largely motivated by Christian ideals and sentiment, led to the Great Reform Bills and the abolition of child labour and slavery. The British, who had led the slave trade and profited enormously from it, realized the errors of their ways, and slavery and discrimination were slowly abolished.

The work of Fox and the Quakers, and then Wilberforce made slave trade illegal in British territories in 1811. In 1833, the Abolition Act was passed, making slavery of any kind illegal throughout the British Colonies. It wasn't until 1865 that the United States Congress passed legislation to abolish slavery, but it took almost another century before Civil Rights became a real issue.

As early as 1793, largely through the efforts of John Graves Simcoe, legislation was passed in Upper Canada *"to prevent the further introduction of slaves and to limit the term of contracts for servitude within this province."* Finally, following the British lead, John Beverly Robinson, the Attorney General of Upper Canada declared in 1819 that *". . . the Negroes are entitled to personal freedom through residence* [in Upper Canada] *and any attempt to infringe their rights will be resisted in the courts."*

One of the great tragedies of United States history is that a Civil War cut the nation in two and that a major cause of that conflict was the issue of slavery. As a result of these problems, many slaves found ways of escaping and made their way into Upper Canada (Ontario) and Nova Scotia.

By 1860, an estimated minimum of 30,000 had made Upper Canada their home. There are a few early accounts of escaped slaves making their way into Reach Township. However, none took up permanent residence here until 1866, the year of Edwin's birth, when an escaped slave named Samuel Stoutt (sometimes spelled Stout) arrived and decided to make Port Perry his home. His personal route on the "Underground Railway" had led him through New Jersey to New York, Kingston, Madoc, Toronto and Uxbridge, and finally to Port Perry.

Samuel Stoutt was a man of just under average height and of a stocky build. When he arrived in Port Perry, he immediately made his way to one of the local barber shops and asked for employment. He quickly established himself in the tonsorial art.

He had another talent which helped him to gain acceptance in this pioneer community: he was an extremely proficient musician and was apparently able to play well on any kind of wind or brass instrument. He helped to organize a town band and was its first leader. Because of his musicianship, he became known throughout his long life in Port Perry as "Professor" Stoutt.

The Campbell family would have met and no doubt chatted with Stoutt on Sundays as he also became a member of the Presbyterian Church. In the church, Stoutt met and in 1876 married an English girl, Elizabeth Organ. Elizabeth was considerably younger than himself, possibly as much as 30 years his junior. He rented a house on Lilla Street (now Simcoe Street) just north of Scugog Street (Highway 7A) on the east side not far from the home in which Donald and Christina would spend their declining years. In the Simcoe Street home, Samuel and Elizabeth had five children. Stoutt continued to work as a barber until the end of the century. His loving and faithful wife Eliza died in 1907. Samuel's age is difficult to determine. His birth date has been recorded in various documents as 1810, 1812, 1815 and 1817. When he died on May 4, 1911, his obituary declared that he was a centenarian and "for years he has held the honour of being the oldest man in Port Perry and vicinity."

The arrival of Samuel Stoutt in Port Perry, his attendance at the Presbyterian church on Sunday, his popularity in the barbershop and his celebrated appearance at the head of the town band were all symbolic reminders that here in Canada a level of freedom existed that was almost unthinkable among their neighbours to the south.

Changes

In spite of the pious attitudes of Canadians, there were changes taking place across North America and these changes were being observed by all responsible citizens including Donald and Christina Campbell. By the time that Edwin had reached his impressionable and formative teenage years, two distinct trains of thought had evolved in Canada. The two divergent paths led to anxious debate and a generational divide. On the one side there were those, particularly of the older generation who found solace in the wounds of their fathers and forefathers and, in Port Perry with the daily presence of Samuel Stoutt reminding them, dwelt in the disdain of anything to do with the United States. The other side, mainly the young and adventurous, reinforced by the actions of General George Meade following the legislative leadership of President Johnson, looked to their neighbours to the south as a nation determined to reform itself, but more importantly, the United States was seen as a source of economic opportunity. Indeed, Michigan became home for a significant number of Canadians. They formed the largest foreign population group in that state until well into the twentieth century.[13] In the first half of the nineteenth century, relative to Upper Canada, the abundance and readily available good, cheap land, (and easier credit) drew many Canadians to Michigan. The growth of small industries in southern Michigan, the lumber trade of the central and northern parts of the state and the introduction of mining in the Upper Peninsula, combined with the expansion of agri-

---

13 Richard J. Hathaway, "From Ontario to Michigan: The Migration to and Settlement of Canadians in the Great Lake State", *Families*, 18 (no. 4, 1979) p 169.

culture and improving transportation links, made the state an attractive lure to Canadians.[14]

On August 16, 1866 a new newspaper appeared in the local stores. Edward Mundy decided to launch the *Port Perry Standard*. Mundy was an experienced publisher having worked for owner James Holden at the *Ontario Observer* in Prince Albert and later produced the *North Ontario Advocate* in Uxbridge for five years prior to his new venture. One motive behind Mundy's creation of a new newspaper was clear. Joseph Bigelow had begun to take an interest in supporting the promotion of a railway from Whitby to Port Perry and he needed a platform for his ideas. The rival *Ontario Observer* in Prince Albert supported the railway but its editorials raised serious questions about the funding, and frequently criticized Bigelow. Politically, the *Observer* tended to be conservative in its editorial views whereas the *Standard* was inclined toward the liberal view. Bigelow gave Mundy encouragement for his newspaper by offering second floor accommodation for the newspaper in his Queen Street building in Port Perry.

Edwin's Youth

An event of particular significance to Donald and Christina Campbell occurred in Port Perry in 1868. That September James R. Youmans opened the Port Perry Grammar School. This opening would no doubt have been discussed at the Campbell's dinner table. The opportunity for their bright children to take their education beyond the local one-roomed country school was a lure not to be overlooked.

Youmans' school started out as merely an upstairs room in a log cabin school perched on the top of Port Perry's Borelia Hill. He left Port Perry in December 1871 and was replaced by Dugald McBride. McBride's arrival coincided with a legislative event in Toronto. "An Act to Improve the Common and Grammar Schools of Ontario" was passed. The Act

---

14   Marcus Lee Hansen and John Bartlett Brebner, <u>The Mingling of the Canadian and American Peoples</u>. *(New Haven, Yale University Press, 1941), pp. 13,14.*

stipulated that from the time of its enactment, Grammar Schools would be referred to as High Schools.

Dugald McBride had begun his teaching career in 1856 in Elgin County and then moved to Port Hope. In his first year at Port Perry he had only 19 students and taught all subjects to five High School grade levels.

As soon as he had been hired, McBride set about convincing the local Board of Education to build a larger and more efficient building to complement the growing community. After a lengthy debate regarding the cost of such a structure, played out enthusiastically in the press, McBride won out and the Board was convinced. When completed in 1873 the elegant two storey school was by far the most imposing structure in the all of the adjacent townships and beyond. The school was officially opened with a large parade and a ceremony graced by all the local dignitaries and representatives from the Ministry of Education for the Province of Ontario. The High School again occupied the upper floor of the building, but this time with four classrooms and a staff room. The ground floor was occupied by the elementary school under the leadership of Alexander Rae.

At the time of the opening Dugald McBride taught the classics and his assistant Duncan Crawford taught mathematics and sciences. Later in the year Crawford left and was replaced by James McKenzie. He was joined by Professor Harrington who taught music, J.L. Dowling who taught art, and the principal of the elementary school who also taught English and Geography in the Secondary school. This staff stayed in place until 1879 when Charles Pedley took over the responsibilities in art and music. These were the teachers who would mould the young Duncan Campbell and two years later, his younger brother Edwin.

Illustration # 1: Port Perry Union School opened in 1873 with Port Perry High School occupying the upper floor and the elementary school on the lower floor.(Photo Courtesy Scugog Museum Archives, Port Perry)

The Ontario Ministry of Education evaluated its schools by administering a semi-annual set of examinations for its intermediate students in the High Schools across the province. On July 27, 1876 the *Observer* announced with pride that when the results were compiled, Port Perry High School had the highest percentage of students passing the exams in the entire province!

> *This splendid result for the pupils of the Port Perry school speaks well for their intelligence and perseverance and is creditable to the highest degree to their excellent teacher Mr. McBride to whose superior talents and skills as a teacher these results are largely attributable.*[15]

Two weeks later, the Port Perry Board of Trustees paid for an advertisement in the *Observer:*

> *The Trustees have much pleasure in announcing that the school is well equipped and in a high state of efficiency in all its departments. In the Classical Course every effort will be made to ensure the thoroughness in training so essential to the future success of students preparing for the entrance Examinations in Law, Medicine or the Universities and Theological Colleges.*[16]

The advertisement concluded with the statement, *"At the recent Intermediate Examinations this school stood first of all the High Schools in Ontario."*

By 1880 the student body had grown to 127 and Dugald McBride's reputation as a teacher and principal had gained provincial recognition. From that time onwards until his retirement in 1910, on a per capita basis, more of Dugald McBride's graduates went on to become graduates of the Ontario Medical Schools than any other Secondary School in Ontario. This was due in no small part to his skill as a teacher of Latin. A good understanding of Latin was a considerable asset when studying medicine.

On August 2, 1882 the *Observer* noted, again with justifiable pride:

> *The result of the Matriculation Examinations held in June last at the Toronto University has been made known and a magnificent result it is...that the Port Perry High School still occupying first place in the foremost rank of the High Schools of the*

---

15 *Ontario Observer* (Port Perry) July 27, 1876.

16 *Ontario Observer* (Port Perry) August 10, 1876.

> *Province. It is not at all surprising that parents anxious for the thorough education of their more advanced sons and daughters should seek to place them within the influence of such superior advantages as are to be secured at the Port Perry High School.*[17]

In his 1913 volume, **On the Shores of Scugog**, Samuel Farmer wrote the following about the school's principal:

> *There are preachers doctors, lawyers, engineers and businessmen scattered here and there throughout the world, who if they could, would tell how much they owed to this self possessed man, who calmly but persistently piloted them through the turbulent waters of school life. The frivolous pupils had a hard time with Dugald McBride. The calm self pitying, sarcastic contempt meted out to them was a wholesome tonic to those who at heart were right: but with the hopeless ones the words rankled until they engendered resentment. In later years many grew to know that rebuke was just and really kindly.* [18]

Other teachers at Port Perry High School who would have a profound and lasting effect on Edwin's life were the Art teachers. Upon Edwin's arrival at the school, Charles Pedley taught art and music. He was replaced in 1883 by William Rees.

With the discipline and scholasticism meted out by McBride and his staff it is not surprising that among Edwin's personal schoolmates at Port Perry were an unusual number of boys who would also make their mark on national and international affairs. That Edwin would develop a lasting friendship with a core of teenage friends is not unusual. That each of these friends would each achieve remarkable success in his chosen field and that they would become scattered across North America and beyond and yet continue their relationship is quite extraordinary. These friends,

---

17   <u>Ontario Observer</u> *(Port Perry) August 2, 1882.*

18   Samuel Farmer, <u>On the Shores of Scugog</u>, *(Port Perry, Star Print, 1913), p.35.*

some fellow students at Port Perry High School, others visitors to the community, all would have an impact on each other's lives.

Dr. H. A. Bruce

Stewart Bruce and his wife Isabella Morrow had farmed in Cartwright Township immediately to the east of Reach. Stewart Bruce, true to his environment in Cartwright Township, was a staunch Orangeman.[19] The Bruces, like the Campbells, moved to Port Perry primarily to enable their children to attend Port Perry High School. They moved from Cartwright in 1873 and purchased a farm in Prince Albert. Their third son Herbert Alexander Bruce was two years younger than Edwin but the two became friends at school. That friendship was reinforced by the fact that Edwin attended the St. John's Presbyterian Church with his parents and siblings. Herbert served as the organist at that church for a short time. Herbert wanted to follow Edwin to medical school but when he graduated from Port Perry High School in May 1884 he was only 15 years old, too young for university. Instead, he became an apprentice to S. E. Allison, the druggist in Port Perry. Three years later he followed Edwin to Medical School in Toronto and graduated in 1892. Bruce and Campbell remained in contact throughout their lives and would call upon each other at various periods in their lives. In his memoirs, Dr Bruce recalled fond memories of Port Perry and his school days there.[20] He noted with admiration, his teachers, particularly the math teacher George Stone, and Principal Dugald McBride. He also made a detailed reference to his school friends including Dr. Edwin Campbell.

Llewellys Barker

Another childhood friend was Llewellys F. Barker who was not actually from Reach Township but, through Herbert Bruce, he developed ties with

---

19   H.A.Bruce, <u>Varied Operations</u> (Toronto, Longmans Green and Company, 1958), p. 15.

20   Ibid, pp 8-25.

the community. Barker, the son of a Baptist minister, was born in 1867 in Brooklin a few miles to the south of Port Perry. The Reverend Barker visited Port Perry many times as a minister, preaching at the Baptist Church located at the north east corner of Rosa and Queen Streets directly across the road from Port Perry High School. This building was originally a branch of the Mechanics Institute, the early form of Public Library in Ontario and was acquired by the Baptists in 1866. It was also just across the road from where Donald and Christina Campbell would eventually settle.

When preaching in Port Perry, Rev. Barker usually brought his son Llewellys with him. It was on these occasions that Barker, Bruce and Campbell, similar in age and interests, became close friends

While working at Allison's drug store before attending medical school, Herbert Bruce took advantage of a new invention which Mr. Allison had acquired. Allison's was one of the first businesses in town to make use of Alexander Graham Bell's telephone. Bell applied for patents for his machine in 1876 and the first telephone exchange in Canada was established in Hamilton in 1878. The fact that Mr. Allison had a telephone installed in his store in 1882 places him in the early days of the telephone's history. In his memoirs, Dr. Bruce makes the valid claim that he was one of the early telephone operators.[21]

Upon early graduation from Pickering College High School, Llewellys Barker went to work at Gibbard's drugstore in Whitby where there was also a telephone. Bruce and Barker spent many pleasant moments talking to each other on Bell's new gadget.[22]

Bruce, Barker and Campbell continued their friendship while in Medical School. Barker and Campbell were classmates, with Bruce three years behind them. Upon graduation, Barker worked at the Toronto General Hospital and then moved to Johns Hopkins University Medical School in Baltimore, Maryland in 1891. Later Edwin was to call on Llewellys at a critical point in his life.

---

21   Ibid., p. 21

22   Ibid.

Hamar Greenwood

Another childhood friend of Bruce, Barker and Campbell was Hamar Greenwood. As a young man, H. A. Bruce took organ lessons at the Ontario Ladies College in Whitby and came in contact with Thomas Hubbard Greenwood. He was the son of a prominent Whitby lawyer and mayor, John Hamer Greenwood.

Greenwood's father was a frequent visitor to Port Perry in the sessions of court which took place in its Town Hall. He advertised his services regularly in the *Observer* in the 1860s and 70s. His son Thomas and daughter Florence often accompanied him to Port Perry and usually stayed at the Bruces' home while his father administered justice. Here, the boys would enjoy each other's company. Thomas later assumed the name Hamar.

Greenwood attended Whitby Collegiate and upon his graduation in 1887 decided to be a teacher. When an opening occurred at the Manchester Public School, just a mile west of Port Perry, in 1888, Hamar taught there for a year, spending his leisure times with the Bruce family at Prince Albert. The Manchester school was located a few hundred yards west of the four corners of Manchester on the north side of the road.

Hamar then went on to the University of Toronto to study political science. While a student there, he would frequently meet up with his Port Perry friends. After graduation he worked for a brief time at the Department of Agriculture but gave that up and worked his way to England on a cattle boat. He decided to become a lawyer and financed his way through law school in London by giving Temperance lectures and by suing a bus company after an accident. He later entered politics in England and was first elected to Parliament in 1906, preventing him from attending Edwin and Margery's wedding. Under Prime Minister Lloyd George he was appointed to the cabinet.[23] Edwin frequently visited him when he travelled to Britain.

Hamar's sister Florence spent much time in England with her brother and on one occasion met Leopold Amery, a rising politician, elected to the

---

23   Ibid. p. 22

House of Commons in 1911. The two married shortly afterwards. Amery became a member of the Cabinet in 1919 and was appointed as First Lord of the Admiralty in 1922.

Sam McLaughlin

Probably one of the more important friendships which Edwin developed during his youth was with a young cyclist from the hamlet of Enniskillin, a few miles south of Port Perry. The name of the cyclist was Sam McLaughlin, a hyperactive youngster who found an outlet for his boundless energy in cycling and one of his favourite rides was north to the Ridges and then down into Port Perry.

In his declining years Sam McLaughlin wrote of Edwin Campbell as his lifelong friend. How close they became during their youth is a matter for speculation but what is clear is that they did meet and strike up a friendship during their teens. They had much in common; their grandfathers had emigrated from Britain, Edwin's from Scotland and Sam's from Ireland although his ancestry was also Scottish. Edwin's older brother was in medical school and Sam's uncle was a doctor. More importantly both families were Presbyterians, although the McLaughlins appear to have been a little stronger in their commitment to the church, due in part to Sam's father serving as an elder in the church, and both boys had fathers who were members of the Masonic Order.

The McLaughlins had joined in the perilous 1830s migration from Ireland to Canada. The McLaughlin patriarch, William McLaughlin and his wife Jane made their way from County Cavan in Ireland to Cavan Township, Upper Canada. Their journey was marked by horror as tens of thousands succumbed to cholera and today lie buried on Gross Isle close by the Quebec landing. The McLaughlins were among the few fortunate families who managed to escape the scourge.

They made their way by boat from Quebec to Cobourg settling eventually just west of the village of Tyrone on the seventh Concession of Darlington Township, a few miles south east of Port Perry. The following spring William and Jane McLaughlin's son John put a down payment on a two hundred acre property beside his parents. He married Eliza Rusk in 1835 and their first son Robert was born in January 1837. The census of 1851 recorded John and Eliza with their five children: Robert, William, James, John and Mary Jane, all Presbyterians.

There was no Presbyterian Church in Tyrone but one had been built in Enniskillen a few miles to the west. The Free Kirk at Enniskillen was a busy, well attended institution and the McLaughlins took an active part in its leadership with William and John among its elders.

At an early age, John and Eliza's son Robert became fascinated with wood and what he could make with it. As a teenager he took over a corner of his father's barn and carved axe handles. He also took an active interest in painting and sketching. As a sideline from farming he sold his axe handles and with the money he made, he bought tools to improve his skill. Robert, as the eldest son, knew that he would inherit the rights to the family farm while the other children had to plan more carefully for their future. Their third son James earned a place at the Toronto Medical School, graduated and opened his practice in Bowmanville in 1864. That was the year that Robert married pretty Mary Smith, a neighbour and daughter of another Scottish immigrant.

Wagon Making

At the time of his marriage, Robert had a flourishing business selling his handmade axe handles and whiffletrees. Wiffletrees were an essential part of horse drawn vehicles. Around this time a bound set of Volume II of *The Coachmaker's Illustrated Monthly Magazine* fell into his hands. The volume was an older issue, published in Ohio in 1856 but it stimulated Robert's craftsmanship and artistic nature. Inside were drawings, plans for all manner of buggies and sleighs.

He applied some of the ideas in the magazine to develop his own design for a cutter following the instructions for curving boards, building the frame and moulding the iron runners. The final product was a work of art, painted a vermillion colour. He even paid J.B. Keddie to create the upholstery in green twill for the vehicle. As soon as the cutter was seen on the roads it became the talk of the region and neighbours immediately offered to buy it. He kept his original but started building more cutters to fill the demand. When he showed his cutter at the Bowmanville Fair, he knew that he had a decision to make. The demand for his cutters meant that he would have to construct larger facilities in which to build them and add wagons to his inventory, but more importantly, he had to decide whether or not to focus on his carriage making and let his farming take second place.

In 1869 he moved four miles west to Enniskillen, built a new log house and a larger carriage works. Here he employed three men; a body and wheel maker, a blacksmith and an apprentice to assist in all the aspects of carriage making. Robert did the wood finishing, painting and varnishing himself. His insistence on exceptional quality rather than fast production meant that demand for his carriages grew so much that by 1887 he had added four more men to his payroll including a man to carry out the bookkeeping and accounting.

In the house in the village, Mary had given birth to George William in 1869, Robert Samuel in 1871 and Elizabeth in 1874. Unfortunately Mary became a victim of tuberculosis, 'consumption' as it was then called. Robert called on his doctor brother James to help her. He even hired a maid, Miss Sarah Jane Parr to assist in her care. Unfortunately Mary died on March 10, 1877.

Robert's deep sense of loss was compounded by the responsibility of raising five children ranging in age from three year old Elizabeth to ten year old John James. To ease his burdens Robert married Sarah Jane Parr on January 17, 1878. Since the Presbyterians expected mourning to last at least a full year, he knew that the congregation at Enniskillen would look upon the union with some disdain. As a result, the marriage took place not in Enniskillen but in Oshawa. The hasty marriage and the resulting rejection by the congregation produced another result; Robert decided to move his family and his carriage works to Simcoe Street in Oshawa. The social implications were obvious; it would give Robert and Sarah a chance to start their new relationship in a new church. The business move was a strategic but extremely controversial one. His brother James tried to encourage him to relocate in Bowmanville, to the east, a more sedate and settled community where Dr. James had a respected practice and would welcome his brother as a neighbour. Oshawa on the other hand was a rougher community, but to Robert it presented more opportunities. Oshawa was closer to Toronto and had only one other carriage maker. Bowmanville had six. Another factor helped Robert in his decision: the president of the Western Bank in Oshawa was an Irish Presbyterian, John Cowan. Cowan also owned the Ontario Malleable Iron Company, a company with which Robert had done considerable business since his beginnings in carriage making.

By combining the $3,000 from the sale of his property in Enniskillen and a $3,000 loan from the Cowan managed Western Bank, Robert was able to build a three-storey brick factory on the main street, Simcoe Street, and move his family into a comfortable home close by.

Always anxious to improve his carriages Robert designed a new chassis for them. His invention incorporated new mechanisms for the springs, couplings and the turning system. He patented it in 1880 as "The McLaughlin Patent Buggy Gear" and within a year, after showing it at fairs, demand for it stretched across the province. By 1884 he employed 16 men at his factory, but then, tragedy struck on July 21; his factory was destroyed by fire.

His oldest son Jack (John) was a top student at the Ontario College of Pharmacy, graduating in 1885. Rather than return to Oshawa he moved immediately to Brooklyn, New York. Here he became involved in the latest addition to drug stores, the soda fountain. This was at a time when Coca Cola had just been invented. In an attempt to lure his eldest son back into the fold, Robert established a new company, the McLaughlin Carriage Company with Jack as one of three partners but Jack refused to become involved. Instead he later returned to Canada, settling not in Oshawa but in Toronto where he established a wholesale soda fountain company and later founded the Canada Dry Company, manufacturers of ginger ale.

Robert Samuel (Sam) McLaughlin

Robert's second son George became an apprentice in his factory at age 14 as soon as he had finished his schooling. Robert Samuel, who became known as Sam in order to differentiate him from his father, in seeing his brother slaving from early morning to late at night six days a week, preferred the freedom of his bicycle and had no interest in his father's business. After three years of apprenticeship George was assigned in 1884 to the office where he took on a variety of accounting duties, assisting 23 year old former teacher Oliver Hezzlewood who was also hired that year as the official bookkeeper. George carried out his responsibilities with meticulous detail.

For Sam, the bicycle and what it had to offer became an obsession. He would pedal to Toronto and back in one day, a total distance of over sixty miles of poor roads. He also made frequent visits, usually on weekends, to see Edwin and his friends in Port Perry. Sam won many awards at bicycle races across the province but eventually he had to consider his future more seriously.

When Edwin Campbell graduated from medical school in 1887 Sam realized that he also had to find a career. Shortly after Sam had said his goodbyes to Edwin as he headed off to Michigan, he followed his brother Jack's encouragement to become involved in their father's business. Sam became an apprentice in the upholstery shop in the factory. That same year his father began a major expansion of the facilities. The expansion included an engine house and boiler to provide steam to power the saws, sanders, drills and lathes.

By 1890 Sam had completed his apprenticeship and on the invitation of his friend took a position in Watertown, New York with the H.H. Babcock Company. He stayed there until he felt that he had learned all he needed to know about upholstery and then moved on to other companies in the area. He returned to Oshawa but not before visiting New York City. On his return he applied what he had learned in New York State and improved the operation of the upholstery section of his father's factory. With George proving his worth in bookkeeping and Sam in upholstery, Robert made his sons junior partners in the expanding factory in 1892. George was sent across the country to visit farm equipment dealers who acted as sales representatives for the McLaughlin buggies and cutters. Such was the growth that in 1896 George was sent to Saint John, New Brunswick to establish a branch office. By the end of the century the McLaughlin company laid claim to being the largest carriage factory in Canada manufacturing over five thousand vehicles (cutters, carriages and sleighs) a year and employing 300 men.

Meanwhile, Sam's adventures on his bicycle had led to a further development. On one of his bicycle trips from Oshawa to his uncle's home in Tyrone he accepted their invitation to attend the Methodist Church. Here he became overwhelmed by the presence of a stunning beauty in the church choir, a schoolteacher named Adelaide Mowbray. Her father, a respected Kinsale area farmer and local politician, was a strict tea-totalling Methodist and Mason. Sam was totally besotted by Adelaide and immediately made a date with her for the following Sunday. On the appointed day he abandoned his bicycle for one of his father's shiny buggies behind a well groomed mare. He made the right impression and on February 28, 1898 they were married at Adelaide's parents' farmhouse. The service was solemnized jointly by the Mowbrays' Methodist minister and the McLaughlins' Presbyterian minister. After the service they were whisked off to the Whitby Railway station in a McLaughlin sleigh and from there went on to honeymoon in New York City for a week.

The following year, 1899, the McLaughlin Carriage Company factory was destroyed by fire and a few months after that Robert married Eleanor McCulloch. In 1899 Robert took on the added responsibility as the mayor of Oshawa. Sam took the Oshawa employees to Gananoque to an empty factory where they re-established production.

The mayor of Gananoque to the east offered Robert a comfortable financial incentive to rebuild there. But Robert, now the mayor of Oshawa and faithful to his community, rebuilt a much improved facility in Oshawa and within a few months, buggies were being designed and built in Oshawa again. Two years later Robert made the claim of being the largest Carriage manufacturer in the British Empire. His claim is difficult to verify in such a vast geographic expanse, nevertheless his production of fifteen thousand gears and vehicles a year was impressive.

Doctors in Port Perry

The medical scene in Port Perry while Edwin was still at school also provided some stimulus for his later career choice. Two doctors with whom Edwin became quite close were the Jones brothers. The lives of the Jones family members also provided some ongoing gossip for the citizens of Port Perry.

The patriarch of the Jones family had settled near Perth, Ontario after fleeing the horrors of the American War of Independence, losing all the family possessions to the vigilantes who roamed the newly formed United States. His son George became a prominent Methodist minister establishing himself in the Orono area. The Reverend George William Jones and his wife had at least eight children. One of their sons, George William junior, became a doctor and set up his practice in Prince Albert in 1860. The reverend's two oldest sons, William Milton Jones and Charles Jones owned a successful flour mill in Madoc. Their property was next door to the Richardson farm, where, in 1866, gold was found, precipitating Ontario's first gold rush. In December 1866 a claim was made that gold had been washed from Deer Creek which ran behind the grist mill on the Jones' property.

The Jones brothers sold their property at a considerable profit. Some small amounts of gold were found in that area of Hastings County and the boom town of Eldorado came into existence. Unfortunately most of the claims proved to be fraudulent. Extremely small amounts of gold were indeed found but they were so small that mining proved to be unprofitable. Allegations immediately began to circulate about "salting" gold, i.e. planting gold in order to inflate the value of the property. This was never proven but the communities of Eldorado and its neighbours soon returned to quiet obscurity.

After capitalizing on their Madoc property the Jones Brothers eventually came to Port Perry in 1869 on the invitation of Thomas Paxton and their brother George. They went into partnership with Paxton in buying a clothing and general merchandise business. The Paxtons and the Bigelows at this time were the most extensive land owners in Port Perry and Charles married Mary Paxton, daughter of Thomas Paxton in 1870.

William Jones had graduated from the Eastman Commercial College in Poughkeepsie, New York, before beginning his business career. His training soon paid dividends as his Port Perry clothing and merchandise business became highly successful, rivaling that of Joseph Bigelow. The Jones brothers built an impressive three story brick building close to Bigelow. Their younger brother Richard graduated from medical school and joined George in his medical practice in Prince Albert. In the late fall of 1868, the doctors established a partnership in Port Perry and opened an office. They also opened a drug store.

Their two sisters also settled here; Sarah Jones was a milliner who married Thomas Bedford, and Metta Jones married James Isaacs who was a tailor.

Unfortunately, Charles had been involved in a number of investment schemes and declared personal bankruptcy in 1870, the year of his marriage, but continued to work in the Queen Street store for his brother. A year later, the Jones brothers bought out Paxton to establish Jones Brothers' store.

In the year of Edwin's birth at Saintfield, Dr. George Jones' marriage to Ann Catherine Martin had fallen apart and she left Prince Albert. At that time divorces were subjected to lengthy and detailed processes which required the approval of Parliament. Jones applied for a divorce on the grounds of adultery on August 10, 1868 and Gordon Bigelow, a brother of Joseph Bigelow, was his attorney in the divorce petition. The petition for divorce was not successful.

In October 1869, Dr. George Jones moved to Michigan, where he took up permanent residence as a pioneer in the small settlement of Imlay City. Here he established his practice, and after a year, became an American citizen. Dr. Jones applied for, and obtained, an American divorce. Sometime during this period he began to court Anna Paxton, a daughter of George Paxton and a cousin of Mary Paxton, his sister-in-law.

In January, 1871, Dr. George Jones paid a visit to Port Perry to take Anna Paxton to the United States to become his bride. Edward Mundy, her uncle and the editor of the *Port Perry Standard*, wrote an editorial in which he maintained that Anna was stolen away from her home by Dr. Jones and carried on to the train in a fainting fit. The editorial went on to state that her widowed mother was also involved in the "kidnapping".

Two letters followed in the *Ontario Observer* and were signed separately by Anna and Dr Jones. They denied the *"...malicious fabrications..."*

Editor Edward Mundy of the *Standard* wrote a series of articles in which he slandered the character of the Jones brothers. He made reference to Charles' bankruptcy, the circumstances of Dr George Jones divorce and subsequent marriage to Anna Paxton. He also made reference to the alleged "salting" of land in Madoc.

In January 19, 1871, a letter to the editor of the *Ontario Observer* appeared. It was addressed as a testimonial to C.W. and W. M. Jones and was signed by W. Paxton, W.S. Sexton and "200 others". In it the writers deplored the attitude of Mundy;

> ... we cannot but regard it as a base and cowardly attempt to destroy the reputation and impair the usefulness of two of our most active and enterprising businessmen for the purpose of gratifying personal jealousy and animosity.[24]

Charles Jones' letter to editor of the *Observer* on February 8, 1871, acknowledged his own bankruptcy and then, in defence of his brothers, he castigated Mundy by stating that Mundy had become:

> ... a subservient fool and sycophant, he has managed to drag out a miserable existence... a lying hypocrite... The poor idiot... Steeped in corruption and utterly destitute of moral or religious principles, this subservient fool is ready to pander to anything... a creature without a particle of ability, pretending to

---

24   Ontario Observer *(Prince Albert) January 19, 1871.*

> fill the position of Editor, without possessing the first mental or moral qualification. Ever since he came to this place, his lying chicanery and hypocrisy have been the cause of more religious bickering, social and domestic trouble and rational prejudices than all other evil influences combined.[25]

The vindictive letters continued for three more issues, concluding with ... *the parasite Mundy... giving his readers a column of the basest and falsest verbiage it is possible to conceive of... the puerile effusion contained in the last issue of his notorious smut machine.*[26]

Dr George Jones' brother, Dr. Richard Jones, lived in Port Perry across the road from the Campbell home and continued his medical practice in Port Perry until 1887 when he moved to Toronto. He attended Edwin's graduation from Medical School. Dr. George Jones and his new bride Anna became some of Imlay City's most respected citizens. He and Anna frequently returned to Port Perry and were treated royally on each visit.

> The many friends here of Dr. G.W. Jones of Imlay City, Michigan had the pleasure of a flying visit from him in the early part of the present week. The Dr. looks active, prosperous and well; thoroughly up in every department of his profession while regarding the health of others he does not neglect his own. The Doctor's appearance is a substantial recommendation to his American home for health and comfort.[27]

Presbyterian Church

Next door to Dr. Richard Jones' home was the Saint John's Presbyterian Church. Both architecturally and socially, it was and still is a focal point of

---

25   *Ontario Observer* (Prince Albert) February 8,1871.

26   *Ontario Observer* (Prince Albert) March 1, 1871.

27   *Ontario Observer*, (Port Perry), April 12, 1882.

the community. In the census of 1881 Donald Campbell was listed as age 44, retired and a Presbyterian. Christina was also listed as age 44. The children; Duncan age 17, Edwin age 15, Tryphena age 13 and Donalda age 8, were all listed as Presbyterians. However their names do not appear on the communion roles for the Presbyterian Church of St. John's in Port Perry. This would tend to suggest that they were Presbyterians but not energetically devoted to the church. The same can be said of Samuel Stoutt the former slave. He also listed himself as a Presbyterian in the 1881 census, but only his wife and children were on the church Communion roles. Port Perry High School principal Dugald McBride and his family were also on the communion roles of St. John's.

Port Perry High School

Edwin's brother Duncan passed the entrance examinations to the Toronto Medical School. Upon graduation in 1885 Duncan set up practice in Scott Township to the north of Port Perry, remaining there for four years before embarking on what amounted to a tour of North America, practicing in places as far apart as Niagara Falls and Rossland B.C. before eventually settling in New York State.

Donald Campbell continued to own his acreage on lot 10, concession 13 in Saintfield renting it out to Stewart Graham. (1877 to 1886)

On August 16, 1883 the *Observer* emphasized yet again the accomplishments of the staff and students of Port Perry High School with a heading *Crossed the Rubicon*;

> We have before us a list of the names of eighteen pupils of Port Perry High School who have succeeded in crossing the intellectual Rubicon: eighteen additional proofs of the intellectual stamina of the youths and young ladies of this favoured section of the country, but they also furnish eighteen additional testimonials of the excellence of the Port Perry Schools, the superiority of their teachers and their marked successes as instructors. The Port Perry High School stands prominently

> *forward amongst our higher educational institutions, it is worthy of such prominence, the success of its students establishes its claim.*[28]

The article then goes on to name the eighteen students and among them, enrolled in medicine, are Edwin Campbell and Walter Gillespie. Gillespie was later to marry Edwin's sister Tryphena.

Edwin's mother Christina had a brother Neil McArthur. He and his wife Mary Ann Watson had three sons who all boarded with the Campbells so that they could attend Port Perry High School. All three also became doctors, and attended medical school in Toronto following Duncan and Edwin. Edwin's three cousin doctors, however, were much younger: Archibald Donald McArthur born in 1879, Edwin Campbell McArthur born in 1887 and John Archibald McArthur in 1889. All three are buried beside their parents in the Greenbank cemetery just south of Saintfield where Edwin was born in 1866.

At the age of sixteen, Edwin won accolades outside the intellectual theatre. At a cricket match between Sunderland and Port Perry held on August 16, 1882, Edwin distinguished himself by scoring the second highest number of runs on his team even though he was the youngest player. His feat earned the following praise in the *Observer* published on August 16,

> *E. Campbell carried his bat with 23 to his name, his innings being, for a young cricketer, a masterpiece of cricket. Sincerely do we hope that his successful innings may act as a stimulus to the other young cricketers of this village...the style in which Eddy Campbell "cut" would have done credit to an older and experienced player.*[29]

Cricket had been introduced to Canada by the earliest settlers from Britain and by the late 1860s it had become the game of the summer, attracting

---

28 *Ontario Observer*, (Port Perry), August 16, 1883.

29 *Ontario Observer*, (Port Perry), August 16, 1882.

teams from many local hamlets and villages. A flourishing league had blossomed by 1870, a league which included teams from Greenbank, Sunderland, Wick and Vroomanton to the north, Uxbridge to the west as well as Prince Albert and Port Perry. As a sign of sibling rivalry Edwin's older brother Duncan, home from medical school for the summer of 1882, organized a Lacrosse club in Port Perry. On his team was the young Herbert Bruce, Edwin's friend. That sport lasted only a few summers and by 1890 the cricket league also faded as baseball took over.

It should be remembered that this nineteenth century phase of the Campbell lineage was living through a period when the father's word was law, his will dominant and his opinion undisputable. All of the children in turn left the neighbourhood to establish their own domain. Whether they left as a result of Donald's magnanimity and encouragement or through a sense of rebellion, is difficult to determine. Neither do we know the level of fondness which existed among the Campbell family members, however there was a clear level of loyalty which they showed by joining each other to celebrate moments of joy and sadness, even though they had spread out across the continent. That evaluation was further born out when Edwin later came to the aid of his sister and her husband when they experienced a period of extreme financial difficulty.

Many of the friendships that Edwin had established in Port Perry during his youth would have an impact on his adult life, but Sam McLaughlin, Herbert Bruce and Llewellys Barker would play the most important roles.

Chapter Three

UNIVERSITY AND MEDICAL PRACTICE

Victoria College

The town of Cobourg poised on the north shore of Lake Ontario rivalled Hamilton, Toronto and Kingston as the lake's primary port for the first half of the nineteenth century. The town plunged itself into ambitious projects such as its railway and harbour development and the impressive Victoria Hall. The town even launched its own university, Victoria College, in 1835. Seven years later the university secured a royal charter and was granted the rights to confer degrees in the arts and sciences. But the industrial and commercial development failed to keep pace with the town's demands for funds and by 1860, mired in debt, Cobourg began to settle into a quiet obscurity.

There were two medical schools in Toronto, the Medical School at Trinity College affiliated with the Anglican Church and the Toronto School of Medicine attended largely by non Anglicans. The Toronto School of Medicine (TSM) was founded in 1843 and incorporated in 1851. But in 1854 an event took place which proved to be momentous for Toronto, indeed for Upper Canada. On October 3, Dr Aikins presented a motion to the Victoria College Board in Cobourg. He proposed that the Toronto School of Medicine should be incorporated with or merged into, Victoria College and become its medical department. The Victoria College board quickly responded in the affirmative with Dr. Rolph, Dr. Workman, Dr. Aikins, Dr. Wright and Dr. Barret as the professors. The agreement was ratified on October 18, 1854. Even though the main university building was in Cobourg, classes for medicine were held in Toronto. In 1887, the TSM was reconstituted as the University of Toronto Medical Faculty and three years later Victoria College itself moved to Toronto to become part of the University of Toronto.

In the 1880s enrolment at university was a privilege enjoyed by less than 2% of the population of the youth of Ontario. Dugald McBride's efforts at Port Perry High School resulted in an unheard of range of between 10 and 30 percent of his graduating students enrolling at university. When Edwin entered the halls of the Victoria College Toronto School of Medicine, he had the company of Llewellys Barker and Walter Gillespie as classmates and his brother beginning his fourth and final year of medical studies. H.A. Bruce was to follow three years later.

Medical Studies

This was an exciting period in the development of medicine. In 1846 the American dentist William Thomas Morton had demonstrated the use of ether as an anaesthetic. The following year, at Edinburgh University, James Young Simpson, a professor of midwifery, demonstrated the use of chloroform as an anaesthetic. Joseph Lister, professor of surgery at Glasgow University developed the science of antiseptics and his friend Louis Pasteur in France was discovering the role of micro-organisms in spreading disease. Using these new studies, William Halsted, at Johns Hopkins in the United States was able to successfully carry out major surgical procedures such as the removal of cancerous growths in the stomach. Lister's emphasis on cleanliness through antisepsis procedures was largely embraced by William Aikins,[30] Edwin's teacher in surgical procedures. The use of the microscope to identify bacteria was creating an exciting new approach to medicine. With this method Freidrich Loffler had just discovered the cause of diphtheria and in 1877, in Germany, Robert Koch had isolated the anthrax bacteria and five years later the bacterium which caused tuberculosis. The following year, 1883, he discovered the bacteria for cholera. He was later to receive the Nobel Prize in Medicine for his work (1905). Immediately following these discoveries Professor Ramsay Wright at the TSM introduced courses in which microscopy was used to identify these and other bacteria. Shortly after Edwin's graduation, Wright was sent to Germany to work with Koch and study his techniques.[31]

A doctor who had a particular influence on Edwin was Dr James F.W. Ross an expert in gynecology. Ross was renowned for his meticulous record keeping in all the details of his hundreds of deliveries. Between 1871 and 1891 Ross had detailed records of 2850 deliveries.[32] Later while at medical school, H.A. Bruce acted as a secretary for Ross, recording the details of these deliveries for him.[33]

By the time Llewellys Barker had entered his third year at the TSM he had become an acknowledged expert in anatomy. Ever the opportunist, he was giving demonstrations in anatomy to younger students, for a fee. Edwin took advantage of this opportunity, as did H.A. Bruce three years later.[34] Needless to say, Barker placed first in his graduating class. In 1883, four years before Edwin's graduation, Augusta Stowe received her M.D. from Victoria College and became the first woman to graduate from a Canadian medical school.

---

30 Charles Godfrey, <u>Aikins of the U of T Medical Faculty,</u>(Toronto, University of Toronto Press, 1998), p. 228

31 Charles Godfrey, <u>Bruce: Surgeon, Soldier, Statesman, Sonofa</u>. (Madoc, Ontario, Codam Press, 2001), p. 7.

32 Charles Godfrey, <u>Aikins of the U of T. Medical Faculty</u> p. 197.

33 Charles Godfrey, <u>Bruce: Surgeon, Soldier, Statesman,</u> Sonofa p. 7.

34 H.A. Bruce, <u>Varied Operations</u> (Toronto, Longmans Green and Company, 1958), pp.34,35.

Graduation

May 1887 was a time of unprecedented excitement and promise for Edwin Campbell, for in this month he became Doctor Edwin Campbell with the potential of a lucrative and interesting career ahead of him. He also had the luxury of having a number of practical choices to make. He could stay in Port Perry to join Drs. Jones, Clemens and McClinton in a pleasant community with all his family and friends. He could also consider joining his brother in Scott Township to the north of Port Perry. Another alternative was to reject the comfortable choice of home and accept the invitation to join Dr. Charles Jones in Imlay City, Michigan. Yet another consideration was to shake the dust of Port Perry off his shoes and venture into a completely new environment.

Illustration #2. Dr. Edwin Ruthven Campbell shortly after graduation from Medical School in Toronto.

His first decision was clear: he went home and on May 11, registered himself as a physician in Port Perry. There is no doubt that at some time Edwin had considered settling in his home town, but one issue that weighed against that decision was that Port Perry had reached a period of stagnation. By the end of the decade, the depletion of the timber stands in the Lake Scugog basin, combined with the financial crisis of 1876 which had been precipitated by the collapse of the lumber market in New York in 1875, resulted in Canada's lumber exports dropping to a half of the 1873 level.[35] The consequence of these events was the closure of all but one of Port Perry's waterfront sawmills. The vast timber stands to the north and north east of Lake Scugog were largely under the control of entrepreneurs such as Mossum Boyd at Bobcaygeon. The products of his mills were transported by the Midland Railway south to Port Hope on the north shore of Lake Ontario, thus bypassing Port Perry and the port at Whitby.

From the appearance of the first steamboat on Lake Scugog in 1851, the water traffic on the lake ferrying goods between Lindsay and Port Perry and the various small ports in between enjoyed a steady growth until a decision was made to extend the railway from Port Perry to Lindsay. When the first regular train ran in to Lindsay in 1877, it eliminated the need for steamboat traffic between the two towns. The steamboats were then reduced to operating leisurely day picnics and weekend excursions for vacationers.

As a result of the horrendous fire of 1884 which destroyed the entire downtown core of Port Perry, the ships and trains of Port Perry were given a brief reprieve as they were used to bring building supplies to the community, lumber from Mossum Boyd's Bobcaygeon mill, bricks from the Fox brickyard in Lindsay and goods from Toronto to replace those lost in the fire. The business section was completely rebuilt by the fall of 1885 and Port Perry settled into a comfortable, self sustained existence by the time that Edwin entered his final year of medical school. The village's

---

35   W.T. Easterbrook and Hugh Aitken, <u>Canadian Economic History</u>, (Toronto, University of Toronto Press, 1990), p. 392.

population dropped to around 1600 and remained at that level until the mid twentieth century.

The railway from Whitby to Port Perry, built too late to attract trade into the region, was mired in debt, and the number of daily runs to Whitby was already being reduced from four to one. The closure of the lumber mills in Port Perry and the lack of growth in the community provided limited employment and career potential for local youth.

As the economic slowdown became apparent, articles began to appear in the Port Perry newspapers, articles that commented on lure of the west. These articles began to appear on a frequent, almost weekly basis in 1882.

> **Go West Young Man Go West.**
> *... for there cannot be a shadow of a doubt that the new and fertile lands of the West offer facilities for bettering the circumstances of active and persevering young men...*
> *... it pinches pretty hard when our desirable young men leave us to go west. Port Perry has a little too much experience of that of late, several of our young men whom we would gladly retain among us are moving west....*
>
> *It was only a few days ago that we were called upon to bid adieu to an active young man of much promise who is off for the west. Again on Saturday evening last on the occasion of two of our worthy young men going west to locate and several others going west to investigate, large numbers of their fellow townsmen determined to give them a becoming sendoff entertained them to a complimentary supper in the Mansion House here. Messrs H.S. Campbell [no relation] and Robert Ross are leaving for good.*[36]

---

36 <u>Ontario Observer</u> *(Port Perry) January 26, 1882.*

The following article appeared on March 9, 1882:

> **Manitoba and the Great North-West.**
> Parties setting out for Manitoba or any other portion of the great North-West will consult their own comfort and the interest of their pocket by purchasing through tickets at W.H.McCaw's Jewellery Establishment.[37]

And on April 20, the following:

> **TAKING OUR YOUNG MEN**
> The numerous attractions of Manitoba are drawing off our young men, very many of whom we would rather keep among us. On Tuesday 18th inst, Manchester contributed a valuable contingent.[38]

A week later the following item appeared:

> H.G. Coram, the station agent at Port Perry announces that "I have received instruction from the Grand Trunk Railway to check baggage through by all train stations in Dakota and Manitoba."[39]

Such reports would not have been ignored by Edwin and his family in Port Perry.

Dr. H.A. Bruce, in his autobiography, stated clearly;

> At this time, many of my own classmates were finding their way to the United Sates with its opportunities for larger

---

[37] *Ontario Observer,* (Port Perry) March 9, 1882.

[38] *Ontario Observer,* (Port Perry) April 20, 1882.

[39] *Ontario Observer* (Port Perry) April 26, 1882.

> incomes and for a wider variety of medical experience than
> Canada could at that time offer.[40]

This insight provided retrospectively by his schoolmate, may be one of the more critical influences which drove Edwin to the United States, but there are other considerations that may have played a part in his decision. Did he wish to escape the turmoil and confusion which surrounded him in his youth: the Orangemen, the Temperance movement, the attitude of Loyalism and its anti-American sentiment? Or was he driven by some deep genetic urge for adventure or rebellion, the same kind of urge that drove his grandparents to leave their Highland Homes in search of a better life in Canada? Tellingly, time and time again, Edwin made the false claim that he was born in Scotland, even in important legal documents such as passport applications.

Nevertheless, given his own background, Edwin's decision to set up his first practice in the United States was undoubtedly one made after long and serious deliberation. Edwin's friend Sam McLaughlin had a brother John who graduated from the Ontario College of Pharmacy in 1885. Immediately upon graduation in 1885 he moved to Brooklyn, New York and made a successful start to his career there, although he later returned to Canada. The success of Dr. George Jones in Imlay City, Michigan and the respect he earned every time he returned to Port Perry was obvious. Both successes probably had an influence on Edwin's decision. In addition Port Perry was already being adequately served by its three Hippocratic practitioners and a fourth, Dr. Elisha Jessop, joined them in June 1887. Edwin probably saw that the potential for a successful practice in Port Perry was somewhat limited at that time. It is evident that his visit home to his parents and friends in the community did not provide the young physician with motivation to remain.

There was a new and refreshing air of confidence about opportunities in the United States. Its westward expansion, despite the total disregard for the rights of its indigenous peoples, created an air of optimism. The

---

40   H.A. Bruce, <u>Varied Operations</u>. p 68

addition to the Union of Kansas in 1861, Nevada in 1864, Nebraska in 1867 and Colorado in 1876, opened up more opportunities for the adventurous. This optimism was reflected in its annual immigration figures, rising from 400,000 in 1870 to 789,000 in 1882.[41]

Canada had become dependent upon trade for its survival. At the time of Confederation Canada's major trading partner had been the mother country, Great Britain. During the next few decades, as the United States demonstrated its increasing reluctance to interfere with Canada's sovereignty, trade with the United States increased, and by 1883 Canada's imports from the United States surpassed those from the mother country.[42]

For Edwin, this was clearly a time to assert his independence and put aside the antagonism toward the United States that had so dominated the attitudes of his parents and their peers, and consider the opportunities that were available to those courageous enough to take them. He spent the remainder of his life as a resident of the United States. Over the years Edwin paid occasional visits to Port Perry and he would frequently call on his Canadian friends for advice and support, but his true links to the community were severed the day he boarded the train for Michigan.

Dr. Edwin Campbell of St. Ignace

Edwin left Port Perry and made his way to Imlay City, Michigan, to visit Dr. George Jones and then took the train north to St. Ignace. On June 20, 1887 he registered as a physician in St Ignace in the County of Mackinaw, Michigan.[43] He was to remain there for over four years. All the factors which drew the young Doctor Edwin Campbell to open his first private practice in Saint Ignace in the remote northern peninsula of Michigan will remain elusive. The absence of diaries, correspondence or any writings of

---

41 U.S. Bureau of the Census. *Historical Statistics of the United States* (Washington D.C.; Government Printing Office, 1975), Series C89.

42 W.T.Easterbrook and Hugh G.J. Aitken, *Canadian Economic History*, p. 403.

43 *Statements of Medical Practitioners 1883-1889, Records of Mackinac County*, Rg 72-137. Archives of Michigan.

a personal nature from this period of his life can only lead to speculation when considering the reasons for Edwin's move to Northern Michigan. It was obvious that Edwin had decided to reject many of the prevailing attitudes which surrounded him in his youth. He certainly never followed his father's interest in Orangism. On the other hand, his father had rejected the Temperance sentiment of Saintfield and Greenbank, and Edwin followed that pattern. Like his father, Edwin was not a strong Presbyterian; indeed he was not looked upon by any of his friends or associates as a notably religious person. Edwin also followed his father's example by becoming a mason while in St. Ignace. It is quite possible that accounts of life in Saint Ignace evoked in Edwin, a sense of nostalgia for the days of his youth in Port Perry. With a population of around 3,000, almost twice Port Perry's, Saint Ignace had become what Port Perry had been in its past; a thriving lumber town and a bustling port. St Ignace was strategically located in the centre of the Straits of Mackinac between Lakes Huron and Michigan and provided a respite for the steamboats plying the Detroit to Chicago route.

Dr. George Howell of Tecumseh Michigan, representing the Lenawee district of Michigan in the House of Representatives, was concerned about the health and safety of the people of Michigan. He pushed for the standardization of certification and training of the doctors who served its citizens. The bill which he proposed was approved in 1883. All practitioners had to register within three months of beginning practice. Dr. Edwin Campbell registered two months within the law's requirements. In the sworn statement he declared that he had been in practice for one month. After completing his legal requirements he settled into caring for the health of the citizens of St. Ignace. All further records of his practice here appear to have been lost. It is probable that much of his practice involved dealing with the workers of the numerous lumber camps in the area. It later became apparent that his practice was a financial success.

In spite of the absence of further records of his medical practice in St. Ignace there are certain records of his social life. Shortly after his arrival in St. Ignace, Edwin decided to follow his father's footsteps by becoming a mason. He joined the St. Ignace Lodge # 369 and received the first three degrees of membership during his four years in the community. A strange facet of his membership in the masons is that in it he stated that he was born in Inverary, Scotland and not in Saintfield near Port Perry Ontario. This may have been predicated by his decision to join the Scottish rights of the Masons. He repeated this false claim of birthplace again later in his life, yet on all his future travels, particularly on all his many trans-Atlantic crossings, he always declared to customs and travel officials the truth that he had been born in Canada.

One condition of the Masons was that members were expected to have a church affiliation. In St. Ignace the only churches were the Methodist, Roman Catholic and Episcopalian. In the absence of a Presbyterian Church, Edwin changed his affiliation to the Episcopalian church and attended the Church of the Good Shepherd built in 1882.

A Chance Meeting

The more wealthy citizens of Michigan and surrounding states were abuzz with anticipation in the spring of 1887. Even those who merely aspired to wealth joined in the excitement. The Grand Hotel on Michigan's Mackinac Island was about to welcome its first guests. The Grand Hotel was the largest summer hotel in the world with 325 rooms and an enormous, elegant, 660 foot long, white columned verandah with commanding views of the Straits of Mackinac. It was the place to be, and the place to be seen.

On May 24 Clara Durant, wife of wealthy Flint carriage maker William (Billy) C. Durant, gave birth to their first child, a girl whom they named Margery. The Grand Hotel was an ideal place for Clara to spend a relaxing holiday in July and it was an ideal place for her husband Billy Durant to make contacts among the more wealthy citizens of the Midwest.

A pleasant 5-hour train ride to Mackinac City, then a refreshing steam ferry ride to the Island followed by a short carriage ride placed them in the lap of luxury at the hotel. Even today, visitors have to travel by horse drawn carriages to the Grand Hotel as automobiles are still forbidden on Mackinac Island.

In the daytime Clara and Billy could stroll along the huge verandah with their baby carriage and its contents, attracting the admiration of their fellow guests. In the evening after the formal dinner (it remains formal to this day) the gentlemen could retire to a room set aside for their pleasure: the Casino where they could relax with a huge cigar, a glass of bourbon and engage in a few hands of poker, legally.

It was on one of these evenings that the wealthy carriage maker from Flint happened to meet a young Canadian doctor, now situated in St. Ignace, a mere ferry ride to the north of the Island. The doctor spent several summer weekends at the hotel over the next few years. Billy was later to say, tongue in cheek, that the doctor's skill at the poker table was superior to his skill with a surgeon's knife. We will probably never know when the carriage maker suggested to the doctor that he consider opening a practice in Flint, but he did. Dr. Edwin Campbell was later (1894) to open his practice in the growing town of Flint with the Durant family as his favoured patients.

Billy Durant

In September 1886, as Edwin was entering classes for his final year of medical training, a series of events was taking place three hundred miles to the west. These events would completely change the course of Edwin's life and, indeed, the lives of millions around the globe.

Billy Durant had taken a ride in a brand new horse drawn cart owned by his friend John Alger. Durant was immensely impressed with the comfort and steadiness of the ride. When they came to a stop, Billy dismounted and walked slowly around the vehicle studiously looking at all the details of the suspension and the cart's construction details. He was so impressed that he noted the name of the manufacturer and after his meeting, Billy boarded a train for Coldwater, a 120 mile journey where he made his way to the Coldwater Road Cart Company. There he met the owners of the company, Thomas O'Brien and William Schmedlen. After a long discussion, Billy made them an offer for the entire operation including the patent for the innovative suspension which had so intrigued him in his first ride. Before he left Coldwater he had obtained a legal bill of sale without any money changing hands! The next morning, back in Flint, Billy entered the Citizen's National Bank and arranged for a loan of $2000 to cover the cost of his purchase. Later that day he encountered his friend Dallas Dort. Billy told Dallas of his venture and Dallas, captivated by the undertaking offered to buy a half interest in the enterprise. The two shook hands to close the arrangement. On acceptance of the partnership, Dort sold his small share in a hardware business to devote his time and money to the new enterprise. The two young men decided to name their business the Flint Road Cart Company.

Illustration #3: Billy Durant

William "Billy" Crapo Durant was born on December 8, 1861 to Rebecca Crapo and William Clark Durant in New Bedford, Massachusetts. Billy's mother was one of ten children of Henry Howland Crapo and his wife Mary Ann (Slocum). Henry Howland Crapo had been born in Dartmouth Massachusetts, worked at a variety of tasks in order to increase his financial worth and the status of his growing family. His ventures were predominantly in the sales field (real estate and farm produce) but he also took on accounting and even became a town clerk and tax collector in New Bedford.

When Michigan became a state in 1837 it attracted the attention of land speculators and entrepreneurs in the New England states. At the age of 51 in 1854, Henry Crapo joined those adventurous speculators, leaving the comfortable New Bedford atmosphere for the wilds of Michigan. To further his plans he purchased a sawmill in Flint. Four years later he brought his family from New Bedford and plunged into the life of a lumber mill owner in the growing frontier city.

The settlement had begun its days as a fur trading post in 1811, located on a relatively strategic spot on the Flint River which flowed north to Saginaw forming a link on the Detroit to Lake Huron route. By the time of Crapo's venture, Flint had become a progressive and civilized community. It had banks, schools, churches, sawmills and newspapers, a Masonic order, a High School for deaf and blind students, and with a population of over 2,000 it was officially classified as a city in 1855.

Crapo poured his energies into the mill and then into organizing a railroad to link Flint with the main railway at Holly. This enabled him to give year round access to lumber markets across the nation. His business successes led to his election as Mayor of Flint in 1860 and then to the Michigan Senate two years later. He successfully ran as governor of Michigan in 1864 and was re-elected in 1866. All through his political career he continued to administer his lumber enterprises.

Henry Howland Crapo's seemingly boundless energy was costly. He began to suffer from bladder problems and internal hemorrhages in 1867. His condition deteriorated gradually until 1869 when, following surgery, he passed away on the twenty-third of July.

Henry and Mary Ann Crapo had produced nine daughters and one son. The son, William Wallace Crapo had become a successful lawyer in New Bedford, Massachusetts. One of the girls, Rhoda married James Willson, a Canadian who had left his home near Guelph at age sixteen to seek his fortune in the California Gold Rush. His plan was thwarted by illness so he settled into the new field of photography before entering the teaching profession. From there he returned to school to the

University of Michigan and graduated in medicine in 1857 and opened his practice in Flint.

Billy Durant's father William Clark Durant was born in Lempster, New Hampshire in 1827. He drifted through several jobs without the drive or determination of his future father-in-law. In 1855 Durant was a lowly bank clerk and in Henry Crapo's eyes he was a lowly prospect for his daughter. Nevertheless, on November 29 William Durant married Crapo's daughter Rebecca. Two years later a daughter, Rebecca was born and on December 8, 1861 Rebecca gave birth to their second child William Crapo Durant.

After Crapo's move to Flint, the Durants remained in New Bedford but exchanged visits a few times each year. Henry Crapo tried to draw his son-in-law into his remaining business dealings in New Bedford, but became discouraged with Durant's lack of drive and business acumen. Durant made an attempt at stock broking but this ended in disaster. In the end he lost his savings, but more importantly he lost the respect of his in-laws, and particularly that of his father-in-law. He then began to seek solace in alcohol. The Crapos, father and son, made several attempts to save Rebecca's husband from total disaster. None were successful.

In 1869 Durant abandoned his wife and their two children, 15-year-old Rebecca, who went by the nickname of Rosa, and ten-year-old Billy. Rebecca Durant and the children moved to Flint in 1872 to live with her sister Rhoda and her husband, Dr. James Willson. During the ensuing years Durant occasionally wrote to Rebecca and to the Crapos. When William Crapo was serving in the House of Representatives in 1875, he received a letter from Durant asking for a job but Crapo had lost all faith in Durant and refused to help him. Durant died in 1883 in East Lempster when Billy was twenty one years old. It is doubtful that Durant saw his children at all during the last five years of his life.

After being abandoned by his father the dominating male influence in Billy's life became his grandfather. Among the Durant papers are several letters written by Henry Howland Crapo to his grandson Billy; they reflect a caring, affectionate and compassionate grandfather. On the death of Henry Howland Crapo in 1869 Billy's two uncles, William Crapo and James Willson had a strong influence on the young boy.

Upon reaching the age of seventeen Billy left Flint High School and sought employment in his grandfather's lumber mill, the Crapo Lumber Company. No favours of a financial or physical nature were extended to the youth. His first job was outside in the yard stacking lumber at seventy cents a day. To supplement his relatively meager income, in the evenings he worked as a clerk in the Flint Drugstore.

By 1880 the lumber mills of many towns in North America were looking ahead to a somewhat bleak future. The lumber stands around Flint and Port Perry were rapidly approaching complete depletion. No reforestation projects had been undertaken. At the national and continental level this timber dilemma reached the New York Stock Exchange in 1875 when the bottom fell out of the lumber market. One by one the lumber mills of Flint and Port Perry closed their doors and Port Perry had a further problem to deal with. In July 1884 a devastating fire destroyed the entire downtown core of the community. More than eighty stores were burned to the ground

While Port Perry struggled to rebuild and re-establish its economical and commercial base while simultaneously seeking to compensate for the absence of the waterfront lumber mills, Flint also looked for alternative opportunities for its workforce. Wagon and carriage making proved to be the panacea for Flint's ailing economy. Other enterprises, including cigar making, played supporting roles.

Young Billy tried his hand at selling cigars. He met the challenge with amazing success. He then took on the role of secretary of Flint's waterworks where his responsibilities included collecting overdue bills. Again his youthful energy and exuberance came to the fore. His next venture was in the Fire Insurance business. He again succeeded and simultaneously became part owner of the Casino Rolling Rink.

In 1885 it was customary for gentlemen who had plans for marriage to have a home to take their brides after marriage. Billy put a down payment on a house at the corner of Garland and Fourth Streets in Flint. On June 17, 1885, William Crapo Durant married the pretty 23 year old Clara Miller Pitt, daughter of Ralph Pitt, agent of the Flint and Marquette Railway Station in Flint.

Illustration #4: Clara Pitt, prior to her marriage to Billy Durant

Dallas Dort

Dallas Dort, not quite a year older than Durant, had trained to be a teacher but a career in business and commerce lured him away from the classroom. At the time of his decision to join Durant in the cart building business he was the manager of a hardware store in Flint. Durant knew Dort well enough to realize that their combined talents and youthful enthusiasm had immense potential. Further, Dort was able to add $1,000 to the enterprise.

That handshake with Billy on September 28 initiated a flurry of activity. They had agreed that Dort would supervise production while Durant would look after sales, promotion and financing. To begin their venture, they opened a bank account and then rented a small warehouse in which to establish their factory. All the equipment and supplies in Coldwater were immediately shipped by rail to Flint. But before that had arrived Durant had arranged for an example of their cart to be shipped to Madison, Wisconsin to the Agricultural Fair where he would begin his sales campaign.

At the fair he demonstrated his cart so successfully that he earned a Blue Ribbon for the cart. He then parlayed his Blue Ribbon into a contract to deliver 100 carts to a Wisconsin dealer. From Madison he traveled east to Milwaukee to further demonstrate and promote the cart. He returned a week later to report his success to Dort; a total order for 600 carts. In its first year of business, 1886, the Flint Road Cart company sold 4,000 of its two-wheeled carts. Unable to meet that level of production, they contracted W.A. Paterson, another Flint cart manufacturer, to build carts to the Dort-Durant specifications. Paterson was also a Canadian who had learned the art of carriage making at his uncle's shop in Guelph Ontario and then set up his own factory in Flint in 1869. At the time that Durant and Dort approached Paterson to produce carts for them, he was the largest producer of carts in Flint.

Slowly Dort and Durant gathered around them a core of dedicated and capable workers. Among them was Charles W. Nash, born in 1862 into a poverty stricken family in DeKalb, Illinois. Nash and his wife Jessie Hallock moved to Flint in 1889 and he found work in a hardware and grocery store. In town he came into contact with Dort and Durant and was hired to work in their Flint Road Cart company in 1891. He started work in the cushion department and became superintendant of that department in a matter of months. When the factory was reorganized in 1898, his leadership abilities were noted as he was appointed superintendant of the entire factory.

In 1892 the company bought an abandoned farm machinery plant and in it they began production of wagons under the name of the Webster Vehicle Company. Two years later they established the Victoria Vehicle Company in what had been Durant's uncle James' general store. Confusion arose between Durant and Dort's Flint Road Cart Company and the rival Flint Wagon Works. In light of this problem, the company was completely restructured in 1895 and renamed the Durant-Dort Carriage Company with the Webster Vehicle Company and the Victoria Vehicle Company as its subsidiaries. The quality improved and more sales followed. At the peak of its production, 1906, the year's output reached 56,000 vehicles at the Flint facility.[44]

Meanwhile Clara had given birth to two children. Margery arrived in 1887 and a second and final child Russell Clifford was born in 1890. It was during this period that Durant began to take his small family on summer holidays to Mackinac Island and met Dr. Edwin Campbell.

Illustration #5: Billy's First Wife Clara Pitt with their children: Clifford (left) and Margery (right).

---

44 Lawrence Gustin, <u>Billy Durant: Creator of General Motors</u>. *(Grand Rapids, Michigan, William B. Eerdmans Publishing Company, 1973), p. 48.*

In Flint during Christmas of 1895, Durant came up with the idea of building a low priced cart to be sold for cash only. Dort reluctantly agreed but was somewhat more supportive when Durant hired Alexander Brownell Cullen Hardy as the plant manager. A.B.C. Hardy was a mutual friend who was currently manager of the Wolverine Road Cart Company. The new low priced Durant-Dort cart was named the Diamond Buggy.

Durant and Dort came to the realization that by controlling all the supplies and component parts used in the building of the carts they could be more efficient and cost effective. Everything from the various types of wood, the wheels and axles, to the paints and varnish and even the brackets for holding buggy whips- full control of these items and materials would result in a cheaper vehicle. Durant took on the responsibility of finding some way of taking full management of the suppliers.

In 1897 he created the Flint Gear and Top Company. The following year he bought the Imperial Wheel Company in Jackson. Two years later he bought a farm north of Flint in order to establish a noisy Flint Axle Works. He also took control of mills and timber stands in Arkansas and Tennessee. With the creation of the Flint Varnish Works in 1901 he had made the manufacture of his wagons no longer dependent on other suppliers for components and accessories. To further speed up production he moved all his factories to Flint.

The time and energy involved in managing and coordinating the factories, their products and the numerous plant managers, placed an ever increasing strain on a seemingly tireless Billy Durant. He in turn placed pressure on all around him including the close friends that he employed. Even Dort himself left the company in 1898 but returned to the excitement and stress two years later.

Also among those who succumbed to the pressure was A.B.C. Hardy. Sensing Hardy's fatigue, Durant sent the exhausted man and his wife on holiday to Europe in 1901. Charles Nash was appointed as general superintendent in his place. While in Paris, Hardy attended the Exposition held there and became intrigued with the automobiles on display. His fascination evolved into an obsession and he began an earnest study of the vehicles and their manufacturers, visiting the makers' workshops in the backyard sheds, barns, warehouses and factories of France.

The First Autos

The creation of the first four cycle internal combustion engine is credited to Nicolaus Otto in Germany in 1876. He exhibited his engine at the 1873 Paris Exposition and it earned him several awards. Otto's concept was further developed by a number of German and French engineers in the following decade. By 1885 Gottleib Daimler and Wilhelm Maybach, former engineers for Otto, developed their own engines. Later that year Carl Benz in Stuttgart installed a more refined engine in the back of a tricycle, the first vehicle to be considered as an automobile. This was exhibited at the Paris Exposition of 1889 creating a demand for the vehicle resulting in a number of sales that year. Daimler used his engine to power a four wheeled vehicle in 1886. In France Emile Levassor and Rene Panhard took a Daimler engine, developed and refined it to produce their own cars in 1890. Two years later this company produced what may be the first car advertising catalogue or sales brochure. Levassor changed the centrally engined chassis layout and introduced the first front engine, rear wheel drive vehicle in 1891, setting the trend for today's cars.

While Benz and Daimler manufactured the first practical automobiles and began producing them for sale, the mantle of automobile development and manufacture was quickly taken up by the French. By 1890 France led the world in automobile production. By 1901 there were 130 automobile manufacturers in the Paris district alone. The city became the world's largest market for cars and the world centre for automobile production. Companies such as Panhard, Mors, Renault and De Dion-Bouton were all significant Paris area producers of automobiles. Incorporated in 1893 the De Dion-Bouton company began its operations producing steam engined automobiles but switched to gasoline engines the following year. By 1900 it had become the largest manufacturer of automobiles in the world producing 440 cars and over 3200 engines that year. Later that year the company opened a factory in Brooklyn New York. The second ranking car producer was Panhard-Levassor with Peugeot in third place.

The first reliability run was held in 1894. This event, sponsored by *Le Petite Journal*, a Paris newspaper, ran from Paris to Rouen. The following year the world's first long distance race took place in which 22 automobiles ran from Paris to Bordeaux and back. The winning car was a Panhard-Levassor with an average speed of 15 miles an hour. Eight other vehicles finished the race. Immediately following the event the first car club was organized: the Automobile Club of France. This club had over 2,200 members by 1900.

By 1904 De Dion-Bouton was producing 2000 cars and 40,000 engines a year at its factory near Paris. In 1910 the company became the first in the world to successfully mass produce a V8 engine. Between 1895 and 1901 De Dion-Bouton sold over 15,000 vehicles and in addition, was selling thousands of engines to other vehicle manufacturers. Many of these engines were exported to Britain and the United States. The first Packards, Peerless and Pierce Arrow cars produced in the U.S. were powered by De Dion-Bouton engines, as were several British and German cars. Edwin Campbell's friend Dr. H.A. Bruce became the first doctor in Toronto to own a car. His was a De Dion-Bouton.

Early U.S. Autos

These events in Europe and particularly in France were not unnoticed in the United States, largely as a result of their extensive coverage in the press of the day. Newspapers made references to the advances being made around the world in the realm of motorized vehicles. Magazines such as The *American Machinist* and the weekly periodical, The *Scientific American*, were giving increasing attention to details of steam, electric and gasoline powered engines and their applications as stationary engines or in marine and road going vehicles. The magazines gave explanations and diagrams of how various forms of these vehicles functioned. The *Scientific American* devoted a large section of its magazine to the gasoline engines in 1892. By that time the magazine had a circulation of over fifty thousand. In 1895-96

The *American Machinist* had a series of articles on how to build gasoline engines for the application of road going vehicles; automobiles. Numerous fairs and exhibitions across the world gave attention to the latest developments in engines and transportation methods. In the United States the Philadelphia Centennial Exposition of 1876 had displays of functioning steam driven vehicles. Between 1887 and 1892 Ransom Olds produced and sold over 2000 steam powered stationary engines, sometimes misleadingly referred to as gasoline engines, but the gasoline was only used to heat water to produce steam for the engine's propulsion. The first exhibition devoted entirely to the Automobile was held in London England in 1895 and was attended by a large number of Americans. Five years later, in Chicago in September, the First International Automobile Exhibition and Tournament was held, the first of its kind in North America. This show was followed in November by the National Automobile show in Madison Square Gardens in New York. This was an overwhelming success.

Henry Ford had completed his first vehicle in Detroit in 1896, an event which had not passed unnoticed. In October 1901 he took his latest racing machine and, in front of several thousand people at a track at Gross Point Michigan, reached a speed of 60 miles an hour!

The Duryea brothers built what was probably the first automobile in the United States in 1893. The 1895 Paris-Bordeaux-Paris race stimulated immense interest in the automobile in the United States. Not to be outdone, the *Chicago Times Herald* sponsored the first U.S race a few months later. Although only six cars were entered, and most were European built, only two cars finished the 55 mile event: Duryea's car took first place; a German Benz was the only other finisher. This success led to the first sales of the Duryea car, the first U.S. produced vehicle to be sold. In attendance at the Chicago event were father and son bicycle manufacturers, Thomas B. Jeffery and his son Charles. Enthused by what they saw at the race, they began to experiment with gasoline powered automobiles and built their first successful operating model in 1897. They named their vehicle, "the Rambler" and exhibited two models of their car at the Madison Square

Gardens event in 1900. The following year the Jefferys were manufacturing Ramblers for sale and by the end of 1902 they had sold 1500 vehicles.[45]

On his return to Flint, just before Christmas 1901, A.B.C.Hardy anxiously awaited Durant's return from New York to tell him of his findings.

Edwin leaves St. Ignace

On August 25, 1892 a brief article appeared in the *North Ontario Observer* in Port Perry;

> *Dr. E. Campbell, second son of our worthy townsman Mr. D. Campbell, who has for the past five years been practicing his profession in St. Ignace, Michigan has sold his practice there and intends taking a special course in New York City, after which he will permanently locate in Chicago. The doctor has been highly successful and had a lucrative practice in St. Ignace and vicinity. He has a large balance to his credit in one of the monetary institutions of his adopted country.*[46]

Edwin's departure from St. Ignace marked another significant turning point in his life. As if to underline that turning point, immediately before his departure from St. Ignace, he stood before the circuit court judge on June 10, declared the appropriate oaths in order to sign his naturalization papers and become a citizen of the United States.[47]

Before heading for Europe, Edwin took advantage of the opportunity to visit his family in Port Perry. The occasion was the wedding of his sister Tryphena to a classmate of Edwin's at Port Perry High School and at Medical school, Dr. Walter Gillespie. The wedding took place at his parents' home in Port Perry in November. The service was conducted by the Rev. J. McMeehan assisted by the Rev. Mr. Whiteman. No

---

45   *Daimler-Chrysler Historical Collection, Detroit, Michigan.*

46   <u>North Ontario Observer</u> *(Port Perry) August 25, 1892*

47   *Passport application form, New York, May 4, 1921.*

doubt many guests were asking Edwin if he had any plans to lose his bachelorhood. He was able to inform them that he had no such plans. He then headed for Europe.

Edwin in Europe

Europe was a hive of activity for anyone involved in the field of medicine. In a letter to the editor written by Edwin in the *Flint Daily News* of July 27, 1896, Edwin stated:

> *I sought shelter beneath the Stars and Stripes and located at St. Ignace, Michigan at which place I remained in practice about four and a half years. Then being desirous of gaining further knowledge in my profession, I visited Europe and took special courses at the hospitals of London, Paris and Vienna, after which I travelled several months in Europe, spending some time in the hospitals of Berlin and other cities on the Continent.*[48]

At the Toronto School of Medicine Dr. James Ross had stirred Edwin's interest in the latest research on gynecology. Edwin's friend Herbert Bruce had acted as Ross's secretary for two years recording details of all the births carried out by Dr. Ross. The interests of Herbert and Dr. Ross probably had some influence on Edwin's decision to study gynecology. Upon arriving in England in the winter of late 1892 Edwin registered at the Hospital for Women, Soho Square, London.[49] Here he acted as an assistant while studying gynecology and obstetrics at the hospital.

At the time, Queen Victoria was still firmly on her throne and was to remain there until her death in 1901. The attitudes which the traditional stereotypical view of her era symbolized were slow to change. During the Victorian era female anatomy was firmly secreted away in an array of undergarments encased in rigid corsetry and this in turn was protected by

---

48   *Flint Daily News*, July 27, 1896.

49   *Flint Daily News*, April 3, 1894.

layers of crinolines, all engulfed in flowing gowns. This fashion of the era was emphatically symbolic of the attitudes toward female medical issues. The Gibson girl of the turn of the century, in spite of her statuesque and ephemeral beauty, still retained her highly corseted hourglass figure and this lasted until World War One.

The year 1920 in the United States became a symbol of radical change. The lobbying and protesting of women's rights groups finally brought about a constitutional amendment in Congress giving women the right to vote and with this legislation, the roaring twenties began. The flapper girls swept aside the corsets and gowns and Margaret Sanger's movement gained momentum:

> *"...claiming the right of women to own and control their own bodies- to experience their sexuality free of consequence, just as men had always done."*[50]

Margaret Sanger invented and popularized the term "birth control" and led the movement for the right to have an abortion, moving rights for women beyond the civil and political realm into the social and cultural domain. It is more than ironic that later, Edwin's daughter Edwina married Margaret Sanger's son Grant.

Before all these dramatic changes took place in the early twentieth century, studies of diseases of women were extremely rare. A pioneer in the study of female medical problems in the United States was Dr. J. Marion Sims who founded the first hospital for women in New York in 1855. In London, England, Dr. Protheroe Smith was the key figure behind the establishment of the Hospital for Women in Red Lion Square in London in 1843. In order to satisfy growing demand the hospital was relocated eight years later in larger accommodation at No 51 Soho Square but even this property had to be expanded by taking over neighbouring property in 1852. A decade later the hospital's in-patient capacity had

---

50   Ellen Chesler, <u>Woman of Valor; Margaret Sanger and the Birth Control Movement in America</u>. *(New York, Simon and Schuster Paperbacks, 2007), p. 420.*

grown to fifty beds. It wasn't until the 1870s that surgery such as hysterectomy and removal of ovarian abscesses was carried out. In 1884 the British Gynaecological Society was established, giving more credibility and respectability to the study of female medicine. By the time of Edwin's arrival the Hospital for Women had undertaken even further expansion to include more beds and a residence for nurses. As a result of Edwin's training in London he was well placed in the forefront of such studies. After spending most of the year 1893 at the Soho Hospital for Women, Edwin made his way to the continent and visited hospitals in Paris, Berlin and Vienna. He then returned to the United States and on February 14, 1894 registered as a physician and surgeon in Flint joining the four other doctors registered in the town.[51] Needless to say, he was the only doctor in the area who had any qualified training or expertise in female medicine.

---

51   *Records of Genesee County Professional register, Archives of Michigan V22 Rg 81-56*

Chapter Four

1902 AND THE CONSEQUENCES

Dr. Edwin Campbell of Flint

After his arrival in Flint in 1894 Dr. Edwin Campbell quickly gained the respect of the citizens of Flint. Lawrence Gustin, Durant's biographer says;

> "*Elderly citizens of Flint remember him as a dashing, handsome man and the city's most prominent obstetrician. It was said that to be well born a child had to be delivered by Dr. Campbell. He made his winter rounds in a red sleigh, his lap covered with furs, and all the young ladies and many of their mothers were properly impressed.*"[52]

The fact that Edwin was the personal physician to Flint's wealthiest man, W.C. Durant, and his family did not hurt his reputation. He took up residence at 516 Court Street East and had his medical offices at 426 Saginaw Street, the main street of Flint. The nature of his profession meant that the handsome thirty-year-old bachelor made contact with many of the

---

52   Lawrence Gustin, <u>Billy Durant</u>, pp. 79-81

ladies of the city, giving rise to envy and the usual gossip among the less scrupulous. In July 1896 this gossip became downright malicious.

In August 1895 Edwin took the train back to Port Perry to be present at the funeral of his brother-in-law Walter Gillespie. He died of heart failure at the age of only 29 years of age leaving his wife Tryphena and an infant daughter who had been named after her grandmother Christina Isabella. Dr. Gillespie had died in Cannington where the young family lived. Shortly after his death Tryphena moved back to Port Perry with her infant daughter and lived with her parents. Unfortunately tragedy hit her again that November as the one-year-old Christina died too. In the summer of 1896 Donald, Christina and Tryphena moved to a new home in Port Perry, a comfortable and elegant house at the south west corner of Queen and Crandell Streets, today's 126 Crandell Street. The house, with a sweeping verandah around its east and south sides, had been built twenty years earlier by Caleb Crandell, the son of Reach Township's first white settler, Reuben Crandell. When the Campbells purchased the house the deed was registered in Christina's name. Edwin returned to Port Perry again that summer to see his parents and sister in their new home.

By the time that Edwin returned to Flint after his third journey to Port Perry in a year rumours were circulating that he had been married before his arrival in Flint and had abandoned his wife and children and that his holiday was taken in order to visit them. These rumours were so prevalent that he felt compelled to write a letter to the editor of the *Flint Daily News* to set the matter straight.

> *During my late absence from the city to secure much needed rest, some persons, from motives best known to themselves, have seen fit to circulate and publish scandalous, libelous and malicious falsehoods to my whereabouts and past conduct. Since my return I have searched diligently to find the originator that I might obtain legal redress for the wrongs done me, but have utterly failed to find the source... I feel that I owe it to*

> *my friends and myself, inasmuch as I expect to make my home here, to give a public history of my past.*[53]

He followed with an unusual and false claim;

> *I was born in Inverary Scotland,[sic] on the 12th day of February, 1868, my father being Donald Campbell, a grain merchant, who removed with his family when I was one year of age to Toronto, Canada, where he, with other members of the family has remained, except for a few months each summer, which time is spent at Fort [sic] Perry on Lake Ontario. I attended school at Toronto and Fort [sic]Perry.* [54]

It is not clear why he felt it necessary to continue this false claim to have been born in Scotland. His claim of a birth year of 1868 may have been a misprint. He further mystifies the reader by claiming that his family home was in Toronto. He continued;

> *...I visited various other cities of the United States in search of a permanent location. I decided on Flint in 1894, since which time this city has been my home, and I hoped that my conduct had been such as to entitle me to the respect of the good people of this city.*
>
> *I have never been married: neither have I seriously contemplated the marital relation not because I did not believe such a condition would be for my own good and happiness, nor because I did not believe that a good and pure woman would do me credit as a helpmate, but rather because I believe a physician under thirty years of age had best worship alone at the shrine*

---

53   <u>Flint Daily News</u>, July 12, 1896.

54   Ibid.

> *of his profession. It seems strange that one who feels he has been guilty of no misconduct should be called upon to explain...*[55]

In the press there were no responses to his statement and Edwin continued his duties as a physician. His anguish over the allegations that gave rise to his letter was no doubt relieved by his friendship with Billy Durant and his family. Edwin had taken on the health of the Durant family as his personal focus and spent many hours with them dispensing his medical care but increasingly becoming a part of their social life. In addition Billy spent a considerable amount of time at Edwin's Court Street home sharing confidences of an intimate nature as Billy began to experience problems in his relationship with Clara. Edwin's home had another attraction; once Edwin's housekeeper had left for the evening, Edwin would gather some of his friends together for a few hands of poker. Billy thoroughly enjoyed the challenge of these evenings. In 1899 Edwin moved his practice down the street to 400 Saginaw while maintaining his Court Street residence.

Edwin continued his loyalty to the masons, but not in Flint. He journeyed to Bay City by train, a journey of forty miles to the north to maintain his fellowship. While living in Flint he rose up the Masonic ranks to the 32nd degree.

Autos in Flint

The time and energy involved in managing and coordinating the production of carriages and the personnel involved never seemed to affect the seemingly tireless Billy Durant. Durant's daughter Margery commented,

> *He slept only two or three hours a night. Like Edison he felt that too much sleep was unnecessary for some men. I suppose his intense pleasure and complete engrossment in his work buoyed him up. It was his daily tonic.*[56]

---

55 Ibid.

56 Margery Durant, <u>My Father</u>, p. 63.

Spurred on by his encounters with the development of the automobile in Europe, on his return to Flint, A.B.C. Hardy gave Billy an excited account of his experiences. Meanwhile, in Flint, momentous events were taking place not far away from the noise and smells of the factories. Several of its citizens were reading the newspapers and magazines and following the development of the horseless carriage with interest, and in their spare time were indulging in a universal pastime: they were tinkering.

In a carriage house behind his home in Flint, Judge Charles Wisner, who had built an x-ray machine for Edwin, built a one cylinder engine automobile. Wisner drove his noisy contraption around the streets of Flint disturbing its citizens in the fall of 1900. The following year with the aid of his friends, he built two more vehicles. That same year, 1901, a compatriot of Edwin Campbell, Dr. H. H. Bardswell, added his own backyard creation to the sights and sounds of the community. Not to be outdone, William Paterson bought an electric car to drive around the town. After his sojourn in Europe and a visit to the New York Motor Show, A.B.C. Hardy, now convinced of the viability of the automobile, decided to build gasoline powered cars himself. In the fall of 1901 he established the Flint Automobile Company and began building single cylinder engines. He bought axles from the Weston-Mott Company and bodies from the W.F. Stewart Company in Flint and by late 1903 over fifty of his Flint Roadsters were bouncing around the area. When the Association of Licensed Automobile Manufacturers demanded fifty dollars for every car that he had produced, Hardy abandoned his project and moved to Iowa.

Billy Durant was traveling the country promoting and selling his horse drawn vehicles and increasingly spending time in New York playing the stock market with considerable success. This factor, by design or accident widened the gap between Billy and Clara. Even by the late 1890s he failed to let Clara know where he was going or what he was doing. His office in New York, which he had opened in 1901, became a more permanent base for him and he failed to write to her or to respond to her letters.

Illustration #6: Margery as a child   Illustration #7: Margery as a child

During this period Billy's daughter Margery was enrolled at "The Castle," also known as Miss Mason's School for Girls, located in Tarrytown, New York. The school was located in a series of buildings on an eighteen acre property with a castle-like building at its centre. "The Castle" had been built in 1854-56 for John J. Herrick. Miss C.E. Mason bought the property in 1895 and opened her residential school for girls. The senior or "Upper School" accommodated up to 130 girls who took part in a four year College preparatory program. In the prospectus, Miss Mason stated, *"the girl's mind of today is more alert, more questioning, more swift, than the mind of twenty years ago."* [57] She further stated that one of the aims of the school was to develop, *"Directly by training and indirectly by its atmosphere of refinement, enthusiasm and friendliness, the school is developing the type of woman whose presence gives brightness and joy..."*[58]

Margery's Ride

In addition to the noisy contraptions devised by Bardswell, Wisner, Hardy and others, a few much more sophisticated machines from more experienced manufacturers in Europe began to appear on the streets of Flint. One such vehicle was that belonging to the parents of one of Margery Durant's friends. This vehicle, a French Panhard, was to profoundly affect the lives of the Durant family. In the summer of 1902 Margery was home for the summer vacation from Miss Mason's School for Girls. In her biography of Billy Durant entitled **My Father,** Margery gave an account of her ride in her friend's parents' automobile:

> *"Pops, I've ridden in a horseless carriage!"*
>
> *It was the summer of 1902. I could hardly wait to tell the great news to my father. My eyes must have shone as I cried it out to him. I was in my 'teens and wore a wide blue ribbon on my unbobbed hair.*

---

57   *Drawbridge*, a prospectus for Miss Mason's School for Girls, 1910.

58   Ibid.

The family of one of my schoolmates owned a Panhard—built by the same firm that had first put pneumatic tires on an automobile in 1892. When she asked me to go for a ride my heart missed a beat. An invitation to go up in an airplane today wouldn't have half the thrill in it.

"Of course!" I choked a little saying it.

But what would I wear? What should I wear? Goggles—I had no goggles. But they were terribly necessary: no windshields and dust inches deep on the roads. Oh yes, and a veil; I had plenty of them. A very long veil; one that would go around my hat, under my chin, around my neck—and then stream out behind in the wind! (That streaming out behind was considered very stylish!) A linen duster. Yes, I had one of them, too. We always wore dusters when we drove out in the country Sunday afternoons in the surrey.

I was tying the veil under my chin—getting the side effect of it in my mirror—when I heard a noise. A very loud, very strange, almost frightening noise...

I was used to the clatter of iron-shod wheels on cobble stones; to the thumpety-thump of galloping hooves; to the gay trumpet of a coach; to the whistle-and-puff of a locomotive; and I had heard the hiss-and-chatter of the new-fangled horseless carriage.

But this noise was different. It wasn't a roar and it wasn't a wheeze. It wasn't a puffing, or a pounding, or exactly a raucous rattle. It was a combination of all three! And it was getting closer all the time.

I was torn between a desire to call some older person and ask what the racket was, and a burning curiosity to go and look for myself. Like a woman, I went and looked for myself to see what it was.

I saw the Panhard coming up the hill to get me!

What a gorgeous thing it was! Bright yellow paint; paint, not enamel, such as is used on cars today. Red leather upholstery. Shiny lamps (that burned kerosene). A big complicated steering wheel was stuck at the end of a too-long shaft which projected almost vertically from the floor under the driver's seat. A lot of handles and gauges and other mysterious looking mechanisms.

As I looked I saw that the whole car was trembling as if it had the palsy. I suppose the mechanic who drove it was afraid to shut it off. It roared, too; a fine lusty sound, like a big beast held in leash. My schoolmate and I had to talk in shrieks to make ourselves heard.

"Get in!" She waved her hand and I climbed in the rear door of the Tonneau. (Do you remember those rear doors?) Vibration of the car was communicated to my body. I trembled a little in fear of, and a great deal in rhythm with the machine.

There came a staccato clank of gears. The chain beneath our feet rattled. The car sprang forward, nearly jerking our heads from our shoulders; and we were off.

My schoolmate and I clutched each other. It was terrible and delicious all at the same time. When we swooped down a hill (at about thirty miles an hour) it felt like the dive of a roller coaster. Pedestrians paused and watched us pass. Heads stuck out of windows. Mothers called to their children to come and look—at least I gather they did from the waving of arms and the running of children.

Each time we overtook a horse was an adventure. The horses reared, tried to run away and showed every sign of terror. Once the pandemonium of our progress was so great that a team of fine horses began to jump and lunge in their harness long before we reached them...

We were stiff and half deaf when we arrived back at school. My face was caked with dust and smarting from sunburn.

I could scarcely wait to tell my father the great news: "Pops, I've ridden in a horseless carriage!"

> He made me say it twice. And then with deep emotion he made the priceless retort which for all these years I've treasured. He, William C. Durant, the man who was presently to do more than any other living man to sell the United States on the idea of the automobile as a means of transportation; he who was to make his creed "a motor for every family"; he who in a few short years was to form the greatest merger the automobile industry has ever known, said:
> "Margery, how could you—how could you be so foolish as to risk your life in one of those things!" [59]

The conversations that followed in the Durant household are not recorded, but Margery's unbridled enthusiasm and excitement would undoubtedly have had a profound effect on her doting father. Indeed, her experience that day may well have been the critical event in persuading Durant to investigate his daughter's obsession further, but additional circumstances were also building into a tidal wave that would sweep Durant into the world of the automobile. That tidal wave included Hardy's experiences in Europe and the circumstances surrounding another automobile, one that carried the Buick nameplate.

David Dunbar Buick

David Dunbar Buick was born in Scotland on September 17, 1854 but his parents brought him to the United States two years later. The Buick family settled in Detroit and David eventually apprenticed in the same shop as Henry Ford; the James Flower and Sons Machine Shop. Once the young Buick had completed his apprenticeship he ventured into the plumbing business with William Sherwood. They established the Buick and Sherwood Manufacturing Company, a plumbing supply business. With this business Buick developed and patented a process of fixing porcelain to cast iron, a process which quickly became popular for bathtubs.

---

59   Margery Durant, <u>My Father</u>, pp 3-9.

In 1900 Buick became fascinated with the European development of the internal combustion engine. He built his own L-head engine and in 1901 he sold his interest in the plumbing business and the porcelainizing process in order to venture into the business of building gasoline engines, initially for marine use. He established a company with the unusual name of the Buick Auto-Vim and Power Company. In his first year of operation he realized the potential in using his engine to power a road going vehicle; so, he built one.

Illustration #8: David Dunbar Buick

The Buick Motor Company

There are several credible but differing accounts of the early years of the Buick Motor Company. The accounts differ over the comparative levels of input of David Dunbar Buick, Walter Marr, Eugene Richard and the Briscoe brothers, but there are some common elements in all the accounts.

What is clear is that Marr opened his own bicycle factory in Saginaw in 1896 and then moved to Detroit to continue his design and production of bicycles. In Detroit he began experimenting with gasoline engines building his first complete automobile, a 4 cylinder buggy steered by a tiller, in Detroit in 1898.[60] Eugene Richard was a Frenchman who had trained as an engineer in Philadelphia and had worked with Ransom Olds in his Olds Motor Works. Most engines in North America to that time had been built with the "L" head design. In Europe, engineers had been experimenting with a "valve in head" design which produced more horse power. By 1902 Marr and Richard had teamed up with Buick in the experimentation of engines following the latest European design for the newly formed Buick Manufacturing Company. Buick was in his element in the experimentation phase of his work to the neglect of financial and managerial matters. This proved to be problematic throughout his life and eventually lead to his downfall.

After numerous disputes Marr left the group and worked with Ransom E. Olds in the production of his Oldsmobile before eventually building his own Marr Autocar which appeared at the Detroit and Chicago auto shows in 1903. Eugene Richard also disillusioned with Buick's obsession with development rather than management, parted company with Buick to venture on his own. With the departure of Marr and Richard, Buick entered into a partnership with Benjamin and Frank Briscoe.

The Olds factory in Detroit had been destroyed by fire in 1901. As a result, Ransom Olds looked to various parts manufacturers from whom he could buy reliable parts in order to maintain production of his curved dash Oldsmobiles. He turned to the Briscoe Manufacturing Company

---

60 Beverly Rae Kimes and James Cox, <u>Walter Marr. Buick's Amazing Engineer</u>, (Boston, Racemaker Press, 2007), pp. 18-20.

to produce parts. Briscoe recalled; *I made samples and soon after secured an order for 4,400* [cooling systems] *together with an equal number of tanks, sets of fenders and other sheet metal parts.*[61]

The Briscoe brothers decided to invest in the Buick Company and reorganized the company structure which resulted in the incorporation of the Buick Motor Company of Detroit on May 19, 1903.

Again, Buick's desire to experiment rather than place interest in production led to dissention with the Briscoes. Unknown to Buick, Benjamin Briscoe was discussing a partnership with Jonathan Maxwell to create the Maxwell-Briscoe Company in the production of the Maxwell car. Maxwell had been the chief engineer at the Olds Motor Works. Briscoe and Maxwell entered into an agreement whereby Maxwell would design and build the car while Briscoe and C.W. Althouse would finance the project. This contract was signed on July 4, 1903 but three months later Althouse sold his interest to Briscoe and Maxwell.

Benjamin Briscoe heard of James Whiting's interest in automobiles and in the early summer of 1903 approached him with the idea of selling the Briscoe interest in the Buick Company to him so that he could free his money to invest in the Maxwell venture. Whiting responded positively and in his usual methodical way began to investigate the Buick Company and its products. Surprisingly, James Whiting found the potential of the Buick Company to his liking and by September the arrangements were in place for the Flint Wagon Works to acquire the Buick Motor Company, thus allowing Briscoe to reinvest in the Maxwell arrangement. Frank Briscoe, meanwhile, continued running the Briscoe Manufacturing Company.

One condition of Whiting's purchase of Buick was that the production facilities were to be moved from Detroit to Flint. In December a new Buick factory opened its doors on Kearsley Street in Flint and its twenty five employees, including Walter Marr who had been hired back in April 1904. Production of Buick engines began immediately: two cycle engines for stationary use and four cycle units for marine use. A month later the

---

61 Benjamin Briscoe. " *The Inside Story of the Rise of General Motors,*" <u>Detroit Saturday Night</u>, (Jan 15, 1921).

Buick Motor Company of Detroit was dissolved and the Buick Motor Company of Flint was incorporated with David Buick as the secretary of the board and Walter Marr leading the development of a new two cylinder engine. Later that fall Eugene Richard also returned to the company. Before year's end the three were back at work developing their valve in head engine and driving their prototype motor vehicle around Michigan. In September Marr drove a Buick to a third place finish in a race at Grosse Pointe, giving the car its first entry into motor racing history.

Illustration #9: A Prototype of a Buick with Walter Marr behind the wheel, and Tom Buick, David Buick's son as a passenger. Taken in Flint around June 1904.

On July 9, 1904 the citizens of Flint saw the new two cylinder engined automobile with Walter Marr at the wheel and Thomas Buick, David's son as passenger, as it bounced on the roads and made its way to Detroit. The *Flint Journal* gleefully reported,

> "Tom Buick and W. L. Marr of the Buick Motor Works, who left for Detroit on Saturday to give the first automobile turned out by that concern a trial on the road, returned to the city [Flint] late yesterday afternoon... the trip home was made in the remarkable time of 3 hours and 37 minutes, or at the rate of a trifle less than a mile in two minutes..."[62]

At one stage of the run Marr had the car running at thirty miles per hour for a sustained period. The successful, trouble free run gave assurance to the company as it began regular production of the car by the end of the month. It was designated as Buick Model B.

Dr. Herbert H. Hills, in Flint, took delivery of the first production "Model B" Buick in August 1904. The Model B was the first of eighteen or so to be sold that year. But all was not well with the company.

The cost of Buick's experimentations, not surprisingly, had exceeded the development budget. Expenditures in the new factory, the development of the engines and the new automobile had stretched the company's finances to the limit. Whiting discussed the problem with Fred Aldrich, the secretary of the Durant Dort Carriage Company. Aldrich suggested that he contact Dallas Dort with the view of involving millionaire Billy Durant in the automobile production in order to alleviate their financial problems.

Billy Durant took his first ride in Dr. Hill's Buick and was impressed. A few weeks later James Whiting took Billy Durant in his Buick and, with Clara and Margery in the rear seat, they drove around Flint. Not fully convinced, Billy wanted to drive it on country roads outside Flint himself. After his solo ride and a further ride with Whiting, Billy agreed to get involved financially. The amount of influence that his 16 year-old daughter Margery had on this decision is not recorded.

---

62   _Flint Journal_, Wed. July 13, 1904.

Buick and Durant

In October Durant and Whiting worked out the details of Durant's involvement. On the first day of November an agreement was put into place with Durant on the board of directors of the Buick Motor Company with Charles Begole as president. Two days later, as a publicity stunt Billy had as many Buicks as could be found, paraded down Saginaw Street. Whiting resigned as president in order to devote more time to the Flint Wagon. Earlier, Durant had moved the Imperial Wheel Company from Jackson Michigan to Flint leaving the factory in Jackson empty. The Jackson facility was seen as an excellent location for assembling cars.

As expected, Billy enthusiastically took on his favourite role, that of super salesman. He took a Buick to the January 1905 New York Automobile Show along with David Buick, Walter Marr, James Whiting, and H.J. Koehler, an auto dealer. Here Billy gave a lesson in salesmanship to the group. He led them in taking orders for over 1,100 vehicles! This was the impetus the company needed.

Illustration # 10: Margery Durant at the wheel of a 1905 Model C Buick.
(Photo: Courtesy Scharchburg Archives, Kettering University)

In 1905 the engines, transmissions and bodies were being produced in Flint and then shipped to Jackson for assembly. Billy immediately dealt with this inefficiency. He convinced four Flint bankers to pledge $20,000 each to bring the entire production to Flint. He also encouraged other investors to support the move with smaller investments. These included Dallas Dort, Durant's uncles William Wallace Crapo and Dr. James Willson, and of course, his personal physician, Dr. Edwin R. Campbell. The total amount raised was $500,000.

Before the move to Flint, the first cars under Durant's direction came off the line in Jackson and among the first to receive a new Buick was Margery.

> *I was promised one of the first cars. One day my father told me it was ready. You can imagine my feelings as I took the train to Jackson. The car wasn't ready...It grew later and later. I was just about to give up hope when the car appeared, surrounded by half a dozen grinning, grimy workmen. How proud they were. At the driver's seat was one of my father's trusted mechanics, the late Bob Burman.*[63]

Burman drove Margery to Lansing where they stayed overnight with Margery's uncle, Charles Downey. Margery's experience as a teenager remained strong in her memory. She continued,

> *The first Durant built and backed horseless carriage, one of the first Buicks ever manufactured, had proved it could head for a destination and get there! Of course Bob Burman made it possible. He afterward drove me for two years.*[64]

Although Burman continued to be her chauffeur, she learned to drive the Buick on her own. *"I like you to use the car, Margery,"* he [Durant]

---

63   Margery Durant, My Father, pages 49, 50.

64   Ibid, p. 50.

told me. And the way he said it he meant; "Let's make them like the car by proving its usefulness!"[65]

Margery became one of Durant's unofficial test drivers. *Margery was the Buick's most demanding test driver and she and her father logged hundreds of miles along the twisting back roads of Michigan and New York State.*[66]

She made many journeys alone but most were with her father, sometimes sharing the driving, sometimes doing all the driving herself with her father as passenger. Margery would no doubt be regarded with considerable alarm as she became familiar with every aspect of the vehicle and would frequently be seen crawling under the car to investigate a mechanical problem;

> *"And I had broken clutches and flat tires, burned out bearings and short circuits, valve rattles and piston knocks, from one end of the country to the other… I ruined half the dresses I possessed trying to find out why my car engine wouldn't start….In the summer of 1905 my father asked me if I'd like to motor up to Pentwater, Michigan, where he had built a little log cabin for his mother on the shores of Lake Michigan. Would I! I wanted to be driving all the time! There was nothing like it!*[67]

As a result,

> *A pretty girl at the wheel turned heads, and sold Buicks, but, … Margery Durant was leading a rebellion. She was proving to women that they could drive, and they could drive alone, by themselves, wherever they wanted to go.*[68]

---

65 Ibid, p. 77

66 Heather Robinson, <u>Driving Force</u>, (Toronto, McClelland & Stewart Inc., 1995), p.119

67 Ibid. pp. 77-78

68 Ibid. p. 119

Later that year Enos De Waters, an engineer who had worked on the Thomas Flyers in Buffalo and on Cadillacs in Detroit, and Arthur Mason, also a Cadillac mechanic, were recruited to join the company and assist in design and development of the new Buicks. William H. Little was hired as the production manager of the Flint plant. Little had been involved with the production of the Ilion Buckboard Car in Waltham, Massachusetts.

In order to facilitate the moving of Buick to Flint, Durant decided that a new plant was in order. He bought a 220 acre farm on the north side of the city for this purpose. To further consolidate vehicle production, he contacted Charles Mott who owned the Weston Mott Company, producer of axles for automobiles in Utica, New York. He persuaded Mott to relocate in Flint in a new factory beside the new Buick plant. The new Weston-Mott factory began production in Flint in February 1907. The designer of the roller bearings used in the Weston-Mott axles was Alfred P. Sloan, later to be head of General Motors.

Arthur Mason led in the design and development of a new 4000 r.p.m. engine for the Buick. Prior to his development of this engine, the 1905 Model C, engines produced in North America conventionally ran at 1800 r.pm. During Durant's first year at the helm of Buick he increased production from 30 or so to 750!

The publicity that Henry Ford had gained by racing his cars had pushed his sales to more than 1700 cars in 1903. Following the trend set by Ford, Billy also entered cars in races and in the fall of 1904 Buicks won a number of well publicized races such as the Eagle Rock Hill Climb near Newark and the Race to the Clouds at Mount Washington, New Hampshire. With this publicity, Durant and his Buicks were well on the road to acceptability.

By 1906 the Buick Motor Company under Durant's leadership had increased its sales to become the second largest automobile producer in the United States. In January, Buick had an unfinished brand new Model D version on display at the New York Auto Show.

Illustration #11: Billy Durant at the wheel of a 1906 Model F Buick in preparation for the 1906 Glidden Tour.(Photo: Courtesy Scharchburg Archives, Kettering University)

On February 13, 1906 David Dunbar Buick resigned from his position as manager of the Buick plant in Jackson. Later that year he broke away completely from the Buick organization. Meanwhile Billy had made huge profits playing the stock market in New York, but his marriage had virtually broken down. He increasingly neglected Clara as he spent time in New York, Flint, Jackson or on the road promoting his cars. Prior to moving the entire Buick production to Flint, on his many trips to Jackson, Billy frequently took one or both of his children and stayed in the Otsego Hotel. His relationship with Clara had seriously deteriorated, so she was never invited to accompany him or the children. While in Jackson, Margery developed a close friendship with Catherine Lederer who worked in the Post Office and was the daughter of a railroad clerk. One evening Margery was given two theatre tickets by her father. Margery wasn't able to attend so she gave both tickets to Catherine. Catherine invited a friend. As the performance drew to a close the girls were surprised to see Billy walking down the aisle of the theatre. He then drove the girls home dropping Catherine off last. A few days later Billy called on Catherine's mother to ask if he could take Catherine out on her own. Her mother stated that it would be inappropriate given Billy's age (he was 45 and she was 19) and the fact that he was still married. Undaunted, Billy hired Catherine as his personal secretary shortly afterwards.

Edwin and Margery

While in Flint he spent most of his leisure time with Edwin either at Edwin's home or at his own home entertaining Edwin. The time that Edwin spent at Billy's house drew him ever closer to Billy's teenage daughter Margery.

After graduating from Miss Mason's School for Girls in 1903, Margery was enrolled at Mount Vernon Seminary in Washington D. C. Her roommate while at Mount Vernon was Marjorie Merriweather Post daughter of Charles William Post, who had made his fortune by creating breakfast cereals such as Grapenuts and Post Toasties, and Postum, a coffee substitute. Marjorie later became the leading socialite of New York and founded General Foods, eventually becoming one of the wealthiest women in America. Margery graduated from Mount Vernon in the summer of 1905 and returned home to Flint.

> *At the end of each year when she returns home she should have finer manners and greater charm; she should show greater power to think, to will, to plan, and to execute; to feel with others as never before; to hold honor dearer; above all she should have stronger faith, a clearer vision and a deeper love for God and man.*[69]

So stated the prospectus from Miss Mason's Castle School. It is obvious that in Edwin's eyes Miss Mason's objectives had been fulfilled. Extremely attractive, and, at the age of seventeen, she was bright, creative and full of youthful energy and exuberance. Did Edwin see in Margery an opportunity to regain something of his own youth? Sometime in the early part of the year he proposed to Margery and she accepted.

On April 26, 1906 the *Port Perry Star* reported briefly:

---

69   The Drawbridge, op cit. p. 4.

> Flint, Michigan, April 19.
>
> Dr Edwin Ruthin [sic] Campbell, formerly of Port Perry Ont., and a graduate of Toronto Medical College was married at 8 o'clock last night in St Paul's Episcopalian Church to Miss Margery Pitt Durant, daughter of the millionaire senior member of the big carriage firm of Durant, Dort Company. The affair was very elaborate in all its appointments and was attended by a large number of guests from Michigan, New York, Boston and Pittsburg. The happy couple left last night for New York whence they sail on a two months bridal tour of Europe.[70]

Unquestionably the social event of the year in Flint, the wedding was given extensive coverage in the Flint and Detroit newspapers. With the rumours of 1896 behind him, Edwin was highly respected and the most eligible bachelor in town. Margery was young, stunningly attractive, and she was the daughter of the wealthiest man in town.

> No expense had been spared for the ceremony at St Paul's Episcopal Church;
> In elegance of appointment and detail, the happy function was perhaps the most notable hymeneal event in the social history of Flint. The church decorations evidenced a lavish expenditure of artistic taste and furnished an effective background to a singularly brilliant scene.[71]

The *Detroit Free Press* carried almost a full page coverage of the event with large photos of the couple and a brief article, headlined "Campbell-Durant Wedding At Flint. A Brilliant Affair." [72] The *Flint Daily News* coverage of the event also took up most of a full page. It detailed the elaborate decorations using lilies and other Easter floral themes and listed names of many of

---

70 *Port Perry Star,* (Port Perry, Ontario) April 26, 1906.

71 *Flint Daily News,* April 8, 1906.

72 *Detroit Free Press,* April 19, 1906.

the guests. The four ushers were; Arthur Bishop, Dallas Dort, Margery's brother Clifford Durant and Edwin's old schoolmate from Port Perry and the University of Toronto Medical School, Dr. H.A. Bruce. His best man was William B. Powell, a Boston banker. Margery's bridesmaids included her roommate from Mount Vernon, Marjorie Merriweather Post, who had the previous year married investment banker Edward Bennet Close. Catherine Lederer was not acknowledged in the press coverage. Twenty three years later, the now divorced Margery recalled the wedding;

> I was married on April 18, 1906 when I was a little over eighteen years old, to Dr. Edwin R. Campbell of Flint. The wedding was held in the Episcopal Church at 8 o'clock in the evening. I remember as though it were yesterday that the church was filled to the doors and the streets lined with people who apparently came out of curiosity to catch a glimpse of the bride.
> My father took me up the aisle. With his usual enthusiasm for getting a thing done once it was started, he walked so fast that I could hardly keep up with him. At the rehearsal we had been instructed to move slowly and keep time with the music.
> "Don't go so fast dear!" I whispered to him and pressed his arm to emphasize my words. I remember wondering in a flash whether he was in a hurry to get rid of me. But he never has — and I hope he never will.[73]

The wedding certificate stated that Edwin was 32 years of age and Margery, 19. Both statements were incorrect. Whether these mistakes were mere slips of the pen or made on purpose to hide the wide difference in age, we may never know. The facts are that Edwin was forty years old and, as Margery had stated in her biography of her father, she was eighteen.

The marriage may have been looked upon by some as unusual because of the age differences, but many regarded it as entirely romantic. The two left immediately for New York by train and then boarded the first class

---

73   Margery Durant, <u>My Father</u>, pp. 155,156.

section of the Cunarder *Caronia* bound for Liverpool, arriving there on May 2.[74] The *Caronia* was a stately and modern two funneled, 700 foot long vessel. It offered the latest in modern ocean travel having enjoyed its maiden voyage only a year earlier.[75] The steamer was capable of a full 18 knots as it crossed the calm Atlantic. They continued on an idyllic two month tour of Europe, a journey that only the wealthy could afford. The newlyweds holidayed in Paris, London and the south of England and returned to New York on June 10 on board the *Celtic*, an equally luxurious, but older vessel than the *Caronia*.[76]

On their way home to Flint they stopped off in Toronto to visit Dr. H.A. Bruce and then to Port Perry to visit Edwin's family and friends. Back in Flint they took up residence in the newer and larger house that Edwin had purchased, a comfortable home at 415 Stevens Street. Margery had the luxury of a maid and the pleasure of the company of her father, for immediately upon their return from their honeymoon Billy Durant moved in to live with them. Margery had an upstairs bedroom set aside for him. His occupancy of this room during his time in Flint was a clear symbol of the failure of his marriage to Clara, but it allowed Margery the luxury of being with the two most important people in her life, her father and her husband.

The Campbells' ability to afford a maid meant that Margery could do as she pleased during the daytime. She frequently chose to accompany her husband around town as he paid visits to his numerous patients and then in the evening pick up her father at work to bring him home in time for dinner. Margery also did Edwin's bookkeeping and *"in my spare time I pored over his medical journals and great thick books on the practice of medicine. In those days I began the industrious reading I have done all my life since then."*[77]

---

74 New York Passenger Lists, 1820-1957. Microfilm Roll # T715-724, p. 28.

75 Passenger ships and Images, Ancestry.com.

76 New York Passenger Lists, op cit.

77 Margery Durant, My Father, p. 156.

Edwin and Billy

The daily presence of Durant, "Pops" as he was affectionately called by Margery and Edwin, drew them increasingly into his world. As a wedding present, Billy had given Edwin and Margery $150,000 in shares in the Durant Dort Carriage Company. This was more than just a remarkably generous present; it was a lure. During the time that Edwin and Billy had spent together, Billy was well aware of Edwin's quick mind. He no doubt had seen the potential in Edwin's perceptive interest in the affairs of the various factories. The fact that Edwin now had shares in one of Billy's enterprises drew him inexorably into their operations.

Evenings in the Campbell home were rarely free when Durant was in Flint. As Margery recalled,

> *Night after night men came to our house in Flint. All kinds of men: bankers, lawyers, executives, foremen, mechanics. Some came because Durant sent for them. Some came because it was the only way they could get enough of Durant's time to have ten minutes consecutive conversation with him. Some had axes to grind. Some longed to help him grind his bright new gasoline-buggy axe—hoping that they would be permitted to use it later for a little chopping on their own account.*
>
> *There were men at dinner. There were men at the front door. The parlor was often full of men, behind closed doors there were men. Earnest men, emitting an unending stream of facts, figures, suggestions, protests. They sat with their heads forward, elbows on knees. They talked and they listened; but my father mostly listened. When he did talk it was like a violin beginning to play. Those present had to listen. I know: they all said the same thing then that they do now; "Durant is the greatest salesman I ever knew."*[78]

---

78   Ibid., pp. 57, 58.

All this was taking place at Edwin and Margery's home on Stevens Street. They had no choice but to be a part of the dinner meetings and increasingly Edwin was invited into Billy's business related meetings after dinner in the sitting room in their home. There are no written records of the evening business dealings but by the end of 1906 Edwin was clearly involved with some aspects of Billy's enterprises. Within a few months of his marriage, Edwin's name appeared on the board of directors of the Durant-Dort Carriage Works.

Later that summer in Flint, Billy proudly watched as his new Buick factory and the nearby Weston Mott factories neared completion. The Buick plant in Jackson was producing 1400 units a year. With the new four cylinder engine Model D, the first four cylinder engine for Buick, the new Flint plant produced 4641 cars in its first twelve months of operation. This placed Buick in second place in U.S. automobile production. Ford was in first place with four times that number, almost 15,000. By the end of 1906 Buick had 100 agencies across the United States from New York to San Francisco. Most were actually Durant Dort carriage agents who were additionally authorized to sell Buicks. Buick ended the year with the release of a new Model F.

In the fall of 1906 Edwin and Margery joyfully announced to Billy that he would soon be a grandfather. Unfortunately for Edwin, the excitement of his approaching fatherhood was counterbalanced by sad news from Port Perry in October.

> *This entire community were shocked and grieved on Monday morning last to hear of the sudden death, late the previous evening of one of our most esteemed townsmen in the person of Mr. Donald Campbell. ...Mr. Campbell was widely known having in his capacity as a grain merchant been in contact with all the farmers in the community surrounding Port Perry. He was a Presbyterian and a Conservative...*
>
> *He is survived by a widow, two daughters and two sons: Dr. D. Campbell, Rossland B.C., Dr. E.R. Campbell, Flint, Michigan, Mrs. Gillespie, Port Perry and Mrs. Delehart, Butte*

> Montana. He also leaves five sisters and one brother. The funeral which will be private will take place today.[79]

Edwin and his young and pregnant bride made the sad journey to Port Perry to meet with family and friends and to pay their respect to his late father. Sam McLaughlin and Dr. H.A. Bruce made their way to Port Perry to offer condolences. Presumably McLaughlin made the journey from Oshawa in one of his new rigs and not by bicycle as he had in his youth. Edwin and Sam would no doubt have chatted about the carriage business since Edwin was now on the board of directors of Durant Dort. They may have even discussed Billy's latest venture into horseless carriages. While in Port Perry Edwin made arrangements for the impressive monument which marks the Campbell family's resting place in the Pine Grove Cemetery. Of interest is the fact that he had his own name placed on the monument. We shall never know whether he had intended to be buried there too.

McLaughlin Buicks

The following year Edwin returned again to Port Perry to visit his mother, but his primary purpose for his visit to Canada was to meet with Sam McLaughlin to discuss a business venture. In 1904 Hezzlewood, who was now a shareholder in the McLaughlin Company but not on the board of directors, visited the Canadian Cycle and Motor Company (CCM) in Toronto where they had a brand new Packard automobile on display. But the main attraction was Henry Ford who was invited to talk about his most recent exploit; he had driven one of his cars at a speed of ninety-two miles an hour on the ice of Lake Saint Clair near Detroit.

One of the rivals to McLaughlin in the carriage trade, the Walkerville Wagon Works, had announced a deal with Ford. They had signed a contract to buy engines and chassis from Ford and the bodies from the Gray Factory in Chatham and then assemble the cars in their Walkerville factory.

---

79   *Ontario Observer*, (Port Perry), October 11, 1906.

Hezzlewood knew that Gordon McGregor of the Walkerville factory would be at the CCM factory event and he wanted to find out the details of his arrangement with Ford and Gray. He met McGregor who told him that he had already sold five of his Fords. After McGregor took him for a ride in one of his automobiles Hezzlewood became entranced by the agile little vehicle and promptly bought one. On arriving home he became the talk of the town and its neighbouring communities as he spent every spare moment driving the country roads around Oshawa in his contraption, making sure that he passed Sam's house as frequently as possible.

Even though Sam had settled into a stable family life with Adelaide and their three daughters, he had not lost his vibrant enthusiasm for life and was quickly caught up in Hezzlewood's passion for his horseless carriage, particularly when he saw the simplicity of the carriage itself. He knew that he could improve on the workmanship and he had read of a better quality engine and chassis. It was manufactured in Flint, not Detroit. It was built by a man named David Dunbar Buick and he called his automobile the Buick. Sam's friend Dr. Edwin Campbell lived in Flint and his father-in-law controlled Buick.

Initially the McLaughlins in Oshawa had considered building their own complete cars but hiring competent mechanics, designers and engineers became too problematic. Sam contacted Edwin in Flint who in turn made arrangements for Sam to discuss business with Billy Durant. Billy and Sam had met before at various carriage shows as the McLaughlins were the largest manufacturers of carriages in Canada and Durant was his counterpart in the United States.

Edwin's meeting with Sam to discuss automobiles led to a series of meetings which included Billy. Finally an agreement was reached in which the Buick plant would ship its engines and some chassis parts to Oshawa for a period of fifteen years. The McLaughlins would create their own vehicles around the Buick components, however the first McLaughlins were entirely Buicks which had been shipped to Oshawa in parts. The shipment of unassembled vehicles avoided some of the customs duties. As the factory became more efficient, McLaughlin slowly increased replacing Buick's body parts with those designed and produced in Oshawa.

The McLaughlin Motor Car company was incorporated on November 20, 1907 in Oshawa and the first of the McLaughlin Buicks, a Model F, came out of Sam's plant a month later. Billy bought 1000 of the 5000 shares in McLaughlin's enterprise leaving the McLaughlins with a majority of shares and therefore, the controlling interest. This arrangement was quite unusual for Billy as he liked to have complete control of his various interests. The fact he allowed this arrangement is credited to Edwin.

> Dr. Edwin Ruthven Campbell was a pivotal figure in the relationship between McLaughlin and Buick. ...It may have been Campbell who persuaded Durant to let the McLaughlins retain majority ownership of their Canadian Buick plant, a favour Durant granted to no one else. [80]

In the year 1907, the Buick factories production figures at Jackson and Flint reached 4,641, but Ford was ahead with almost 6000 vehicles. We can only speculate about the conversations at the Campbell home at 415 Stevens Street, as Billy, Edwin and others no doubt would have considered strategies to surpass Henry Ford.

Billy's Divorce

On March 18, 1907, Margery gave birth to her first child, a son. Edwin handled the delivery himself with a nurse in attendance at their Stevens Street home. With no hesitation the proud parents named him William Durant Campbell.

In 1973 Larry Gustin's extensive work **Billy Durant**, was published and received wide acclaim as the first authoritative biography of Durant. In the process of compiling his information Gustin interviewed a number of people who knew Billy intimately, including Billy's second wife Catherine who, at the time of the interview lived in relative obscurity in New

---

[80] Heather Robinson, <u>Driving Force</u>, p. 121.

York. Through his interviews he was able to determine many matters of Billy's personal life.

After almost 23 years of marriage Billy followed through on a decision which had been occupying his thoughts for some time. He decided to seek a divorce, although it was agreed that Clara would file the petition for divorce. Edwin worked with Billy and Clara in making sure that all the arrangements would provide for a quick and painless closure to the marriage.

Three witnesses provided affidavits: the Durants' handyman, their maid and Edwin. All three affidavits are identical and obviously all written by Edwin. Clara stated that Billy's failure to let her know where he was or to respond to her letters when she wrote to him in New York, were part and parcel of his *"cruel indifference."*[81] It was also stated in the proceedings that Edwin, as Clara's personal physician had ordered her to spend time in a rest home during the winter of 1907 as a result of her mental and emotional stress.

The Circuit Judge, William Gage, a friend of Billy, had no hesitation in granting the divorce. The decree was granted on May 27, 1908. Gage also ordered that the divorce proceedings not be made available to the press. The divorce settlement determined that Clara should receive $150,000 in the form of cash and securities as well as the Flint family home on Garland Street. There were also rumours of an out of court settlement that may have been as much as $2 million. Within hours of the conclusion of the divorce proceedings Billy headed for New York City. There, the next day, forty six year old Willy Durant quietly married his secretary, Catherine Lederer, the friend of Margery from Jackson, Michigan. In his biography of Durant, Weisberger, when discussing Mrs Lederer's relationship with her new son-in-law, commented:

> *She developed in time a warm relationship with Durant, once she accustomed herself to the idea of a son-in-law of her own*

---

81 Divorce petition Clara Durant versus Durant William C. Durant. *Circuit Court for the County of Genessee in Chancery, March 26, 1908.*

age. Durant himself had just such a son-in-law, and after May of 1908 he and Margery each had, in their spouses, a counterpart of the other.[82]

Strangely, in her biography of her father, Margery never mentioned the divorce. The only reference to Billy's new wife occurs toward the end of the book when she stated: *When he is at home in Deal he is a most thoughtful host to the many friends who visit him and his beautiful wife.*[83]

Soon after the divorce Clara sold her Garland Street house and moved to California taking their 19 year-old son Clifford with her. It appears that Billy never saw Clara again. Clifford did return to the east to attend Pennsylvania Military College. He graduated in 1910 and then returned to California. Billy did not keep in contact with his son for the next few years.

Illustration #12: Catherine Lederer Durant, Billy's second wife. (Photo: Courtesy Scharchburg Archives, Kettering University)

---

82 Bernard Weisberger, <u>The Dream Maker</u>, p. 115.

83 Margery Durant, <u>My Father</u>, p. 328.

It should be pointed out that during Billy's numerous sojourns in New York he was spending a considerable amount of time on Wall Street studying the nature of the stock market and at that time began to develop a confidence in successfully investing in stocks.

Bigger Yet

During all these dramatic events, more than coffee was brewing in the Campbell's kitchen on Stevens Street. Ideas, ambitious ideas, shared between Edwin and Billy, grew from "what if" to "let's do it." By January 1908 Henry Ford had refined his production system to the point that it had set the standard for the world. Other manufacturers would ignore his methods at their peril. Henry Ford introduced his Model T in October 1908. Production of the "Tin Lizzie" spread out across the world. Later, in 1911, Ford opened a plant in Manchester, England and began churning out the Model T for the British and European market. By 1913 this factory alone was producing 6000 cars a year.

Ford's production methods became a blueprint for other forms of manufacturing: the cost cutting simplicity of the design of the engine and other components, and the efficient, moving assembly line. The car remained primitive for its time, but it was relatively reliable, cheap to buy and economical to operate. It was obvious to all but the most cynical that by 1908 the automobile was no longer a fad, fashion statement or recreation vehicle. It had evolved into a practical and reasonably reliable means of conveyance, and Billy, with Edwin's encouragement, was anxious to do with the automobile what he had done with his carriage manufacturing: become the largest in North America. To assist Billy in carrying out these plans it was necessary that Edwin devote his full attention to them. This would necessitate giving up his medical practice.

Over the next few weeks Edwin wound down his business, closing his office above the Genessee County Savings Bank. Lawrence Gustin states, in his book **Billy Durant** ; ... *starting in 1908...he* [Campbell] *became one of Durant's closest business associates.*[84]

In their biography of Walter Marr, Beverly Rae Kimes and her husband James Cox echoed Gustin's statement with:

> *Doc Campbell gave up his medical practice to become his father-in-law's closest business advisor as well as his eyes and ears in Flint.*[85]

Illustration # 13: Edwin around 1910 (Photo: Courtesy Grant Sanger)

---

84 Lawrence Gustin, <u>Billy Durant</u>, p. 81.

85 Beverley Rae Kimes and James Cox, <u>Walter Marr</u>, p. 123.

Chapter Five

GENERAL MOTORS

The Creation of General Motors

Many details of the story of the creation of General Motors are profoundly enigmatic. There are numerous varying accounts and many disagreements, even among the principals. Biases, agendas, fading memories and lack of documentation add to the difficulties facing those looking for the facts surrounding the birth of what was to become the world's largest industrial corporation. The role of Edwin in this epoch making event is even more difficult to determine. The absence of official secretaries recording the events of numerous meetings frequently leaves his role open to speculation. However some documents have come to light that reveal that Edwin played a critical role in the creation and expansion of General Motors.

Durant's memoirs were written during his declining years, but mainly during the convalescence following his stroke in October 1942, long after Edwin's death. This presents some difficulties for the researcher. A stroke can affect parts of the memory resulting in distortion, misinterpretation or even complete obliteration of past events. This may explain why he made no mention of his son-in-law Edwin Campbell in these accounts. Durant's memoirs were published unedited, by Kettering University in

2008 as **William C. Durant, In his own Words.** Margery's biography of her father, **My Father** was written several years her divorce from Edwin and left out most of the details of her ex-husband's involvement in her father's businesses. She reveals further bias by making no mention of her father's own divorce and subsequent marriage to her own friend, Catherine Lederer, probably partially due to Catherine's youth and vitality displacing some of Margery's closeness to her father. Nevertheless a number of other sources enable us to put together what is probably a reasonably accurate picture of the events that led to the creation of General Motors and Edwin's involvement in them. The basic and indisputable fact is that in New Jersey on September 16, 1908, General Motors was incorporated and William C. Durant was the key figure in its incorporation and Edwin was clearly involved in the event.

Sam McLaughin, in his memoirs stated:

> *I was sitting in Mr. Durant's little office in Flint with Dr. Campbell, after Mr. Durant had bought the Buick Company. The three of us were alone there when we started gossiping and talking about things in general. During the course of the conversation we decided we should form a company calling it General Motors and Dr. Campbell was directed to go to Chicago to sell the first million dollars worth of stock; so that was really how General Motors was formed and started.* [86]

This strange account was given by Sam as he reminisced just prior to his one hundredth birthday. It is the only account that places Sam in at the beginnings of the creation of General Motors and has no support from automotive historians. However, its importance may lie in Sam's understanding of the closeness of the three men and Edwin and Billy's dependence on each other at the dawn of General Motors.

---

[86] *Letter to Lee Mays from Sam McLaughlin, July 14 1971. Parkwood, Oshawa, Ontario.*

Benjamin Briscoe

Another major disagreement in the story is over who was the initiator of the idea of an amalgamation which would eventually led to the creation of General Motors, and when the initial discussions took place. Durant's daughter Margery claims that it was her father who initiated the idea. Durant claims that credit for this should go to banker J. Pierpont Morgan; others claim that it was Benjamin Briscoe. Briscoe did play a major part in the initial moves.

As mentioned in Chapter 4, after leaving Buick, Briscoe continued his enthusiasm for the automobile by joining with Jonathan Maxwell to produce the Maxwell car at the Maxwell Briscoe Motor Company. Production and sales gradually increased and in order to expand his production he obtained an infusion of cash from financier J. P. Morgan and moved his factory to Tarrytown, New York. As a result of this development the Maxwell stood fourth in North American production behind Ford, Buick and Reo.

In 1902 alone 52 new automobile manufacturers started business. By 1906 there were 178 companies producing automobiles in the United States.[87] Two years later this number had grown to over 250 companies. Of these, fewer than 50 companies accounted for 75 per cent of national sales. The remaining companies had an average annual production of fewer than 20 units. J. P. Morgan had just created the United States Steel Company by merging 10 steel companies and 149 steel plants. Briscoe came to Flint in late 1907 to meet with Durant and the two discussed the idea of consolidating some of the auto producers following the example of United States Steel.[88] One motivating factor behind this move was the thinking that larger companies and corporations could withstand financial challenges better than smaller independent companies.

---

87   Anthony Yanik, <u>Maxwell Motor and the Making of the Chrysler Corporation</u>. (Detroit, Wayne State University Press, 2009), p.38

88   Ibid., p 47.

The American Banking system suffered from a number of serious flaws that, though not fatal, made it especially vulnerable to financial panics.[89] One of the problems was the different set of regulations regarding capital and reserves that applied to the differing federal and state banks. New York City banks had to earn higher returns from their loan portfolios than other banks.[90]

Precipitated by a number of incidents including the Russian –Japanese War and the San Francisco earthquake, a financial panic gripped the industrialised world in 1907. In April the value of shares dropped dramatically. A number of banks collapsed including the third largest financial institution in New York, the Knickerbocker Trust. ...*the reserves of New York banks fell from a surplus of $11 million to a deficit of $54 million.*[91]

January 1908

Durant gives May 15, 1908 as the date of the initiating conversation between Briscoe and himself. However, along with Briscoe's account, diaries of Ransom Olds[92] and James Couzens, Ford's office manager, mention meetings in 1907 and the follow up meeting of the principals in January 1908. The latter dates seem more credible.

Although the date is not absolutely clear, all are in agreement about the location and the purpose, content and outcome of the meeting. This meeting in late 1907 or early in 1908 took place in Billy's office, and Briscoe proposed a vague plan suggesting the amalgamation of some twenty automobile producers. It is probable that Edwin was present at this meeting but cannot be confirmed. The companies that Briscoe suggested were smaller, low volume producers of more expensive vehicles such as Packard, Peerless, Thomas and Pierce Arrow. Initially Durant was not impressed with the proposal but he did not dismiss the concept.

---

89   Jeremy Atack and Peter Russell, <u>A New Economic View of American History</u>, p. 514.
90   Ibid., p. 515.
91   Ibid., p. 517.
92   Ransom Olds Papers. Historical Collections, Michigan State University.

> Why not modify your ideas Ben and see if you can get together concerns committed to volume production in the medium priced class... I named as my choice Ford Reo, Maxwell-Briscoe and Buick. I suggested that he first see Henry Ford...[93]

Briscoe followed Durant's suggestion and met with Henry Ford and Ransom Olds. Ford was increasing his production almost on a daily basis and was making the final preparations to launch his first Model T. He expressed an interest in the proposal. Ransom E. Olds had started his own company producing Oldsmobiles in Lansing and by 1903 the company was producing 4000 cars a year. The following year he left the company over a management dispute and began a new company producing Reo cars, the name derived from his own initials. In 1907 Olds produced 3967 Reo cars. He also expressed a keen interest in Briscoe's proposal.

After Briscoe's positive reception from Ford and Olds, these automotive giants, along with Durant, arranged to meet in Detroit at the Penobscot building. They and their advisors met in the hotel's reception room, but Billy felt a need for more privacy.

> As I had commodious quarters in the Pontchartrain Hotel and as the lunch hour was approaching, I suggested... that we meet in my room as soon as convenient.... This was accomplished and I had the unexpected pleasure of entertaining the entire party until mid-afternoon.[94]

Among those in attendance were; Benjamin Briscoe, Henry Ford and his office manager James Couzens (Couzens was another Canadian, born in Chatham, Ontario in 1872), Ransom Olds, Herbert Satterlee and Billy Durant with Edwin Campbell as his advisor. There may have been others present. As with all these early meetings, no secretary was present

---

93   William C. Durant, <u>In His Own Words</u> (Flint, Scharchburg Activities at Kettering University, 2008), p.26.

94   Ibid, p 26.

to record the proceedings. It later became evident that J.P. Morgan had instructed his son-in-law, lawyer Herbert Satterlee, to keep all these initial meetings private and away from any press coverage. From various sources it is apparent that the first half of this meeting involved a discussion on the worth of the respective companies, followed by a discussion on the amount of capitalization which would be required to form an amalgamation. A figure of around $3.5 million was considered reasonable. No further conclusions were reached other than the agreement to meet again a week later in New York at the office of Herbert Satterlee.

Even at this meeting in Saterlee's office, no official records were kept. Briscoe, Durant, Ford and Olds emerged as the potential principals of a new amalgamated company. However as discussions progressed and further meetings evolved (May 11, May 31, and June 6, 1908)[95] both Ford and Olds became more entrenched in their desire to sell their companies outright rather than holding stock in the proposed amalgamated new company. And, they wanted to sell their companies for cash. The buyout for Ford and Olds would have required at least six million dollars, an amount that Morgan was not willing to invest in what he saw as an interesting industry but one with many questions about its long term viability.

At the conclusion of the June meeting Satterlee made it clear that Morgan was reluctant to invest the required money. Meanwhile, Durant had obtained a signed agreement from all Buick stock holders that gave him the authority to make decisions on their behalf. On July 1, Satterlee's law firm announced that incorporation papers for a new United Motors Company had been filed and the Buick stock holders agreed to exchange their common and preferred stock for those in the new United Motors Company. The name United Motors was probably the idea of George W. Perkins, a partner in the J.P Morgan Company.

The New York Times on Friday July 31 announced that the Maxwell Briscoe-Buick merger projected an annual production figure of 13,000 vehicles, the highest of any manufacturer in the world. However, the fact that negotiations were now public knowledge as a result of this press

---

95 R.E. *Olds diary for 1908.*

release did not sit well with J.P. Morgan. The source of the press leak is not known. One of the major causes for hesitancy on the part of Morgan and his advisors was that Durant assured them that he was in total control of the shares of Buick and it was apparent that Durant wanted to maintain management of the Buick company after the proposed merger. His assertion that the shareholders would all abide by his wishes was a difficult concept for the Wall Street investors to accept. Morgan insisted that the Buick shareholders should be approached individually for their approval of the proposed merger. Durant disagreed countering that this would delay the process. In a letter from Briscoe to Durant dated August 4, 1908, he stated: *that the people on the corner [Morgan and his associates] are very upset. ...* The letter goes on to suggest that the Morgans requested that, *...a full disclosure to each stockholder must be made whose stock is exchanged...* As a result of this factor and the unwanted publicity, the Morgans withdrew from their interest in the amalgamation. Meanwhile, Billy had been investigating another company that offered potential in a possible merger; this was the Olds Motor Works and not Ransom Olds' Reo Company.

Ransom Eli Olds

Pliny Fiske Olds and his wife Sarah Whipple lived in Geneva, Ohio, where Olds provided a comfortable living for his family as a blacksmith. Their youngest son Ransom Eli Olds was born on June 3, 1864. Six years later the family moved to Lansing where Olds went to work in an iron works. When his health began to fail, Pliny Olds decided to move to the country where he farmed for four years. After his health showed clear signs of recovery he bought a machine shop in Lansing and, with his son Wallace as a partner, established P.F. Olds & Son Company. One facet of the Olds shop was the repair and manufacture of steam engines. While still in school, young Ransom Olds spent much of his spare time in the shop and quickly developed skills in all aspects of the machine shop. Ransom bought his brother's interest in the company during 1885 and became a partner himself. At that time steam for their engines was generated by burning wood or charcoal. Ransom developed a far more efficient burner using gasoline to develop steam. Because of this method of producing steam, the engines became known erroneously as gasoline engines. After successfully using his gasoline-fired steam engines in boats, in 1887 he installed one in a buggy.

Most probably in order to secure outside capital, the P.F. Olds and Son Company was incorporated in 1890. Major investors in the company were Samuel L. Smith and Edward W. Sparrow. Smith had made his millions in copper mining. Around this time, Pliny Olds at age 62 decided to take a back seat in the company's affairs, handing the leadership to his son Ransom. By now the Olds steam engines had acquired such an excellent reputation for their reliability and efficiency that the *Scientific American* magazine featured an article on Olds' "gasoline steam carriage" in its March 21, 1892 issue. A further complimentary article appeared in June 9, 1894.

After attending the Chicago World's Fair in 1893 where he saw gasoline powered engines on display, Ransom Olds returned to Lansing and began work on designing his own internal combustion engine. He and an employee, Madison Bates, filed an application for a patent for a gasoline powered engine on August 24, 1895, and in 1896 Olds drove his first gasoline powered vehicle around the streets of Lansing. Simultaneously he began selling gasoline engines across the country, primarily for marine applications.

In August 1897 the Olds Motor Vehicle Company came into being and produced a handful of his gasoline powered buggies. Olds merged his father's machine shop with his own company and established the Olds Motor Works in 1899 with the financial backing of Samuel Smith. On Smith's insistence, the Olds Motor Works factory was moved to Detroit to become the city's first permanent automobile producer. Henry Ford had incorporated his first company there in 1899 but it failed the following year. Smith's sons Fred and Angus assumed the administration for the Detroit plant while Olds looked after the Lansing based Olds Motor Vehicle Company. Owning the two factories proved to be advantageous when the Detroit plant was destroyed by fire in March 1901. In spite of the fire, production continued and sales demands were met without much difficulty. The company became famous for its "Curved Dash Olds," a tiller controlled, modified cart powered by the single cylinder Olds gasoline engine. By the end of the year over 400 vehicles had been built.

A new factory was opened in 1901 in Lansing while a new plant was being built in Detroit on the site of the original one destroyed earlier. Following the example set by Ford and others, a number of Olds enthusiasts drove their little cars to victory in a variety of racing events such as the first 100 mile endurance race in 1902. The following year, the management decided to concentrate on production of complete cars and sold off its engine-only division which still produced stationary engines.

By 1903, in spite of increased sales (over 2500 for 1902) and the fact that Olds was on the verge of becoming the largest producer of cars in the U.S., the original curved dash Olds was falling behind the latest trends and developments of other North American vehicles. It was obvious that the one-cylinder engine needed more power and improved reliability. Olds was content to continue production of the curved dash vehicles but the Smiths, particularly Fred Smith, wanted to build a more powerful and larger vehicle. Olds, who was at that time the company's vice president and general manager, discovered that Fred Smith had established a research and testing room at the Detroit plant without consulting him. At the January 1904 board meeting, Smith was elected to replace Olds in his administrative positions. Olds, highly angered by the events, walked out of the company.

Ransom Olds was determined to remain in the business of designing and producing automobiles so he established the R.E.Olds Company. This was incorporated on August 16, 1904 with Ransom Olds as president and general manager. When Smith threatened to sue over the use of the name "Olds" in the name of the company, Olds retaliated by re-registering the company as the Reo Car Company on September 27. Within a few months this evolved into the Reo Motor Car Company. A new factory was built on land which Olds had owned for some time. While this was being constructed, Olds and his staff worked in temporary facilities and the first Reo was ready for testing by late October. By featuring a two cylinder engine and seats for five, the new vehicle departed completely from the earlier Olds runabout. 864 Reo cars were produced and sold in 1905 and three times that number in 1906. In 1908 his production exceeded 4,000. Ransom Olds no doubt gained much satisfaction from the fact that the rival Oldsmobile production dropped to 1600 in 1906 and down to just over 1,000 in 1908.

General Motors

After the breakdown of the talks of a proposed merger of Durant, Ford, Reo and Briscoe, Durant took a close look at the Olds Motor Works. By 1908, under Fred Smith's administration, the Olds Motor Works sales had declined to barely a fifth of their 1904 level. Nevertheless Durant saw that the company had an enviable reputation and the factory was in good condition. Durant could also see the untapped potential of the company. He offered the Smiths $2 million in the stock of the proposed International Motor Company. The Smiths immediately accepted.

George Perkins still held the rights to the name International Motor Company so a new name had to be chosen. Durant submitted several names to his legal advisors at Ward, Hayden and Satterlee in New York.

In a letter to Durant dated Sept 10, 1908 from the law offices of Ward, Hayden& Satterlee;

> *Referring to our conversation during the past two days we find it is impractical to use the "International Motor Company" incorporated to us recently under the laws of the State of New Jersey for the purpose of taking over the stock of certain motor companies or to use that name in such connection at present . It will be impossible to secure the underwriting by the parties with whom we have been in touch until the inventories, appraisals and audits of all the coompanies have been completed... We might use the "United Motor Company" were it not for the fact that there is already a "United Motor Car Company in that*

> state. We suggest the name "General Motor Company," which we have ascertained can be used. [96]

On September 16, 1908, this time with no publicity, Satterlee's company followed Billy's instructions to complete the legal incorporation of the General Motors Company. Curtis R. Hatheway a member of the law firm Hayden, Ward and Satterlee, and a partner of J.P. Morgan's son-in-law, filed the articles of incorporation in New Jersey. The reason for the choice of the site for the incorporation was that the State of New Jersey had less stringent regulations on stock issues than Michigan. The incorporators were Hatheway, George E. Daniels and Benjamin Marcuse. Two weeks later Durant and Campbell met with the three incorporators. This time, for legal purposes, the minutes were recorded. Daniels was selected as interim president and General Motors officially bought the Buick Motor Company. This was accomplished by transferring the Buick stock into General Motors stock. The value of the stock was estimated at about $3.5 million. A few days later, October 20, 1908, another meeting was held and William Eaton, a Wall Street investment company officer and former Flint gas company manager was named president. Durant became the vice-president with Hatheway the secretary and Edwin as one of the directors.

In the closing days of the legal creation of General Motors, Edwin and Billy obviously spent some time discussing Edwin's role in its future. Whatever the length and intensity of those discussions, the outcome left no question about their intent. In October, 1909, Edwin sold his medical practice in order to devote his full attention to the support of his father-in-law's plans. In spite of severing himself from medical practice in Flint, Edwin maintained a lifelong interest in the latest medical developments. He continued to pore over medical journals to keep abreast of the current advances and practices in medicine no matter where he lived. Later, when he moved to live in Detroit, New York and California he immediately registered himself with the local medical authorities in order to maintain his

---

96 *Letter to W.C. Durant from Ward Haden and Satterlee, Sept 10, 1908, Durant files, Scharchburg Archives.*

certification. He even registered as a doctor when he took his family on an extended holiday in Bermuda in 1913.

Dr. F.A. Roberts had been in partnership with Dr. Paul Rose for almost two years before he severed that business association and bought Edwin's practice and took possession of the office over the Genessee County Savings Bank.[97] With this event finalised, Edwin's professional life was now focussed on his work with his father-in-law.

When General Motors Company was incorporated in 1910, Edwin was on the board of directors. Billy, with Edwin's assistance, then began a frantic pace of acquiring control of automotive companies and parts suppliers just as he had done in his carriage building days. George S. May is highly regarded as one of the better automotive historians. He evaluates Edwin as follows: *"...Durant's son-in-law, Dr Edwin Campbell, who had now given up his medical practice in Flint to become a kind of glorified errand boy for Durant..."* [98] Since this is the only reference to Edwin in May's book, the comment may seem somewhat dismissive. However, when considered alongside the numerous and critically significant business negotiations in the 1908-1910 phase of G.M.'s expansion, the term "errand boy" assumes considerable significance.

With his divorce out of the way, a young and devoted wife at his side and his son-in-law firmly committed to assist him, Billy was now free to work in planning the most ambitious expansion imaginable. Urging them on were the rivalries of other mergers of automobile manufacturers. In June 1908 the Everitt-Metzger-Flanders Company (EMF) was created by merging the Northern Motor Car Company and the Wayne Automobile Company, both of Detroit. This merger was largely due to the infusion of finances from the Studebaker Company of South Bend Indiana. The following summer EMF bought the Deluxe Motor Car Company of Detroit and began buying up a variety of parts manufacturing companies such as the Auto Crank Shaft Company and the Monroe Body Company of

---

97 *Flint Daily Journal*, Nov. 13, 1908.

98 George S.May, <u>A Most Unique Machine</u>, (William B. Eerdmans Publishing Company, 1975), p. 320.

Pontiac, Michigan. EMF was taken over by Studebaker in 1910 and the Studebaker Corporation came into being the following year. Briscoe established the United States Motor Company and took over a number of businesses at this time but his venture went into receivership in 1912. Briscoe's concept of a conglomerate automobile organization paled in comparison with what Billy and Edwin accomplished during the following months.

The Expansion Begins

Immediately after Edwin's closing of his medical practice in October 1908 and before the year's end, he assisted Billy in the purchase of eight companies. The W.F. Stewart Company was among the first to be negotiated and swallowed up by the newly formed General Motors. Fellow mason, Canadian (from London, Ontario), and son of a Scotsman, W.F. Stewart bought Buick engines and built bodies for them in Flint. As Stewart was already a shareholder of Buick and a director of the company, he needed no persuading to become a part of General Motors. The negotiations were minimal and the legal absorption of his company into General Motors was a mere formality. Stewart continued as a director of Buick after the documents were signed and registered.

The fact that Stewart was also a director of the Union Trust and Savings Bank also helped the cause. In the recent past Billy had developed a number of other financial supporters. He had chosen John Carton as the attorney for the Buick operation as Carton was president of the First National Bank. Billy's uncles William Crapo and James Willson were directors of the Genessee County Savings Bank and became directors of GM.

The purchase of two Ohio companies; the Elmore Manufacturing Company of Clyde Ohio and the Ewing Automobile Company, of Geneva, Ohio, provided GM with a base in that state. Of note is the fact that the Elmore used a carburettor designed by Walter Marr, now one of Buick's chief engineers. Two small automobile producers, both in financial trouble in 1909, were bought up by Billy for General Motors; the Marquette Motor Company of Saginaw and the Rainier Motor Car Company. He and Edwin also negotiated the sale of two truck manufacturers; the Rapid

Vehicle Company in Pontiac and the Reliance Motor Truck Company in Owosso Michigan. The latter two truck companies were amalgamated into the General Motors Truck Company although the GMC logo did not appear until 1911.

While helping the creation of a Buick sales room in Boston, Billy was visited by a Frenchman, Albert Champion, who manufactured electrical parts for automobiles. Durant enabled Champion to set up a workshop in Flint where he designed a new and much more efficient and reliable spark plug for Buick engines. Relative to earlier spark plugs, Champion's design was substantially cheaper to produce. Billy assisted Champion in creating the Champion Ignition Company. This was duly incorporated on October 26, 1908 and Champion began designing and producing various ignition parts in addition to spark plugs. A year later the Champion Ignition Company was absorbed by General Motors. The spark plug side of the company was later renamed the AC Spark Plug Division of General Motors. AC came from Albert Champion's initials.

The Oakland Car Company

One of the major acquisitions in 1909 was the Oakland Motor Car Company. Edward M. Murphy, the owner of the Pontiac Buggy Company, the largest carriage maker in Pontiac, was among those who saw that the automobile would replace the horse and buggy as a convenient means of transportation. In late 1907 he began the creation of the Oakland Company in order to produce horseless carriages and hired Alanson Brush as the designer and chief engineer. Brush was a brilliant machinist who had just left the Cadillac Motor Company after a disagreement with its chief designer and president Henry Leland. Financed by Edward Murphy, around 300 Oaklands were produced in 1908, the first year of its existence. On January 20, 1909 Billy and Edwin negotiated the purchase of the controlling interest in the Oakland Motor Car Company for $210,000. Later that year, Murphy died and by September, Billy and Edwin negotiated the full ownership of the company for General Motors. The Oakland was later renamed the Pontiac.

Another small automobile producer in Pontiac, the Cartercar Company held several patents which Billy thought would be useful. After the death of the owner Byron Carter, Billy and Edwin negotiated the sale of that company from the estate in October. Yet another small automobile manufacturer in Pontiac, the Welch Motor Car Company was also purchased.

The Cadillac Motor Company

Undoubtedly the most strategic purchase in 1909 was the Cadillac Motor Company, the remnant of one of Henry Ford's failed enterprises. There is a lingering impression that Henry Ford's success in automobile production was a smooth and ever increasing phenomenon. The facts quickly dispel that impression. Henry Ford had developed an automobile by 1899 and in order to produce and promote his car, a large number of investors including William Murphy, supported the incorporation of the Detroit Automobile Company on July 31, 1899. Murphy was the son of Simon J. Murphy a multimillionaire lumber and mining entrepreneur. Although the Detroit Automobile Company may have started production of as many as twelve automobiles, none were completed. The failure of the company to successfully complete and market a reliable vehicle led to the legal termination of the company in January 1901. Meanwhile, supported financially by Murphy, Henry Ford continued optimistically to experiment with the automobile.

By the spring of 1901 Ford was putting finishing touches to a racing car. At Grosse Pointe Michigan on October 10, an afternoon of car races had been planned at a dirt track owned by the Detroit horseman's club. Pope Steam cars, gasoline engined cars from White, Duryea and Olds and electric cars produced by Baker and Stearns were among the numerous vehicles competing in races of differing lengths. In one race Alexander Winton drove his gasoline powered vehicle over the one mile distance at an average of just under 50 m.p.h. The climax of the day's program was a planned 25 mile event open to all vehicles of any weight and size. As the afternoon progressed, time constraints reduced the final race to ten miles. Only two competitors accepted the challenge; Winton in his 70 horsepower vehicle and novice Henry Ford in his lighter and less powerful vehicle. The race got off to an exciting start but Winton's car developed heating problems allowing Ford to win comfortably.

Buoyed by Ford's well publicized success at the Grosse Pointe event, Murphy recruited investors to join him in launching a second Ford based company, the Henry Ford Company in late November 1901. Ford was hired as the chief engineer and encouraged to design a reliable passenger car. Rather than fulfill his expected role he continued his obsession with his racing car much to the annoyance of the investors, particularly William Murphy. Murphy's frustration led to a confrontation resulting in Ford's departure from the company that bore his name in March 1902.

Shortly after Ford's departure from his second company, a machinist named Henry Leland approached Murphy and the management of the Henry Ford Company with a proposal. He brought with him his own much improved version of the one-cylinder Olds engine. Leland suggested that this engine should be the basis of their car. Henry Leland, born in Vermont, had developed his skill as a machinist at Springfield Rifles in Springfield Massachusetts and at the Colt Revolver Factory in Connecticut. In 1890 he moved to Detroit where he met Robert Faulconer who had made a fortune in the lumber business and was looking for a new investment opportunity. Leland convinced him that a precision machine shop had considerable investment potential. On September 19, 1890 Leland, Faulconer and Norton was incorporated. Charles F. Norton was another machinist but he left the partnership in 1903.

Leland's company was immensely successful as a manufacturer of castings and precision gears and eventually expanded into the production of gasoline engines for marine application. When the Detroit Olds Motor Works factory was destroyed by fire, Leland's company was commissioned to produce 2,000 engines for the Olds runabouts. By this time the Leland factory employed over 160 workers including machinist Alanson P. Brush. By improving the quality of the machining, Leland and Brush managed to achieve ten horse power from the original three horse Olds engine. Leland showed the more efficient and powerful engine to Fred Smith at the Olds Motor Works but Smith rejected it because the entire original vehicle would have had to be redesigned to accept the increase in horsepower. This rejected engine was the basis of Leland's proposal to Murphy and the investors of the Henry Ford Motor Company. Impressed, Murphy accepted Leland's proposal. The ailing Henry Ford Motor Company was reorganized, refinanced and renamed. In August 1902 it emerged as the Cadillac Automobile Company, named after Antoine de la Mothe Cadillac, the founder of Detroit. A few months later the first Leland powered Cadillacs were ready for sale and four were on display at the New York annual automobile show. By the end of the following year over two thousand vehicles had been produced.

Initially Leland was content to manufacture engines and sell them to companies such as Cadillac. During 1904 he also sold 3000 engines to a fledgling car company named Studebaker. In late 1904 Murphy and the management of Cadillac, approached Leland to become manager of Cadillac production and president of the company. He accepted, and the Cadillac Automobile Company and the Leland and Faulconer Machine Company were merged and reorganized as the Cadillac Motor Car Company.

Under Leland's leadership and his fanaticism for precision, the company's reputation for quality grew quickly and the company expanded its production. He and Brush developed a new four cylinder engine in 1905. When Cadillacs with this engine were entered in the prestigious Royal Automobile Club's competition at Brooklands near London England in 1908, the engines won the Dewar Trophy for first place in quality and reliability. This award finally gave international status for U.S. automobiles and earned Cadillac its reputation for excellence. By the end of the year, production for Cadillac had exceeded the 2300 mark. Early in 1909 Billy Durant with Edwin beside him began negotiations to buy the company. The owners of Cadillac, Wilfred and Henry Leland had a good product and they knew it. They demanded $4.5 million for the company. Only by juggling the finances of Buick and General Motors in a series of complicated manoeuvres were Billy and Edwin able to meet the demands of the Leland brothers.

The acquisition of Cadillac had stretched Billy and Edwin's financial position close to the limit. Nevertheless they continued their aggressive campaign to take control of as many companies as they could. They took a close look at several auto parts manufacturing companies and then negotiated the sale of Detroit companies: the Northway Motor and Manufacturing Company, the Michigan Auto Parts Company and the Welch-Detroit Company. In Flint they negotiated the acquisition of the Michigan Motor Castings Company and the Weston Mott Company, manufacturer of wheels and axles. The Dow Rim Company and the Saeger Engine Works of Lansing who manufactured engines, transmissions and gears were also brought into the fold. The Tipless Lamp Company and the Novelty Incandescent Lamp Company, both producers of various types of automobile lamps were also acquired by Billy and Edwin for General Motors that year. The Heany Lamp Company and the Heany Electric Company were purchased in January 1910.

In anticipation of international expansion, Billy and Edwin negotiated the purchase of a Canadian company, the Bedford Truck Company of London, Ontario. In addition, Edwin and Margery, now seven months pregnant, journeyed home to Port Perry in September for a visit. From there Edwin slipped down to Oshawa to see Sam McLaughlin and negotiated, for Billy, the purchase of a forty percent interest in the McLaughlin Motor Car Company. In addition he visited his cousin Dr. Archibald McArthur who had just established his medical practice in the neighbouring village of Blackstock. He had just purchased the house and practice of Dr. Robert Harris. The home was an imposing and elaborate Italianate residence which is still referred to as the Medical Hall.

In order to be at the heart of the economic centre of the United States Billy opened an office at 101 Park Avenue in New York. Ironically Billy and Catherine still had no home of their own. Billy frequently travelled on his own but if they travelled together to Flint they usually stayed with Edwin and Margery. For privacy they occasionally stayed at the Dresden Hotel and while in New York they stayed at the Murray Hill Hotel. It would be several years before Billy finally acceded to Catherine's need for a permanent home.

Henry Ford Again

Late in 1909 an event which could have changed the history of the automobile forever, slipped through Billy's hands. In late October, Billy convinced the board of General Motors to give him the authority to try to purchase Ford. Billy took the train to Detroit and spent a day walking through the Ford plant with Ford's business manager James Couzens. (In his memoirs, Billy always misspelled his name as "Cousins." [99]) Billy asked Couzens to arrange to have Henry Ford meet with him in New York to discuss details of a sale. Ford fell ill and gave Couzens the details of his (Ford's) proposal for the sale. In essence the company could be purchased for $8 million, of which $2 million was to be in cash, and $4 million over three years and the balance in an arrangement involving shares in Couzens' favour.

The following day Billy made his way to the head office of the National City Bank of New York and met with Mr. Vanderlip, president of the bank. He explained his reason for the visit: to apply for a loan of $2 million. Vanderlip called in his assistant McRoberts to put the matter in the hands of the board of directors of the bank for approval. Billy then returned to Edwin and Margery's home in Flint to await the bank's decision. Unfortunately the bank's board rejected Billy's loan application.

> "The answer, by long distance telephone, not favourable, with the explanation that the business [Ford's production of automobiles] was new, that the bank had just recently been severely criticized for a sizable transaction with the Amalgamated Copper Company, and the committee felt that it would be unwise to have it understood that they were sponsoring an automobile venture....I made no further attempt to secure the $2,000,000 and notified Mr. Ford that the purchase could not be financed at the present time.[100]

---

99   William C. Durant, *In His Own Words*.

100 William C. Durant . *In His Own Words*. Pp. 48,49.

Henry Ford's two earlier failed ventures into automobile production gave little confidence to the potential investors even though his third company, the Ford Motor Company was now a successful six year old company.

Two years later, Billy and Couzens were discussing the development of the automobile and Billy asked Couzens what he thought Ford was now worth. Without hesitation he replied *"Three Hundred and Fifty Million Dollars, the value based upon ten times the earnings which last year amounted to $35,000,000."*[101]

But Ford was not the only company that he failed to buy in 1909. Billy set out to buy the E. R. Thomas Company, manufacturer of the Thomas Flyer which had won the 1908 New York to Paris road race. Here again, the purchase of Thomas required cash, something that was in short supply in the Durant organization.

With the immense success of the Buick the board decided to build a new and more efficient engine plant in Flint. In March, 1910, Billy floated a $1 million stock issue. As an indication of the public's confidence in Billy's ventures, the stock was completely sold out by the end of the month.

The failure to acquire Ford and Thomas in 1909 did not deter Billy and Edwin from trying to acquire other companies, but the memories of the financial panic of 1907 still lingered. Billy and Edwin could offer stock in Buick and GM as the key negotiating commodity, but sellers wanted cash. Nevertheless Billy and Edwin initiated a move to acquire control of the Willys Overland Company.

The first Overland automobile was built by Claude Cox in Terre Haute, Indiana in 1903. At the time Cox was employed by the Standard Wheel Company. In 1905 a factory was opened as a division of the Standard Wheel Company in Indianapolis and devoted solely to the production of Overland cars. Three years later the company was bought by John North Willys who developed the car and expanded production to nearly 5000 cars in 1909. In August 1909 Billy and Edwin approached Willys with the intent of acquiring his company, but, as Ford had done, Willys asked for cash, not GM stock. Billy and Edwin were forced to abandon their plans

---

101 Ibid., p. 49.

to acquire the company. In 1910, with over 15,000 cars produced, Overland became the third largest automobile producer in the U.S. The company was later (1912) renamed the Willys–Overland Company.

Buick Racing

Toward the end of the first decade of the twentieth century an expression came into common use in the automobile trade; "Win on Sunday, sell on Monday." The expression, probably originating from tire producer Harvey Firestone, resulted from sales figures for automobile and automobile parts producers who were involved in the immensely popular automobile races of the period. They found that there was a distinct link between the publicity derived from participating in, and hopefully winning car races on Sunday and filling the show rooms with potential buyers on Monday. Indeed, research has found that the link exists even today.[102]

Durant discovered this phenomenon as early as 1904 when, as previously cited, Walter Marr drove a Buick to its first recorded racing success. In addition, that year a Buick won a hill climbing race near Newark, New Jersey. He used an account of this event in his sales catalogue for 1905. He then proceeded to enter his cars in a number of races using one of his test drivers, Bob Burman as his race car driver with remarkable success. Burman also continued to act as Margery's chauffeur. Billy entered a Buick in the second annual Glidden tour and drove it himself.[103] The free publicity derived from these racing successes proved to be a key factor in many sales.

While all these foundation stones were being placed in position, Walter Marr continued his experimentation in the Buick factory and particularly in the development of racing engines and chassis. In 1909 Billy hired William Pickens to manage the Buick racing program with Marr as the

---

102 Press release from <u>Foresight Research</u>, "Survey Says: Motorsports Sells Cars and Trucks." Rochester, MI, August 3, 2010. This study was quoted extensively in the automotive trade press as well as in the regular press.

103 <u>New York Times</u>. July 8, 1906.

engineer and designer, and its four drivers: Bob Burman, Lewis Strang, George Witt, and a newcomer to his program Louis Chevrolet. [104] The team attended numerous races across the country recording and incomparable record of victories. Burman's duels with Barney Oldfield and his Mercedes became legendary. If their weekly competitions weren't on the front pages of newspapers, they led the sports sections.

Louis Chevrolet was a Swiss born mechanic who immigrated to Canada in 1900 with his brothers Gaston and Arthur. Louis went to work as a mechanic in Montreal. The following year the brothers moved to New York and Louis found employment with the French owned car company De Dion-Bouton. He gained his first racing experience as a driver garnering several victories for the FIAT Company. With his success he gained the attention of Durant and was hired as a race driver for Buick.

Illustration # 14: 3 Members of the Buick Racing Team. Left to right: Bob Burman, Arthur Chevrolet, Louis Chevrolet. (Photo: Courtesy Scharchburg Archives, Kettering University)

---

104 Beverley Rae Kimes and James Cox, <u>Walter Marr, Buick's Amazing Engineer</u>, p. 110.

Illustration #15: Bob Burman at the wheel of a 1908 racing Buick.
(Photo: Courtesy Scharchburg Archives, Kettering University).

Upon joining Buick, Chevrolet immediately started to win races with remarkable regularity. In 1909, driving Buicks, he set several World records while competing with fellow Buick driver Bob Burman and Mercedes driver Barney Oldfield. So successful was he that he wrote auto racing news items for the *New York Times*. [105]

Illustration #16: Louis Chevrolet at the wheel of a Buick. Here he has his characteristic cigarette in his mouth, a habit that Billy Durant despised.
(Photo: Courtesy Scharchburg Archives, Kettering University)

---

105 A Years' Record on Road, Track and Beach. New York Times, Jan. 2, 1910.

The strain of working in the engineering department on weekdays and then travelling across the country on weekends proved to be too demanding for Walter Marr. In his exhausted condition he succumbed to tuberculosis in the summer of 1909. Edwin's recommended that he and his family move to a dryer climate. In late summer the Marr family settled in Denver but Edwin, in anticipation of Marr's full recovery and eventual return to work, kept up an extensive correspondence with him, informing him of all the latest developments at Buick. Some of Edwin's correspondence from this period has survived, including a three page personal letter to Marr written in the fall of 1909. In it Edwin, as a director of Buick gave details of the expansion of the Buick plant and problems that they were facing:

> It has been very hard this year to get I beam axles and we have had to resort to the steel castings and the manganese bronze, which is rather expensive. ...The new Motor Plant has been moved into and you will hardly know the plants when you get back. [106]

The following March Edwin wrote to tell Marr that *"Chevrolet's working very hard at the racing models and it looks as if, barring accidents we will be able to do some stunts with your old motors this year again."*[107]

For Billy, a particularly important event in 1909 was the hiring of personal secretary in order to free Catherine from that responsibility. She had served him faithfully in that capacity prior to their marriage and continued to serve him in that role afterwards. However, with the hectic pace of the expansion of General Motors, she was overwhelmed beyond her capacity and as she accompanied Billy around the country she was unable to keep up to date with the correspondence. In her place Billy hired Winfrid Murphy.

---

106   ERC to Walter Marr as cited in Kimes and Cox, <u>Walter Marr. Buick's Amazing Engineer</u>, page 124.

107   Ibid., p. 125.

Winfrid Murphy was a shorthand expert who had worked in the Republican State Committee and then for Oldsmobile. It was while he was in this latter position that Billy used Murphy's stenographic talent while attending a meeting in Lansing and, impressed with his skill, hired him as his personal secretary in December 1909. One of Murphy's first tasks was to tackle stacks of correspondence; some at the bottom of the pile had lain unanswered for almost a year.

For Edwin, the greatest personal event in 1909 was the birth of a six pound baby girl on November 12. She was duly named Margery Edwina. Throughout her life she used her middle name Edwina. The arrival of Edwina necessitated a larger home for the Campbell family. Sometime in early 1910 they moved to 422 East Kearsley in Flint, a residence large enough for the Campbells, their three servants and accommodation for Billy and Catherine when they visited. The census for 1910 gave the servants' names as Julia Murphy age 25, Dora Yorton age 30 and Louise Yasidy age 22. [108]

Illustration #17: Billy Durant (left) and Edwin Campbell (right) with Edwin's children: Edwina on Billy's knee and William on his father's knee. (Photo: Courtesy Alex Sanger)

---

108   *Thirteenth Census of the United States 1910. Genessee County, Flint, Michigan*

Chapter Six

PROBLEMS

Financial Problems

General Motors produced fewer than 8500 cars in 1908, over 14,000 in 1909 and at the end of 1910 they had an annual production of over 30,000 cars. Although these figures produced gross sales of $29 million in 1909 rising to $49 million in 1910, net profits only rose slightly.[109] But all was not well. It was discovered that the patent on the Heany Company's lamp was entirely fraudulent and General Motors had to absorb a loss of more than $12 million! Billy was left with the reputation as a bungler for not investigating the company adequately. But more importantly, he and Edwin had overextended General Motors ability to absorb companies and, to complicate matters, the bookkeeping and accounting had not kept up with the rapid acquisition of companies.

Flink commented:

> *Compounding these blunders* [the purchase of money-losing Heany, Carter and Elmore] *Durant was so optimistic about*

---

109   Lawrence Gustin, <u>Billy Durant</u>, p. 136.

> *demand that he failed to build up cash reserves, relied on cash from sales to pay his operating expenses...* [110]

To a large degree, each plant was left to manage its own affairs. Due to the failure to establish a centralized bookkeeping system, Billy and Edwin were the only individuals who fully understood the financial structure of the company. In Billy's days with Dallas Dort, all his business associates and all who did business with him placed complete trust in his integrity and judgement. He also kept all his banking dealings in Flint. The rapid expansion of General Motors and its multimillion dollar acquisitions involved loans from over 200 banks, investment companies and financial institutions including three Flint Banks and extended all the way to New York.[111] The company's board room was also located on Wall Street. In describing Durant's loss of GM again in 1920 James Flink stated, *"In many instances the accounts could only be explained orally by Durant or his son-in-law, Dr Edwin R. Campbell."* [112] This was also the case in the 1910 dilemma that Billy and Edwin faced.

Billy's wild spending spree in acquiring so many companies in such a short time had gained considerable publicity across the country. It was also widely known that Billy had paid more for the worthless Heany Lamp Company than he had paid for Buick or Olds. In addition, the November rejection by the National City Bank of New York for Billy's application to borrow $2 million to buy out Ford was an indication of the attitude of some bankers toward the automobile. At a convention of national bankers in Texas in late 1909, Billy recalled:

> *"A member of the group...delivered a fiery speech saying...that many concerns engaged in the manufacture of automobiles were not properly financed; that the bankers were responsible*

---

110   James J. Flink. *The Automobile Age,* (Cambridge Mass, The MIT Press, 1992), p. 65.

111   William C. Durant, *In His Own Words, p. 58.*

112   James J. Flink *The Automobile Age,* p. 108.

> *for a situation that if not carefully watched might result in an industrial and financial panic..."*[113]

The statement from the bankers was somewhat reflective of the attitude which prevailed throughout the banking system in 1910. All were still suffering from the aftermath of the 1907 financial panic. Margery, in her succinct fashion, summarized the event as follows:

> *The panic came in the last part of October 1907. The bickering among the top men of the Steel Corporation, the "undigested securities" of a hundred other corporations, the writhings of a thwarted unionism and the blind optimism of men without vision, combined to topple the house of cards that bankers and brokers had built... Credit was practically suspended for days... Those in the automobile industry were desperate.... The weak ones were crushed. Strong ones went down fighting.*[114]

It should be emphasized that this panic gripped the entire industrialized world. In addition to the causes cited by Margery, other contributing factors included the Russian –Japanese War, the San Francisco earthquake and the fact that U.S. bankers had invested heavily in copper ventures notably the Amalgamated Copper Company and these had collapsed. In addition, *"the reserves of New York banks fell from a surplus of $11 million to a deficit of $54 million."*[115] These events led to runs on banks and Trust companies causing the collapse of several financial institutions including one of the largest Trust companies in the U.S., New York's Knickerbocker Trust Company, and the near collapse of the Trust Company of America and the Lincoln Trust Company.

The American Banking system suffered from a number of serious flaws that, though not fatal, made it especially vulnerable to financial

---

113   William C. Durant, <u>In His Own Words</u> , p. 56.

114   Margery Durant, <u>My Father,</u> p. 96.

115   Ibid., p. 517.

disasters.[116] One of the problems was that the regulations regarding capital and reserves applied to federal banks differed from those applied to state banks. Under this policy New York City banks had to earn a higher return from their loan portfolios than other banks. [117]

As a result of the financial panic, Congress passed the Aldrich-Vreeland Act in May 1908. One provision of this act was the establishment of a National Monetary Commission with the purpose of studying the banking and monetary systems both internationally and in the U.S. Investigations into U.S. banks led to a general tightening of credit and, within the banks themselves, a closer look at their own outstanding debts.

Following these guidelines, General Motors' major creditors met in New York to scrutinize the company's finances. By late March 1910, the tightening of credit had begun to affect Billy's own cash flow. Sales dropped dramatically and, largely due to his over-extension of Buick and Durant Dort finances, he could not afford to pay his workers. He was forced to close his factories until he could arrange for more loans. The creditors met again on May 1 and decided to call in their loans to General Motors.

Billy called on Edwin, A.B.C. Hardy and Arnold Goss to comb the country to call on all their banking contacts to try to arrange for loans in order to keep the business moving. Some money was found to keep suppliers temporarily at bay and to reopen the plants, but a broader solution was needed.

GM Rescue Package

In July 1910 Billy and Edwin strategized to create a board of directors for General Motors, one that would fit in with Billy's policies and attitudes towards the company, following the patterns that he had developed at the helm of the Durant Dort Carriage Company. The revised board of directors for the year included Sam McLaughlin.

---

116 Jeremy Atack and Peter Russell, <u>A New Economic View of American History</u>, p.514.

117 Ibid., p. 515.

In September Billy sold off three of his recent acquisitions; the Marquette Company, the Michigan Auto Parts Company and the Welch-Detroit Company. Later that month Billy and Edwin met in New York with several of the bankers involved in GM financing. Billy advanced his plea that GM had earned over $10 million in the previous twelve months and that a loan of $15 million was not unreasonable in order to keep the company functioning well and making a profit. The bankers then held their own meeting and the following day came forward with a proposal. J. and W. Seligman and Company of Boston offered to put forward a loan of $20 million. Of this amount $5 million was interest, but the most humiliating condition was that the bankers would take control of the company for a five year term. Billy would be allowed to remain as vice president but all his allies, including Edwin, Sam McLaughlin, Curtis Hatheway, and Wilfred Leland, would be removed from the board of directors. Billy and Edwin came to the painful realization that at that time it was the only viable way to save their baby: General Motors. Reluctantly the arrangement was accepted.

A new board of directors was created consisting of lawyers, accountants, bankers and investors. They included: Anthony Brady, an investment tycoon, director of several banks, trust companies, railroads and major holdings in the American Tobacco Company and one of the wealthiest men in the United States; Emory Clark president of the First National Bank of Detroit and directors of that bank; A. H. Green Jr., M. J. Murphy, and Thomas Neal; noted financier and accountant J. H. McClement; Albert Strauss of the Seligman Company of New York, a banking and loan company; Nicholas Tilney, a successful New York broker; James Wallace, a director of several banks including the Bank of America and Central Trust of New York; banker James Storrow of Boston;. From the new board a five-member trust was established and empowered to control the company's stock for the five year period. The five members of the voting trust were Brady, Storrow, Strauss, Wallace, and Billy Durant. Storrow was appointed president.

The banking credentials of the new board succeeded in creating confidence on Wall Street, but Billy soon lost faith in the board as it decided, against his wishes, to indiscriminately sell off some of the newly acquired companies and shut down others. The prominent companies sold off included the Ohio based Ewing Automobile Company and Elmore Manufacturing Company. The board shut down production of the Cartercar with its unique friction drive transmission. Also cancelled was the Buick racing program, leaving the now healthy Marr to concentrate on the development of conventional vehicles. In his spare time he experimented with the construction of airplanes.

Leading these moves was president James Storrow. The principals from these events have all passed into the panorama of industrial and corporate history, rendering it impossible to determine if any of Storrow's actions were carried out purely for vindictive reasons. Edwin certainly viewed it in that light. Later, when Billy and Edwin were developing a strategy to regain control of GM in 1915, Edwin was prompted to write to Billy and instruct him to make sure that Storrow was not on the board in order to *"... pay back a little of the humiliation you have gone through..."* [118]

The new board of directors continued to look for ways to reduce costs and to streamline production even further. Appearing to want to appeal more to the carriage trade with larger, more expensive vehicles, led by Storrow, they proposed to halt the production of the cheapest and smallest of their models, the Model 10 Buick. Billy vehemently tried to prevent this move, only to find that Storrow had convinced the entire board, with the exception of McClement, to go along with his suggestion. Billy argued that General Motors would eliminate its opportunity to offer true competition for Henry Ford. He explained to them that Ford's success was largely dependent on his reliable, low priced vehicle. But the new board of directors, with the exception of McClement, had no interest in Billy's ideas. Later that year, to add to Billy's frustration with the new board's decision to drop the Buick Model 10, Willys-Overland passed Buick to become the second largest producer of cars in the United States.

In his memoirs, Billy stated the obvious:

---

118 ERC to WCD., Sept 12, 1915. Scharchburg Archives

> *Many of the men...never having had experience in, or with, automobile design and production, with ideas of their own as to how business should be run, trained in banking rather than practical lines made my position a difficult one, and I realized that I was up against a real problem... I had been given a title and a position... but the support, the co-operation, the spirit, and the unselfishness that is needed in every successful undertaking was not there.* [119]

Margery reiterated his opinion:

> *"He felt that the danger of these so-called experts lay in the fact that each was specialized in a single line. None had any broad view of the motor industry."* [120]

With the discontinuation of the Model 10, Billy realized that a line had been drawn. This unpleasant relationship between Storrow and Durant would later explode into a dramatic confrontation.

As Billy and his family celebrated his forty-ninth birthday at Edwin's home on December 8, 1910, his despair must have been palpable at the dinner table on Stevens Street. He and Edwin were both at loose ends, frustrated, annoyed. Something had to be done.

The Chevrolet

Once the Storrow-led Trust was firmly in control, GM slowly worked its way back into solvency, but the board's lack of understanding of automobile manufacturing carried a problematic cost: a gradual decline in plant efficiency and vehicle quality. The board "... *spent as little as possible modify-*

---

119 William C. Durant, <u>In His Own Words</u>, p. 58.

120 Margery Durant, <u>My Father</u>, p. 131.

ing the production lines to emulate Ford's moving assembly lines. They had not kept pace with the industry's growth..."[121]

Billy Durant was a man of action and soon lost interest in struggling to cultivate allies among the bankers who controlled General Motors. Accepting that their mandate was to manage the company until 1915, he desperately needed to get back into the heat of automobile design, production and sales and, more specifically, to find a way to eventually get back at the helm of General Motors. Billy mused:

> With no idea of being disloyal it seemed to me that it would be better to let the new group handle the business to suit themselves and if I ever expected to regain control of General Motors, which I certainly intended to do, I should have a company of my own, run my own way. In other words, another one-man institution, but taking a leaf out of Henry Ford's book — No Bankers.[122]

Of interest to Billy was the fact that Louis Chevrolet had personally modified Marr's Buick engines even further for his successful racing machines. He even mentioned to Billy that he would like to produce his own cars. Sometime in late 1910 Billy and Edwin approached him with the idea of designing and building a new car for them to compete with the low priced Ford. Although Billy had lost control of General Motors, he had lost none of his personal wealth. He arranged for Chevrolet to have the use of a building in Detroit in order to work on a car of his own design. With Billy's financial support he quickly set about his task.

---

[121] Edward Cray, *The Chrome Colossus: General Motors and its Times*. (New York, McGraw Hill, 1980), p.140.

[122] William C. Durant, *In His Own Words*, p. 59.

Whiting and Little

At the same time, Billy was renewing his friendship with James Whiting, Charles Begole and William Ballenger. Whiting had expanded his Flint Wagon Works and was building a small car which he had named after himself; the Whiting. Begole had been the president of Buick and Ballenger had been its treasurer. These two were now working with Whiting in his fledging venture into automobiles. Billy and his son-in-law realized that this enterprise would fit into their plans by providing a suitable plant for their plans for Chevrolet's vehicle. Billy approached Whiting with an arrangement to buy his company and all the remaining unfinished Whiting cars. The deal was signed in December 1910.

Arthur Mason, a former Buick engine designer was hired to set up engine production in the former Flint Wagon Works. With Begole, Ballenger and William Little, a former Buick general manager under Durant, the Little Motor Car Company was incorporated on October 30, 1911. Their mandate was to build a small car using the Mason engine. Billy's old friend A.B.C. Hardy was placed in charge of the plant. When finished, the car was to be considered as a possible contender to fill the void left by the demise of the Buick Model 10 and to compete head on with the Ford.

Edwin and the Chevrolet Motor Company

In order to accommodate Louis Chevrolet's vehicle, plans were made for a third company to be financed by Billy. Edwin took care of many of the details of the creation of the company and on November 3, 1911, that new corporation came into being. With Edwin Campbell, William Little and Louis Chevrolet as the incorporators, the Chevrolet Motor Company of Michigan was established. Over the next few days, Billy and Edwin met with the principals and the company was firmly in operation with Little as president, Billy as vice president, Curtis Hatheway as secretary, Ballenger as treasurer and Edwin as a director. While Chevrolet was busy working on the design in a building on Detroit's Grand River, they made plans to purchase the former Corcoran Lamp Company factory on West Grand Boulevard in Detroit. This was a much larger facility and ideal for the manufacture of their cars. There was also a large and luxurious office attached to the factory which was ideal for the headquarters for Chevrolet.

Since Edwin was to take a major role in Chevrolet, he and Margery made plans to move to Detroit and made numerous trips to the city to look for a suitable house close to the West Grand Boulevard plant, eventually settling at a large and comfortable home at 2040 Woodward Avenue. With her three servants looking after the home, Margery continued her custom of picking up her father after his day was finished and bringing him home for dinner. Whenever Billy was in Detroit he usually stayed with Edwin and Margery. As Margery would later write:

> *I saw him intimately in those days* [1911-1914]; *lived in the same house with him; talked business with him; often listened to his business conferences with other men.* [123]

Following the pattern for the structure of their initial success at General Motors, they decided to create a holding company. The Republic Motor Company was incorporated in July 1912 as a holding company for the Mason, Little and Chevrolet production.

The first Chevrolet emerged for its first road test in March 1912. Louis Chevrolet proudly took an auto reporter for a ride and at the conclusion asked him to stand a pencil on the hood of the car. Chevrolet then revved the engine up to 2,000 r.p.m. and the pencil remained standing. The reason: Louis had learned from his failure at his first attempt at the Indianapolis race when his Buick failed to finish due to a broken crankshaft. For his new vehicle he had spent hours carefully balancing the crankshaft so that it would run smoothly and without effort.[124] Eight months later the

---

123 Margery Durant, My Father, p. 139.

124 Beverly Rae Kines and Robert C. Ackerson Chevrolet; A History from 1911,. (Kutztown, Pennsylvania, Automobile Quarterly Publications Marque History Book. Second edition, 1986), p. 17.

first production model emerged. The publicity photos showed Billy's son Clifford at the wheel with his wife in the front passenger seat. The car was labelled the Classic Six Chevrolet.

Illustration #18: The First Chevrolet built in Detroit, 1912, with Billy's son Clifford at the wheel and Clifford's second wife, Adelaide Frost beside him.
(Photo: Courtesy Scharchburg Archives, Kettering University)

Another company, the Sterling Motor, a division of The Republic Motor Company was incorporated in September with Billy, Edwin, Dallas Dort, Little and Hatheway, as directors. The Sterling division was given the responsibility of producing the six-cylinder engines for the Little-Chevrolet cars.

Although sales reached a modest but acceptable 2,999 cars, the Chevrolet was a disappointment for Billy and Edwin. It was not what they had in mind. Its six-cylinder, 299 cubic inch engine provided more than adequate power, but the car, with its 120 inch chassis, was too big and more importantly, it was too expensive to produce and certainly offered no competition for Henry Ford. But at least it was a starting point, so production of the vehicle began and Margery took delivery of one of the first production vehicles.

Early in 1913 plans were made to phase out the Louis Chevrolet designed six-cylinder car and to introduce a smaller six-cylinder Chevrolet called the Light Six alongside a new four-cylinder engine car. The smaller six-cylinder Chevrolet had a 112 inch long chassis and its engine was reduced to 271 cubic inches. The four-cylinder engine was of a 171 cubic inch displacement on a 104 inch chassis. These cars, introduced to the public in late 1913, were referred to as Series H cars. They displayed, for the first time, the famous "bow tie" emblem, a creation of Billy's, and the hallmark of Chevrolet still being used today.

Illustration # 19: The Early Chevrolet logo. (Courtesy General Motors)

The stories of the origins of the Chevrolet "bow tie" logo are numerous and varied. Margery's version is as credible as any and serves to underline the importance of so many unrecorded but central events that took place at the Campbell's dinner table in Stevens Street. Margery stated:

> "As in the case of the Buick, my father drew name-plates on pieces of paper at the dinner table. I think that it was between

> the soup and the fried chicken one night that he sketched out
> the design that is used on the Chevrolet car to this day." [125]

The move to offer less powerful and cheaper cars did not sit well with Louis Chevrolet and, after further disagreements; Louis Chevrolet parted company with Durant, much as David Buick had done in the early days of the Buick car. Chevrolet returned to his true love: racing.

Shortly afterwards, in January 1913, Benjamin Briscoe's United States Motor Company went into receivership. Briscoe had experienced a devastating cash flow problem when he over-expanded, just as Billy had done in his creation of General Motors. Briscoe resigned and the assets were bought by a newly created Maxwell Motor Company.

Doubling Production

In January 1913, the Campbell family, with Billy in tow, took a much needed holiday in Bermuda in order to allow Edwin and Billy to spend a relaxing time together while planning a framework for future action for Chevrolet for the remaining two years of the banker trust control of GM, all this while far away from the pressures of Flint, Detroit and New York. Billy took his mother, Rebecca, on the holiday, but strangely Catherine did not accompany them. On January 20th Edwin registered himself as a doctor in Hamilton, Bermuda. [126] In mid April they left Bermuda and April 17 they disembarked from the *SS Arcadian* in New York with a determination to put their plans to work.

By the summer, the strategy of Edwin and Billy was obvious; they were building the Chevrolet company into a viable competitor for GM. With Edwin and Margery's encouragement, Billy focussed his entire attention on the Chevrolet and resigned from his role as treasurer of the old Durant Dort Carriage Company. There are no apparent unpleasant circumstances in the relationship between Billy and Dallas Dort however, Billy and Dort

---

125   Margery Durant, My Father, p. 146

126   Directory of Deceased American Physicians.

parted company. Billy resigned from the Durant Dort Carriage Company and Dallas Dort withdrew from his involvement in Chevrolet. Shortly afterwards Dort ventured into car production himself and established the Dort Motor Company.

The Chevrolet Company absorbed Sterling just before the end of the year, and most importantly, had taken control of the entire Republic Motor Company phasing out the Republic name and the Little Company. In response to an increased demand for the smaller Chevrolets Billy and Edwin reorganized vehicle production with the emphasis on the smaller four-cylinder vehicle. To meet the growing demand for these vehicles, Edwin went to California to oversee plans to establish a west coast division of Chevrolet. He met with Billy's son Clifford with the authority to appoint him as an officer in the west coast division. The next step in this phase was to set up a new plant for the production of the small Chevrolet in Oakland, California. While in California, Edwin bought a comfortable home at 340 California Avenue East in Pasadena to use as a base for his time in that state. Back in Flint, through the Chevrolet Company, Billy took over the Imperial Wheel Company.

By the end of 1914 the decision was made to completely drop Louis' original larger and unprofitable Classic Six Chevrolet. The following year, the Light Six failed to generate large sales (only 500 for the year) so it too was dropped from production. The Series H four-cylinder cars proved to be steady sellers. Almost 7,000 of the models were sold in 1915. In January 1915 a new model, the 490, was introduced at the New York Auto Show at an advertised sale price of $550 and competed directly with Henry Ford's Model T. The designation of the model number was Billy's target: to manufacture his new Chevrolet and sell it for $490. Designed by Alfred T. Sturt, another former Buick employee, it was, like Ford's model T, reliable, economical and attractive. It even had electric lights and a starter as optional extras. By the end of the year over 13,000 of the 490 had been sold. The following year, 1916, an astounding 70,000 vehicles bearing the Chevrolet nameplate were sold. With this production level, the Chevrolet name was rapidly gaining acceptance; however, it still had a long way to go to compete with Henry Ford's sales of over three hundred thousand Model Ts for 1915 and reaching the half million level for the 1916 fiscal year.

Illustration # 20: Margery in her own 1915 Amesbury special Model H Chevrolet, in Central Park New York. The car sold for $985 but the wire wheels were an extra $125. (Photo: Courtesy Scharchburg Archives, Kettering University)

Chevrolets in Canada

During a fall visit to New York in 1915, Sam McLaughlin joined Edwin and Billy for dinner at Pabst's Restaurant. *"It was my custom, whenever I was there* [In New York City] *to have lunch with Edwin Campbell."*[127] They were joined by Nathan Hofheimer, a major investor in Chevrolet. Hofheimer, a German immigrant, had made his fortune by investing in the international liquor trade, initially in New York. He then organized a huge syndicate of British investors who bought out several major Kentucky distilleries in 1892. Billy mentioned to Sam that he was thinking of arranging to have Chevrolets assembled in Canada. Hofheimer suggested to Billy that

---

127   R.S. McLaughlin, as told to Eric Hutton, "My Eighty Years on Wheels," <u>Macleans Magazine</u> Part Three, October 15, 1954.

Sam should be given the opportunity to assemble the cars in Canada. Sam stated that he certainly was interested but in order to do so, there were two problems to overcome:

> "First, how do we stand with our Buick contract if we took on another line of cars? More important, could we persuade the Governor [his father, Robert McLaughlin] *to sell the carriage business. Certainly if we undertook to make a car with the volume Chevrolet promised in Canada, we couldn't go on making carriages. And if the Governor decided against abandoning the business that was his life, we couldn't take on Chevrolet.*" [128]

The McLaughlins were short of production space as they were assembling McLaughlin Buicks and carrying on the carriage making in the same facility in Oshawa. The following day Sam's brother George came to New York to work out more details. The two then returned to Oshawa and had no difficulty in convincing their father that the Chevrolet was a worthy proposition and that they should sell off the carriage production. Within two months, the carriage business had been sold to Jim Tudhope and his Carriage Factories Ltd., of Orillia, Ontario. Tudhope established the right to continue to manufacture the carriages with the prestigious McLaughlin label for another year, after which the McLaughlin name reverted back to the McLaughlin family and the Tudhope name was used on the carriages. Production of Canadian Chevrolets began immediately with Billy as the majority shareholder.

More Chevrolet Expansion

With the Detroit production of 20 Chevrolets a day, Billy and Edwin expressed their dreams to double that figure but realized that they needed

---

128   Ibid.

bigger and more spacious production facilities. On March 21, the *New York Times* reported;

> The sale of an industrial plant of more than average importance has just been made by Joseph P. Day who has sold the factory and land at Tarrytown on Beekman Avenue formerly occupied by the Maxwell-Briscoe Motor Company. The land comprises about twenty acres and the buildings contain about 150,000 square feet of floor space... The new owner is the Chevrolet Motor Company of New York City, of which William C. Durant is president. The company will use it for the manufacture of a new light automobile.[129]

To accomplish this, more capital was needed and the only way to gain more capital was to go against Billy's aversion for bankers. Putting aside this mistrust, early in the year Billy and Edwin conferred with close friends in the financial world. Nathan Hofheimer introduced Billy and Edwin to Louis Kaufman, president of the Chatham & Phoenix Bank of New York. He, Billy and Edwin had also developed a close relationship with Pierre S. du Pont and John Raskob, treasurer of Du Pont de Nemours & Company. Du Pont was also on the board of directors of the Chatham & Phoenix Bank. Billy and Edwin discussed their strategy with them.

> Late in the summer of 1915, Mr. Durant arranged a meeting with Mr. Raskob and Pierre S. Du Pont. John Thomas Smith, a New York attorney ... and Dr. Edwin Campbell, Mr Durant's son-in-law, attended with him. Other conferences followed. Arthur G. Bishop, president of Genesee Bank in Flint, recalled a session at the Du Pont office in Wilmington. The deal [Durant and the Du Pont interests would buy shares and then each would have a 50% interest in the company] *was closed and the Flint men elated. They were then invited to the*

---

129 *New York Times* March 21, 1915.

> Du Pont estate for dinner. "Let's not go," Dr. Campbell whispered to Mr. Bishop. "They might change their minds." The doctor was afraid the small town delegation would be too far out of its element and make a poor impression.[130]

They went anyway. With finances in places, Billy and Edwin began another growth plan, but this time being careful not to repeat the failings of their 1908-1910 over-expansion under the General Motors banner. Realizing that many potential buyers from New York and other centres in the New England area would enjoy visiting the factory which produced their cars, Billy negotiated the lease of a factory on land which occupied a full city block in downtown New York. It was located on 11th Avenue from 56th to 57th streets, in Greenwich Village, a short walking distance from the south-west corner of Central Park in the heart of New York City. The *New York Times* noted;

> Most of the property formed part of the old Chandler estate now owned by the heirs, and this has been taken on long leaseholds, while parts of the plot, which runs back to a depth of 200 feet in each street have been purchased.
>
> The Chevrolet Motor plant now covers the block front directly to the block front directly to the north between Fifty-sixth and Fifty-seventh Streets and with the improvement of the new block front with a modern factory and service building, the facilities of the company in this city will now be more than doubled.
>
> In addition to this deal, the company is making large additions to its plants at Tarrytown and at Flint, Mich. Within a short time the Chevrolet Company expects to be turning out 800 cars a day.[131]

---

130 Frank Rodolf as quoted in Lawrence Gustin, <u>Billy Durant</u>, p 166.
131 <u>New York Times</u> October 17, 1915.

Walter P. Chrysler

Meanwhile at GM a number of significant developments were taking place at the administrative level. In 1910, Billy suggested that Charles Nash, Billy's former superintendent of the Durant Dort Carriage Company should be promoted to the presidency of Buick. Storrow accepted this proposal. In return Storrow was allowed to hire Walter P. Chrysler as an assistant to Nash at Buick.

Chrysler came from an engineering background as his father was a railroad engineer in Kansas where Walter was born. He fulfilled his apprenticeship as a mechanic at Union Pacific. In 1908 with a salary of $350 a month he saw a new $5,000 Locomobile car, became infatuated with it and bought the vehicle. He promptly took it home and dismantled it to see how each part was produced.[132] He then applied to work at the American Locomotive Company (ALCO) in Pittsburgh. Within two years he was promoted to works manager. His reputation for efficiency and productivity attracted the attention of James Storrow, who was a director of the American Locomotive Board at the time.

When he was elected as president of GM, Storrow realized that although Nash was an excellent administrator, his main manufacturing experience was with workmen building carriages out of wood and he had little experience in handling the machine side of affairs from a manufacturing standpoint. Chrysler filled that void and was hired to assist Nash. As a result of his disciplined control of Buick and his ability to reduce costs, Nash was elected as president of General Motors itself in 1912. In his place, Walter P. Chrysler was promoted to the head of the Buick division.

Showdown Approaching

The bankers' five year control of GM was set to expire at the end of September 1915. With their own success now obvious, Durant and Campbell faced a problem in regaining control of GM: the bankers

---

132   Richard M. Langworth and Jan P. Norbye. <u>The Complete History of Chrysler, 1924-1985.</u> (Greenville, S.C. Crescent Publishing Company, 1985), p. 9.

trust could vote themselves back in control for another term. Billy and Edwin realized that control of the company and the voting control could only be wrested from the bankers by taking control of the majority of the stock of General Motors. In order to bring this about they spent the next weeks contacting shareholders and offered to either buy their GM shares or arrange for them to be sold to the Du Pont group. In addition they encouraged their close friends to buy GM shares. In 1915 Sam McLaughlin increased his own holdings from $77,000 to $208,000.[133] The showdown between Billy and the GM Board was approaching, but more importantly to Edwin and Margery, there were storm clouds looming in their own relationship.

---

133   Heather Robertson, *Driving Force* page 156.

Chapter Seven

THE CAMPBELLS MOVE TO NEW YORK

Diamond Jim Brady

Everything that Diamond Jim Brady said or did from about 1895 until his death in 1917 was followed closely in the press.

> ... *Diamond Jim Brady had a unique official position in the world of Broadway...He was Broadway's master of reels, its oracle and arbiter, its greatest host, its premier angel and philanthropist, its outstanding playboy, its most benevolent, authoritative pander.* [134]

James Buchanan Brady developed the nickname "Diamond Jim" as a result of his apparently insatiable penchant for diamonds.

> ... *his gaudy sets of enormous gems — he had thirty sets, each composed of twenty items, and collectively they included more*

---

134   Lloyd Morris, <u>Incredible New York</u>, (New York, Random House, 1951), p. 263.

than twenty thousand diamonds of varying size and shape, as well as six thousand other precious stones. [135]

He had risen from the streets of New York's Lower West Side to become one of that city's wealthiest and most gregarious and flamboyant characters. He made much of his immense wealth through the stock market, particularly as a result of his knowledge and understanding of railways. Not all of his dealings on the stock market were beyond question and he had many detractors. However he dispelled many of those detractions through his philanthropic endeavours, supporting numerous Broadway plays and musicals and giving generous donations to several charitable organizations including the Johns Hopkins Hospital.[136] Diamond Jim's extravagant parties and gatherings were the highlight of any social season and were always given full and extensive coverage in the *New York Times*.

By 1914 Billy Durant was already a long established and familiar face on the New York Stock Exchange, indeed he was one of the more powerful and influential forces on the floor of the exchange, and his son-in-law was increasingly becoming a familiar face there too. During their frequent visits to the exchange Billy and Edwin would rub shoulders with many of the richest men in the United States including James Brady. As the 1913-1914 social season came to an end Diamond Jim held what was arguably the culminating event of that season. He took over the entire Greenbrier resort at White Sulphur Springs, West Virginia for a few days in early May, 1914. This resort was the most luxurious and exclusive in the entire country. On Thursday May 3, the first of the invited guests began to arrive. They included Brady himself along with: Mr. and Mrs Henry Taft (brother of Republican President Howard Taft); leading Democrats and former Congressmen John Thayer and Cornelius Pugsley; Fred Housman, one of the major brokers for the J. P. Morgan Company; Robert Livingston Gerry, a director of the Farmers' Loan and Trust Company and Francis Ormond French, President of the Manhattan Trust Company. Also

---

135 Ibid.

136 *New York Times*, August 13, 1912.

among the invited guests were numerous Southern multi-millionaires, including Theodore H. Price, all of whom had made their fortunes on the stock market by speculating in cotton. All brought their wives, all that is except Brady himself; he never married, but he did have a mistress, singer/actress and former department store sales clerk, Edna McCauley, who accompanied him on all social occasions. From the press coverage of the event, we are not told whether or not McCauley was accompanied by her ever-present companion, singer/ actress, many-times-married Lillian Russell and her lover, copper millionaire and turf baron Jesse Lewisohn. The press does however make mention of the early arrival of Dr. and Mrs. Edwin R. Campbell.[137]

As the long weekend progressed there were luncheons, parties and dances. It is not difficult to imagine the radiant 24 year-old Margery gliding elegantly through the sea of matronly bejewelled dowagers of the high society of the entire eastern seaboard and beyond. Margery Campbell, her beauty, grace and youth, particularly her youth, the envy of all. Thus Margery and Edwin made their social debut in New York society.

Noticeably absent from the carefully selected guests were Billy and Catherine Durant. We do not know whether they were invited or not. If they had been invited, it is most likely that they declined the invitation as Catherine was notoriously shy and uncomfortable among people who were not of her own choosing. Two years later, when the Durants took possession of Raymere, their stately home on the New Jersey shore, they entertained frequently and lavishly, and Catherine was a gracious hostess but her guests were carefully selected from those among whom she was at ease.

The Plaza Hotel

In March 1914 Billy took possession of an apartment at 565 Park Avenue in downtown New York. Within a few months, at Margery's insistence,

---

137 *New York Times*, May 4, 1914.

she and Edwin and their family made plans to move to New York too. Margery explained:

> *In the autumn of 1914 my husband and I moved to New York and took an apartment at 635 Park Avenue on the corner of 66th Street. I chose this address in order to be near my father who lived a little further up the same avenue. I could no longer drive him to the factory as I did in the old days; or stay up half the night in an outer office while he held a business conference. But he and I were still comrades in arms, so to speak; and we found the greatest pleasure in each other's company.*[138]

The Campbells' arrival in New York plunged them into the whirl of the dynamic cultural and social life of the city. This was the prelude to the "Roaring Twenties." It was in stark contrast to their lives in Detroit and an even greater contrast to the way they began their married life in Flint. Of their life in Flint, Margery wrote: *"I liked Flint and I still do. I had friends and acquaintances there. It had been my home, but I had never entertained very much."* [139] At the Plaza and later at their apartment, they entertained regularly and were included annually in the city's social register beginning in 1915.[140]

Arriving in New York, they found that the Park Avenue apartment was not finished so they moved into a suite at the Plaza Hotel. The Plaza Hotel was to continue to play a major role in their lives. They initially remained there for three months while awaiting the completion of their apartment and returned again in 1917 for a six month period while their Park Avenue apartment was again remodelled. After their divorce four years later, Edwin moved into the Plaza and maintained a suite there until his death.

The first Plaza Hotel was opened on the present site in 1890. It was torn down in 1905 and work began on a new hotel designed by Henry Hardenbergh, renowned for his design of the Waldorf Astoria, at the time

---

138   Margery Durant, <u>My Father</u>, p. 211.

139   Margery Durant, <u>My Father</u>, p. 164.

140   <u>New York Social Register 1915</u>, New York: The Social Register Association.

the most luxurious hotel in the city. When the new Plaza Hotel opened in October 1907 it was advertised as "the World's Most Luxurious Hotel." It was certainly the most expensive and elegant building erected in the city, and its reputation quickly replaced that of the Waldorf. At its opening, millionaire Alfred Vanderbilt, son of Cornelius Vanderbilt II, was the first to sign the register and take possession of his exclusive corner suite overlooking Fifth Avenue, Fifty-Ninth Streets and Central Park. He was joined later that day by several millionaires including: John Drake, a major financier of the Plaza, Benjamin Duke, of the wealthy textile and tobacco family and brother of the benefactor of Trinity College of Durham, N.C., after whom the college was renamed Duke University; financiers John Gates, George J. Gould, Mrs. Oliver Harriman, C. K. Billings, Mrs. James Henry Smith and Mrs. Young Heyworth, all of whom occupied corner suites above or below Vanderbilt. Many also had mansions in and around the city but used the Plaza as the place to be when entertaining or relaxing after a night in the centre of town. Either socially or in business circles, the Campbells would have become acquainted with most of them.

The *New York Times* announced, *"With the assured distinction of sheltering as permanent guests, the largest millionaire colony in the city, or as a matter of fact in the entire world, the new $12,000,000 Plaza will be viewed by official invitation today."* [141]

The hotel had several dining rooms including The Grill, the least formal of the hotel's restaurants. It was frequently used as a setting in F. Scott Fitzgerald's novel **The Beautiful and Damned**. He also used the Plaza's Tea Room and a hotel suite as settings in **The Great Gatsby**. After their marriage in 1920 the Fitzgeralds lived in an apartment at 38 West Fifty-Ninth Street, close to the Plaza. This enabled them to visit their favourite restaurant, the Grill at the Plaza on most evenings. The Fitzgeralds may very well have come in contact with the Campbells.

On November 15, 1907 there was a scandal in the Plaza when Mrs Patrick Campbell (no relation), a star of British stage (George Bernard Shaw wrote **Pygmalion** for her), lit up a cigarette in the Plaza dining room.

---

141 *New York Times*, October 1, 1907.

This caused a furor in the press. A screen was placed around her table so that the sight of a lady smoking would not disturb the other guests. Her provocative act lead to the banning of smoking in the New York City Subways the following year.

In the 1940s, Kay Thompson created a fictitious, precocious six-year-old named Eloise who lived at the Plaza. She has been the subject of several books and has become an institution at the Plaza. Eloise could very well have been based on Edwin and Margery's children William and Edwina; however the dates of Thompson's involvement with the Plaza belie such a conclusion. The hotel was expanded again in 1921.

635 Park Avenue

Three months later their apartment was completed. Located at the southeast corner of 66th and Park Avenue, the 13-story building at 635 Park Avenue represented the height of luxury when it was built in 1912. The Campbells' immense 5000 square foot apartment occupied the whole of the sixth floor. To greet visitors, the Campbells had their own 13 foot diameter circular foyer. The living room was over 30 feet long and 19 feet wide, the dining room was 27 feet long. It had five bedrooms, providing accommodation for several servants. In the 1920 census, the Campbells had living with them: waitress Annette Peterson age 32, cook Berna Westergren age 36, chambermaid Augot Abelson age 39, kitchenmaid Aina Hirkcanta age 30 and ladies maid 37 year old Alma Jussila. For the children: a governess, 25 year old Lenore Reno and a nursemaid Elsie Anderson age 17. Coincidentally, all seven servants were Scandinavians. [142] Although the Census lists all seven as living at 635 Park Avenue, it is not clear whether they all lived directly in the Campbell suite or in separate accommodation in the building.

---

142   1920 United Sates Federal Census 1920 Manhattan Assembly District 15, New York Roll T625-1213; page 7A.

Illustration #21: Edwin and Margery with the children in Detroit, just before their move to New York. Edwina is in front of Margery and William is on his father's knee. (Photo: Courtesy Alex Sanger)

Edwin and Margery settled into an intense social life. Margery expressed herself this way:

> *It was a great event for us to come to New York. I particularly felt the need of a broader environment. I felt the city with its opportunities to hear the best music, see the best in art and enjoy the finest lectures, was where I belonged. The cosmopolitan life about me satisfied a hunger I long had felt.*[143]

---

143 Margery Durant, <u>My Father</u>, p. 212.

Kandinsky

Both Edwin and Margery took a keen interest in the arts. For some strange reason, in stark contrast to his traditional, classical art schooling at Port Perry High School, Edwin became fascinated with the abstract expressionism which dominated the current interest in art. Edwina noted, *"He frequented the gallery at "21" run by Alfred Stieglitz, watched Georgia O'Keefe blossom, and became interested in the work of Kandinsky, who was exhibiting at New York's Armory Show in 1913."*[144]

Opening in mid February 1913 and lasting for a month, a trend-setting exhibition of modern art was held at the New York Armory. The exhibition received rave reviews, with the work of Russian artist Wassily Kandinsky at the centre. Kandinsky is regarded as the pioneer of modern abstract art, leading the way for Picasso. During the show, Edwin, impressed with his work, commissioned Kandinsky to paint four panels for the foyer of their Park Avenue apartment. The artist completed the panels in Germany. At the outbreak of hostilities in 1914 it became difficult to ship artefacts from Germany. To get around this problem, the paintings were initially shipped to Sweden where they were first exhibited. Edwin finally received them in the summer of 1916. The four panels each over five feet in height were arranged about two-and-a-half feet apart in the huge foyer of their apartment. Edwina commented; *"The panels were hung in the foyer and occasioned much comment from friends, ranging from bewildered admiration to 'My God, Ed, have you lost your mind?'"*[145]

The Lambs

Immediately after moving into the Plaza, Edwin began visiting The Lambs, a club created in New York in 1874 and incorporated in 1877 for those interested in arts and letters, but primarily in the performing arts. It followed on the ideals established by a group of the same name in

---

144 Edwina Campbell, <u>My First 90 Years</u>, page 13

145 Ibid.

London, England, founded a few years earlier honouring Charles Lamb, the writer who hosted actors and writers at his home in London. In New York the club provided a meeting place for those involved or interested in stage and screen in the city. New plays were often given their first reading here. One of the more significant happenings in the history of musicals is that Alan J. Lerner and Frederick Loewe, later creators of **Brigadoon**, **Camelot** and **My Fair Lady**, met at The Lambs before their fame and began their collaborations at the club, giving presentations of their works for its members before putting them on stage.

Potential members had to be introduced by existing members and their application reviewed by an executive. New members were then inducted by The Shepherd (the president). In 1917 Edwin was inducted into the Lambs. His Shepherd, the president of the Lambs at the time of his induction, was William Courtleigh a successful movie actor. He had an extensive list of movies to his credit in the 1920s. Edwin and his Shepherd had another distinction in common, they were both Canadians. Courtleigh had been born in Guelph in 1867, a year after Edwin. Courtleigh owned a large estate on Boston Post Road in Rye, N.Y. His son, William Courtleigh Jr. was also a movie actor who featured in several movies before falling victim to the flu epidemic of 1918, dying at the age of 26.

Edwin would have no doubt met most, if not all, of the members of the Lambs at some time or other. Some of the more prominent members at that time, and the dates of their induction to the Lambs were: actors Lionel Barrymore (1900) and Douglas Fairbanks Sr. (1905), comedian W. C. Fields (1918), movie star Charlie Chaplin (1925), singer Al Jolson (1919), composers/songwriters George M. Cohen (1911), Irving Berlin (1913), Jerome Kern (1919), Oscar Hammerstein (1921) and George Gershwin (1924) and movie director and producer Louis B. Mayer of Metro Goldwin Mayer (1919). Other notables from outside the entertainment industry, such as aviator Charles Lindberg (1927) also became members. Many were guests of Edwin and Margery at their Plaza suite and later at their Park Avenue home. Irving Berlin was known to have come to their Park Avenue apartment and played their piano on several occasions. Today The Lambs is located just off Fifth Avenue on Fifty-First Street.

Sleepy Hollow Country Club

During their initial stay at the Plaza the Campbells were introduced to Percy Rockefeller who encouraged them to join the Sleepy Hollow Country Club. Rockefeller was the nephew of John D. Rockefeller, wealthy industrialist and founder of Standard Oil. Percy Rockefeller and his father William Rockefeller, John D's brother, were on the board of directors of the club at the time. One of the most prestigious country clubs in the United States then and today, the Sleepy Hollow Country Club was originally the stately country home of Colonel Shepard, husband of Margaret Vanderbilt. In 1910 the home on its 338-acre estate was bought by Percy's father William Rockefeller, and turned over to the organizers of the Sleepy Hollow Country Club. Its first directors, along with the Rockefellers, included the Campbells' neighbours at the Plaza: the Astors, Harrimans and the Vanderbilts, as well as other wealthy socialites of the city. The Club had a variety of sports, cultural and recreational facilities including an 18 hole golf course, riding trails, tennis courts, a ballroom and a library. The Campbells bought a membership in the club while still at the Plaza. Percy Rockefeller was soon to play a key role in Edwin and Billy's strategy to regain control of General Motors.

To complete his move to New York, Edwin registered himself with the physicians of New York on October 6, 1915.[146]

Socialite Margery

Margery's immersion into the vibrant social life of New York included her passion for music. She took singing lessons from *"the best vocal coaches of the day."* [147] Edwina, a competent pianist often accompanied her on the piano *"... she sang Italian and French operatic arias — in public no less!"* [148]

Edwina continued:

---

[146] *Directory of deceased Physicians, 1804-1929.*

[147] Edwina Campbell Sanger <u>My First 90 Years</u>. (Lunenburg, VT., Stinehour Press, 1999), p. 11.

[148] Ibid.

> Meanwhile, mother was joining an elite group of well-to-do New York women who lived a busy and varied life. Between one activity or another, she was out nearly every afternoon and evening — teas dances, charity costume balls, settlement house work, art shows, plays and of course music — opera every Monday night, Philharmonic every Friday afternoon. As an admiring 10-year-old, one of my great pleasures was to help mother select her evening gown and accompanying jewelry for the festivities.[149]

Shortly after her arrival in New York, Margery became a member of the Colony Club, the earliest New York club for women only. With exclusive admission requirements accessible only to the wealthy in the city, it was patronized by several of the Campbells' fellow residents at the Plaza, including the Astors, and the Harrimans. The first Colony Club building was located at 120 Madison Avenue. Just before Margery's arrival in the city, the Club announced that it was to build a new "club house", the finest in the world. In 1916 the new facility, housing meeting rooms, a swimming pool and a large gymnasium, opened on Park Avenue. The original Colony Club was founded by Florence Harriman, Anne Morgan and their friends as a gathering place for women with interests in the arts and humanitarian concerns. Many of its members were involved in the suffragette movement. During World War One, Margery joined the members in knitting socks and scarves and making and rolling bandages for the soldiers overseas.

Dr. Bruce Visits

The decade which followed the outbreak of "The War to End All Wars" witnessed the advent of numerous events which would shape the evolution of the western world. Central to those events were indi-

---

[149] Ibid., p. 14.

viduals whose lives, by uncanny coincidences, would cross the paths of the Campbell family.

When Britain declared war on Germany in August 1914, Canada, with its sense of loyalty to the mother country immediately joined in the fray. Edwin's old friend and classmate Dr. H. A. Bruce, disappointed that he was not called upon for his medical services with the Canadian armed forces, paid his own way to the front in France to volunteer his services. After a short stay, he returned to Toronto and was given the position of Inspector General of Medical Services with the duty to investigate the quality of care given to the Canadian wounded in Europe and submit a report to the Canadian Ministry of Militia. Bruce's scathing report cited major administrative problems. His report made sweeping recommendations but in Ottawa it became a political football and he resigned because of the ineptitude of the government and the ministry.

He was offered, and accepted a position as Consulting Surgeon to the British War Office. In this capacity he was invited, in 1916, to Washington to speak on the organization of medical care to the Council of National Defence. On his arrival in New York he and Edwin met briefly to renew their friendship. After his return to the conflict in Europe his organizational and surgical successes with the British attracted the attention of the French Army Medical Organization who asked him to tour their facilities and again, produce a report.

In June 1918, in response to a request from the United States government through the British, he was invited to the United States to give a number of presentations on the organization of medical care for the Armed Forces. On arrival in New York he was greeted again by Edwin and stayed briefly with the Campbells at their Park Avenue suite. Dr. Bruce's major presentations included those to the American Medical Association in Chicago and the Medical Surgical Association in Cincinnati.

In February 1919, while still in England, Dr. Bruce married a nurse, Angela Hall. Later that spring, Dr. Bruce was again invited to address the American Surgical Association at their annual convention in Atlantic City. On his way he stopped off in New York to introduce Edwin and Margery to his bride. It should be pointed out that when the American College of Surgeons was founded in May 1913, Dr. Bruce was a founding member.

Marital Problems

As events in Edwin and Billy's plans to regain control of GM gathered momentum, Edwin and Margery's simultaneous move to New York, and Margery's subsequent immersion into the hectic social life created difficulties for the couple. Their daughter Edwina observed:

> *" He... [Edwin] thoroughly disapproved of women indulging in cocktails, flirtations, and cigarettes...The gap grew wider, the arguments more acrimonious. On many occasions my mother and father fought so violently that my brother and I hid in the linen closet out of earshot.*[150]

Illustration #22: Edwin and the children, Edwina is leaning on her father's knee and William is behind. (Photo: Courtesy Alex Sanger)

---

150   Edwina Campbell Sanger, <u>My First 90 Years,</u> p. 16.

Illustration #23: Margery and the Children, William (left) and Edwina (right). (Photo: Courtesy Alex Sanger)

At some time prior to Edwin's journey to California, the couple quietly separated unofficially. Edwin moved to Bretton Woods while Margery remained in New York. In December 1915 Edwin wrote to Billy apologizing for the strain that his marital problems were placing on Billy during his demanding negotiations with the bankers.[151]

Immediately after Edwin's return to Detroit, he wrote to Billy telling him that he and Margery had met and were trying to resolve their differences:

> ...she came over and had lunch with me and in a short time we both acknowledged we were to blame and are going to make a real start this time. ..I am on my way to Pasadena and will get

---

151   ERC to WCD December 13, 1915, Durant Papers, Scharchburg Archives.

the house already [sic] and they will be out early next month. I think it is much better to get away from New York for the time being and get a right start — Margery agrees with me in this.[152]

He continued by apologizing again: *I am sorry our troubles came on just at the time when you were carrying so much, but it has cleared the air and everything will be better than ever.*

The remainder of the handwritten five page letter contains Edwin's instructions to Billy for dealing with investor "Hof" (Nathan Hofheimer) and his son, and advice regarding stocks;

Warning — Don't get involved in stock deals so that they can embarras [sic] you, for remember they are all powerful and can do it if they choose — so- do be careful You are in a strong position today and don't let your foot slip.

Following this he gave Billy explicit directions for his income tax:

In making out your income tax- don't forget to put in the $65,000.00 on the 1300 shares of GMC which stood in Margery's name and the $415,000.00 which I turned over to you for stock which still stood in my name...

Edwin concluded the letter:

Do take good care of yourself for so much is depending on you. Surround yourself with strong men- let the sycophants go, for they are only like vultures, around when the table is set and away when all the food is eaten and the table is bare...I have only had one ambition since 1910 and that was to see you back in the business world where you belong at the head... Give my love to Katharine and thank her very much for me for

---

152 ERC to WCD January 2, 1915, Durant Papers, Scharchburg Archives.

> the interest she has shown in my trouble — Tell her to take care of POPS.

Edwin, Margery and the children spent a comfortable winter in their Pasadena home. However, on returning to New York the marital problems soon began to re-emerge as Margery again plunged headlong into the social life of the city. Despite these personal setbacks, Edwin continued his efforts to have Billy back at the head of General Motors. That time was rapidly approaching.

Chapter Eight

BILLY'S RETURN

The Battle Begins

The members of the banking trust in control of General Motors were enjoying profitable returns for their investment and had no intention of relinquishing this after their initial control of five years had elapsed. The profits for 1915 were in excess of $14 million and it was clear that they could double in the following year even though General Motors market share for automobile sales had dropped from 20 percent of the U.S. market when the Board of Trustees took control in 1910, to less than eight percent by 1915. The Board proposed to the shareholders that on the September 16 meeting they approve leaving themselves in control for a further three years. Billy and Edwin had other ideas.

The only board member with whom Billy and Edwin had developed a close relationship was accountant James McClement. As September approached Edwin clearly had designated McClement as his proxy and wrote to him almost daily. McClement also represented the stock held by Percy Rockefeller, Edwin's friend at the Sleepy Hollow Country Club. It was obvious that Edwin, Billy and McClement did not trust many of the executives in the existing GM hierarchy particularly Storrow. Edwin wrote to Billy;

> *I am very glad you are taking the position on Storrow that you are. I hope you have absolute control and can rely on it. You and McClement must not miss a meeting for fear they will put*

> *something over on you. Say, it will be happy days in the village if we can ever get in position where we can even up old scores with some of the sons of bitches.* [153]

It is interesting to note Edwin's use of the pronoun "we" in this letter. Through this letter and subsequent correspondence it becomes obvious that Billy and Edwin had decided who would best fit into their plans for Billy's return to full control of General Motors. Storrow, Nash and the bankers were clearly not among them.

On September 12, Edwin wrote to Billy:

> *It seems to me if you can really get control of the GM Co., it would be a great mistake to have Storrow, Strauss or any of the Detroit crowd on the board... if Storrow is left on he will dominate it. He controls Nash absolutely and the only way you can get along with Nash is to take his prop out from under him.* [154]

Billy replied the next day:

> *Nash is acting like a baby and Storrow is so disconcerted that he is willing to resort to blackmail to secure even decent representation. It is clearly a matter of conspiracy between the two and an attempt on the part of both to save their faces.* [155]

The Battle With Storrow

As September progressed, with the stakes now elevated, Storrow's tactics in his power struggle with Durant became increasingly devious. In order to give Billy all the support he needed, Edwin was simultaneously writing

---

153   ERC to WCD, September 10, 1915. Scharchburg Archives.

154   ERC to WCD, September 12, 1915. Scharchburg Archives.

155   WCD to ERC, September 16, 1915. Scharchburg Archives.

to James McClement to make sure that Billy would be firm in his dealings with the board, and particularly with Storrow. From a letter from McClement to Edwin, dated September 15, the machinations and increased subterfuge become apparent. Storrow was obviously mounting a serious "no holds barred" campaign to keep control of General Motors. He even started a smear campaign alleging that Billy and McClement had conspired to misrepresent the number of shares they had under their control:

> *Dear Doctor:-*
>
> *I have yours of the 12th... Immediately after arriving in the city, I telephoned to Mr. Durant, and went up to see him, and had a few moments with him, in which he outlined in a very general way the situation as it now exists. From this I glean that he and Mr. Storrow could not come to terms, and that Mr. Durant concluded that he would make a contest for control.*
>
> *While in the west Mr Durant wired me asking the number of shares of General Motors I owned or controlled. No doubt you are familiar with this telegram and my answer. Mr. Durant informed me that in his negotiations and conferences with Mr. Storrow, that I was made the subject of a bitter attack by Mr. Storrow. Also that Mr. Storrow arbitrarily refused to consider my going on the Board, and also was unreasonable and arbitrary in every position which he took.*[156]

McClement continued by commenting on a claim by Storrow that he (McClement) did not represent one of the major stockholders in General Motors, Percy Rockefeller. Storrow appears to have been unaware of Edwin's close relationship with Rockefeller. McClement's letter continued:

> *Mr Durant seemed quite concerned about this matter,... so while Mr. Durant was present, I called Mr. Cutler of Mr. Rockefeller's office... and ascertained just how much stock*

---

156 J.H. McClement to Dr. Edwin R. Campbell, September 15, 1915. Scharchburg Archives.

> they had at this time (4400 shares of preferred) and had him confirm to Mr. Durant that I did represent them in the voting of this stock and also confirming the fact that so far as their interests were concerned, I had always represented them in regard to their interests in General Motors.

McClement went on to reveal that Storrow had sent an emissary, a Mr. Allen, to the Rockefellers' office to try to take the control of the Rockefeller stock interest away from McClement. To Allen and Storrow's annoyance Rockefeller insisted on having McClement continue to represent his interests. Rockefeller's assistant, Mr. Ivy Lee, informed McClement that *"Mr. Allen had made some serious representations in regard to Mr. Durant's character ... and deploring any movement having in view Mr. Durant's control of the company."*

Storrow and the bankers could see their grasp on General Motors, their money tree, slipping away. A number of clandestine meetings took place prior to the planned September 16 main meeting of the entire General Motors board. Edwin remained at Bretton Woods.

Key Meetings

Once Durant, along with McClement and the Kaufman and Du Pont interests, had an adequate number of shares in their possession, they met with the GM board at the September 15 directors' meeting in room 282 of the Belmont Hotel in New York. It should be pointed out that the Billy's friendship with du Pont had been kept from Storrow, and since du Pont was a powerhouse in the banking world, Storrow viewed him as a neutral party in the conflict, a view that Billy, Edwin and du Pont himself wished to maintain. When McClement arrived at the hotel he was told that a private meeting of Storrow and Nash, Durant, Kaufman and du Pont was already underway. It was later revealed that in that private meeting an attempt at a compromise between Durant and Storrow had been made. Finally it was agreed that the Storrow and Durant factions would each name seven members for the board and, supposedly neutral du Pont would name a further three members, establishing a new seventeen member board. Even though Storrow and Nash were still on the board and controlled seven votes, they were no longer holding a voting majority. Billy had won the first battle of the war.

A week later Billy and Edwin made their next move. The Chevrolet Company of Michigan consisted of a number of companies and factories, some still only vaguely connected to Chevrolet. The factories were located in New York City and Tarrytown, New York; Flint, Michigan; St Louis, Missouri; Oakland, California and in Canada. Billy and Edwin wanted to bring them all together under one larger new company.

On September 23 Billy convened a meeting of the Chevrolet directors. Edwin had recovered adequately to attend. At the meeting a new company was incorporated; the Chevrolet Motor Company of Delaware.

> *With very broad powers, including the right to hold, own, and deal in securities, it acquired all the stock of Chevrolet Motor Company of New York, Chevrolet Motor Company of Michigan, Chevrolet Company of Bay City, Chevrolet Company of Toledo, Ohio, Mason Motor Company of Flint, with contract interests in Chevrolet Motor Company of Canada Ltd., Oshawa, Ontario and Chevrolet Motor Company of St. Louis.*[157]

With Billy Durant as president, A. B. C. Hardy as vice president and Edwin as second vice president, this was the first and only time that Edwin ever took on a role above the level of a directorship during his involvement with Chevrolet or General Motors. On October 1st the *New York Times* announced:

NEW MOTOR CAR COMBINE *Chevrolet Company's $20,000,000 stock sold in a Few Hours. The Chevrolet Motor*

---

157 Arthur Pound, The Turning Wheel, (Garden City, New York, Doubleday, Doran Company Inc. 1934), p. 150.

> Car Company has been formed, through the coalition of two concerns of the same name, one incorporated in New York and the other in Indiana, with a capital stock of $20,000,000. [158]

By now it was clear to Billy and Edwin that the way was opening up for Billy to quietly increase his control of GM stocks. In December Billy privately offered some of his friends who owned GM stock, five shares in Chevrolet for each share in GM. Later in the month he offered the same deal to any GM shareholder. A letter from Billy to Edwin indicates that this offer continued until Valentine's Day, February 14, 1916.[159] On December 23, 1915, Chevrolet stockholders supported Billy's move to increase the company's capital from $20 million to $80 million.

Meanwhile at the November 16 annual general meeting of GM's Board of Directors, Kaufman, du Pont and Raskob were officially elected to the Board and Pierre du Pont was elected as Chairman. At the same time, Storrow supporters, Joseph Boyer, Robert Herrick, E.D. Metcalf, M.J. Murphy, N.L. Tilney and Jacob Wertheim were all removed. Storrow remained on the board with Nash as president, but Billy and Edwin waited for the opportunity to unleash a surprise that they had for them. Storrow and his allies would have begun to clearly understand the strategy of Billy and his son-in-law just before Christmas when the *New York Times* announced:

> **DURANT AGAIN HOLDS CONTROL OF MOTORS.**
>
> W.C. Durant, who was practically ousted from the General Motors Company in 1910, when a committee of bankers took over control of the company as part of an agreement under which they financed it through difficulties, has now turned up in control again. He and his friends now hold more than half of the capital stock, and they will demonstrate it tomorrow,

---

158 *New York Times*, October 1, 1915.

159 WCD to ERC, April 7, 1916, Scharchburg Archives.

> when ownership of a majority of interest will be transferred to the Chevrolet Motor Company.[160]

The lengthy article went on to summarize the events of 1910 and the bankers' role in it, mentioning that the bankers had all been paid off when the five year notes matured on October 1, 1915.

On the last day of the year the *Detroit Times* revealed to the public the next phase of Billy and Edwin's strategy:

> A majority of the directors of the General Motors Company are opposed to the scheme of W. C. Durant to have the Chevrolet Motor Company take over control of the big holding company. And a statement advising the shareholders of General Motors against becoming involved in the scheme by trading General Motors stock for Chevrolet has been expected for several days...

There! He had done it. He had shown his ace; a proposal to use Chevrolet to buy out General Motors! The article continued, indicating the difficult road ahead for Billy and his friends and associates:

> It is expected now in financial circles that some moves will be made to show Durant just where he stands when it comes to a fight in the big game. He has an active opponent in this one deal, anyhow, of James J. Storrow and there is probably no man in the country outside of New York and not more than two or three in New York who have any edge on Storrow when it comes to financial power or influence.[161]

---

160 *New York Times,* December 22, 1915.

161 *Detroit Times,* December 31, 1915.

The Next Battle

Billy's opening salvo was reported on New Year's Day, 1916 in a lengthy article, again in the *New York Times:*

> A fight for control of the General Motors Company has been precipitated by the proposal of W.C. Durant, President of the Chevrolet Motor Company and the largest single interest in General Motors, to acquire control of the latter company for the Chevrolet.[162]

The article claimed that Billy and his associates controlled nearly two thirds of the stock of G.M. It went on to state that

> ...efforts are now being made by other interests in General Motors to block the proposed sale of that company to Chevrolet.
> ...It has been suggested by some shareholders that it would be well to form a three years' voting trust beginning in November 1916 ... A majority of the present board favours this plan. With a sufficient number of shareholders wishing to unite in forming this voting trust, action to that end will be taken. The statement was signed by Samuel F. Prior, Albert H Wiggin, Thomas Neal, Charles S. Sabin, James R. Storrow, C.S. Mott, Albert Strauss and Emory W. Clark.
> ... It was said that there has been no dissension in the General Motors Board... Some of the board members believe that Mr. Durant and his associates actually control enough of the General Motors stock to make the plan effective [Chevrolet taking over GM] but others think that enough holders of the preferred can be rallied to block the exchange of more than half of the General Motors stock. If that can be done, the Chevrolet

---

162 *New York Times,* January 1, 1916.

> interests can be outvoted when the next election of directors of the General Motors is held.[163]

In early March, the Storrow faction mailed out a flyer to all GM stockholders urging them to reject Durant's takeover bid. It contained the following declaration:

> We believe that the continuation of the present conservative management is essential during the next few years and that those who have been largely the creative influence of the great success of the Company should be retained. We do not believe that control by the Chevrolet Company would result in any improvement in the management of the company. We urge both preferred and common stockholders immediately to sign the enclosed paper stating that they are in favour of having a voting trust formed. [164]

This statement was followed by a list of the usual Storrow supporters who had already agreed *"to act as Voting Trustees"* and at the top of the list was Charles Nash. Included on the list of signatories were New York bankers and investors C. W. Blossom and G.B. Collinge.

On March 26 Billy wrote to Edwin in Pasadena commenting on this flyer and its attempt to solicit support for the New York bankers trust in opposition to the Chevrolet takeover bid.

> *Emory W. Clark's latest attempt to organize a new Voting Trust was somewhat of a joke... Mr. Clark enlisted Mr. Howard Bayne* [son of S.G. Bayne, President of the Seaboard National Bank] *in this attempt. ... at the time it* [the flyer] *was issued I think that Mr. C. W. Blossom and Mr. G. B. Collinge were the owners of about 1375 shares of General*

---

163   Ibid.

164   Circular, Durant Papers, Scarchburg Archives..

> Motors stock but at the date ... of March 17th, they did not own a single share, the stock having been purchased by your humble servant. [165]

Regarding Nash being on the list, Billy had this to say: *Nash ... appears to have gotten himself in bad. I am through side-stepping and four-flushing and expect to reach an agreement and have the atmosphere cleared once and for all* [Nash's resignation].

He then continued with details of a further acquisition, two plants of the National Cycle Manufacturing Company:

> *The plants will be used to make the motors for our new car, with Allace Willett in charge of production under the direction of Mr. Mason. The new car is a "peach" — the best designed car I have ever seen. It is a good looker and a wonderful performer...*[166]

A few days later Edwin wrote from California to Billy enclosing a check for a further $58,000 to pay for more GM shares and gave Billy further strategic advice:

> *I do not believe I would turn in much of the General Motors Common into Chevrolet until after the November election* [GM directors] *as I am sure they will try to prevent you from voting and you cannot afford to take any chances — It will not do to lose at this time — don't forget you are up against the biggest money trust in the world when you run up against the Storrow outfit and at the same time, a gang that will use every effort to down you and do it in any way that they can. So every move you make must be well thought out and don't do anything unless you have the very best legal advice — no matter what it*

---

165   WCD to ERC, March 26, 1916. Scharchburg Archives.

166   Ibid.

> costs. They [Storrow et al] *get the best talent and you must do the same. It has been my dream since 1910 that you would get the G.M. back in your own hands and for heaven's sake don't make any mistakes — It is a big stake and a big game — so keep cool and don't get tied up where they can pinch you.*[167]

Bob Burman

In the midst of this flurry of critical correspondence an event occurred which saddened the Durant and Campbell families. On April 8, Edwin went to Corona in California to watch Bob Burman drive in a race. In this event he was not driving a Buick, instead he was at the wheel of a French Peugot. Burman rolled his car at high speed on one of the corners killing himself, his mechanic and two spectators. Two days later Edwin wrote to Billy:

> *I saw the run at Corona (where Bob Burman was killed) and I hope that you will take the opportunity to write to Clifford and tell him he must quit the racing game — it is not only demoralizing but it takes too much time away from the business — the association is not the best.*[168]

He concluded his letter with the following advice and encouragement:

> *Don't get up so early Don't take cold Don't work so hard Don't see so many people Keep cheered for the promised land is in sight.* [169]

---

167 ERC to WCD April 11, 1916, Durant Papers, Scharchburg Archives.

168 ERC to WCD April 10, 1916, Durant Papers, Scharchburg Archives.

169 ERC to WCD April 10, 1916, Durant Papers, Scharchburg Archives.

Nash and the Rambler

On April 18, General Motors Chairman Pierre du Pont received Nash's letter of resignation, effective June 1, 1916. But behind closed doors, Storrow, Nash and Chrysler were hatching their own plans for their exit from General Motors. The three, completely bitten by the automobile manufacturing bug, were arranging to purchase the Packard Motor Company. When those negotiations broke down, Storrow bought the Thomas B. Jeffery Company in Kenosha, Wisconsin. It produced the Rambler which by 1902 was the fourth bestselling car in the United States.[170] In 1904 it became one of the first automobiles to be controlled by a steering wheel instead of the conventional tiller. Jeffery died in 1910 leaving the company in the hands of his son Charles. After surviving the sinking of the Lusitania in 1915 Jeffery lost much of his interest in automobile production. The eventual selling price is not clear but is estimated at a minimum of $5 million.[171] Nash walked away from General Motors on June 1 and immediately joined Storrow in control of the Jeffery Company. Nash became its president and Storrow, its Chairman of the board. The following year the Company was renamed Nash Motors. Notably absent from the administration of the Jeffery Company was Walter P. Chrysler.

Billy and Edwin both valued Chrysler's abilities. In a letter to Billy a year earlier, September 1915, Edwin had encouraged his father-in-law to try to keep Chrysler: *If you get control and can hold Crysler* [sic] *it would not make any difference about Nash going.*[172] When Billy and Edwin heard of the looming Storrow-Nash-Chrysler alliance Billy quickly approached Chrysler to see if he could be persuaded to stay with GM. Billy's opening offer was $500,000 a year. Sensing some hesitancy on Chrysler's part Billy followed:

---

170   George S. May, <u>A Most Unique Machine,</u> p. 289.

171   James J. Flink, <u>The Automobile Age</u>, p. 68.

172   ERC to WCD September 24, 1915. Durant Papers, Scharchburg Archives.

> *Now Walter, you just put aside, for the time being, all your plans of getting into business for yourself. I don't blame you for the ambition, but I ask you for just three years of yourself.*[173]

Billy also offered Chrysler the presidency of Buick and a seat on GM's board of directors. Chrysler could not refuse the offer. Nevertheless he added his own conditions:

> *I can accept only if I am to have full authority... I don't want interference... don't go to anybody else and don't try to split up my authority. Just have one channel between Flint and Detroit: from me to you. Full authority is what I want.*[174]

Billy agreed to the conditions.

Victory at Last

As Edwin was in California at the time of the decisive upcoming June 1 meeting he wrote a series of letters to Billy insisting that Billy should become president of General Motors.

On May 1 he wrote:

> *Just heard today that Nash had sent in his resignation...well I think it is a good thing as it was impossible to get along with him since his head had got swelled. It seems to me that the best thing for you to do as soon as it can possibly be done is for you to take the presidency of the General Motors Co....*
>
> *You are the only one who can hold the different companies together. There is no one else who can do this job... The other chaps have been in power for six years and of course have their*

---

173 Walter P. Chrysler, with Boyden Sparkes. <u>Life of an American Workman</u>. *(New York, Curtis Publishing, 1938), p.145.*

174 Ibid.

> *friends in power and this situation will have to be handled very carefully and you are the one to do it, so don't make the mistake of putting a figurehead in for president: it must be you and you only. It will give you back all your lost prestige. Now don't let anyone talk you into doing anything differently.* [175]

Billy immediately responded:

> *My Dear Doctor,*
> *Your several letters received. You can depend on it that I am keeping my eye on "the bunch." If they stab me again, it will be while I am looking right straight at them.* [176]

Edwin returned to New York on June 1. The following day the *New York Times* reported that Billy had followed his son-in-law's directions:

> **DURANT SUCCEEDS NASH**
> *Head of Chevrolet Co. Elected President of General Motors.*
> *Directors of the General Motors Company, meeting at the Guaranty Trust Company yesterday, accepted the resignation from the presidency of Charles W. Nash. W. C. Durant, president of the Chevrolet Motor Company, who was deposed from the management of General Motors in 1910 when the company's affairs were administered under the direction of a committee of bankers, was elected President.* [177]

The article erroneously stated that Nash was to remain on the board of directors but correctly announced the resignation of Strauss. The resignation of Storrow at the meeting was not reported until June 4.[178]

---

[175] ERC to WCD May 1, 1916. Durant Papers, Scharchburg Archives.

[176] WCD to ERC, May 4, 1916, Durant Papers, Scharchburg Archives.

[177] New York Times, June 2, 1916.

[178] New York Times, June 4, 1916.

In an interview with Catherine Durant over half a century later, Lawrence Gustin reported that, to celebrate his victory on the evening of June 1, Billy took Catherine out for dinner at a fast food restaurant. When he told his wife of his victory she is reported to have said, *"Oh Willie, at least we could have gone to the restaurant in the Plaza."*[179]

The Restart

In his lifetime, Billy Durant's ambitious projects made hundreds of millions of dollars, not only for himself, but also for his investors. His main aim in life was not to make money; it was to be successful. He spent much of his lifetime in New York "playing the stock market," again not to make money but to win at the game. He did win, over and over again, but he also lost occasionally; that was part of the game. When he won, he shared his successes with those who had faith in him. During the time that the bankers controlled GM, they made huge profits for themselves, but to Billy's annoyance, they did not share these profits with the smaller investors. Once he had regained control of GM, he took delight in making up for this omission, personally mailing many of the cheques himself. One of the first cheques he mailed was to Sam McLaughlin. He sent the cheque with an accompanying letter to Sam on May 5, 1916. Sam immediately responded;

> *This is to acknowledge formally your letter of May 5 enclosing cheque for $20,196.88 being my share of the profits of the Syndicate which has recently been closed... You have certainly been Kindness itself to George and to me, and I am sure you have not the least doubt as to our appreciation...*[180]

Prior to taking back full control and just before becoming president of General Motors, Billy with Edwin's assistance, had established yet another

---

179   Lawrence Gustin, <u>Billy Durant</u>, p. 180.
180   R.S. McLaughlin to WCD May 9, 1916. Durant Papers. Scharchburg Archives.

holding company, United Motors, in order to solidify the organization of a number of parts manufacturing companies that they had acquired. These included bearing manufacturing companies Hyatt and New Departure, automotive electrical companies Dayton Electrical Laboratories (DELCO) and Remy Electric, Jaxon Steel products and the Perlman Rim Company. The President of the Hyatt Company was Alfred P. Sloan who was then promoted to president of United Motors and in 1918 became a member of Billy's Executive Committee. Sloan later became president of GM. The President of Delco was Charles F. Kettering who had invented self starters for cars which were first used in the 1912 Cadillac. Kettering was also to play a major role in the future of GM management.

On June 4, the *New York Times* announced that Durant had taken control of the Willys-Overland Company for $90 million.[181] Billy had met with John Willys, president of the Willys-Overland company and tentatively agreed on a deal to combine its holdings with United Motors to make an even greater conglomerate with assets approaching a quarter of a billion dollars. The proposed name of the new company was The American Motors Company. A few days later, the *Times* announced that the agreement had been abandoned and:

> ... *efforts had been made all day Tuesday to iron out the difficulties, but that the manufacturers, bankers, and lawyers could not agree, leaving the only thing to be done; the cancellation of the project.* [182]

The failure of this merger appeared to have no effect on Billy. His business plans moved on without missing a beat. On October 13, General Motors Company was incorporated as the General Motors Corporation. Under the new organization the corporation was set up as a series of divisions each with a president and general manager, all of whom were given a seat on the board of the General Motors Corporation. Initially the controlling

---

181 *New York Times* June 4, 1916.

182 *New York Times* June 15, 1916.

interest of GM was still held by the Chevrolet division enabling Billy to make all the major decisions himself, usually after consulting with Edwin. Toward the end of the year Billy was able to proudly announce to everyone that GM was one of the most successful companies in the United States: *"Motors Now Earns $2,250,000 A Month,"* [183] ran the headlines. The same article went on to announce that Durant was now the president of the immensely successful company and Pierre S. du Pont was the chairman.

When the United States entered the World War in 1917, there was a dramatic drop in GM sales, resulting in an accompanying fall in the value of the company's shares. Billy approached du Pont about increasing his company's investment in GM. The Du Pont Company's involvement in paints, plastics and explosives had huge potential for GM. Pierre du Pont needed no prodding. In December, 1917, the Du Pont Company invested heavily, spending in excess of $25 million buying up almost 24 percent of GM and Chevrolet stock.

Chevrolet Relinquishes Control of GM

One of the conditions placed on Durant by the Du Pont investment was that Durant would create a single structure bringing Chevrolet and United Motors into the General Motors organization and that John J. Raskob would oversee the financial aspects of the company while Billy would run the production and remain as president of the General Motors Corporation and chairman of the Executive Committee.

As a young secretary, John Jakob Raskob had caught the attention of Pierre du Pont who hired him as his personal secretary in 1901. Raskob quickly rose through the ranks and became the treasurer of the Du Pont organization in 1914. Always an admirer of Durant's entrepreneurial and financial skills, Raskob immediately fell into Billy and Edwin's plans for expansion. With du Pont's encouragement, the capital shares of GM were increased to $200 million. United Motors was also absorbed, bringing its

---

183 *New York Times* Nov 22, 1916.

president, Alfred P. Sloan onto the board of directors of GM and making him a member of Billy's Executive Committee.

A series of meetings was held in early 1918 to bring about another massive transformation of Chevrolet and General Motors. The eventual outcome was the subject of an extensive article in the *New York Times* with the headline:

CHEVROLET COMPANY TO WIND UP AFFAIRS
Plant Will Continue to be Operated as a Division of General Motors [184]

The article gave the background of Chevrolet's origins, explaining Chevrolet's current control of GM and how through Durant and du Pont, General Motors was to be doubling GM's capitalization in order to take over Chevrolet's interest in GM. The article continued:

> *Mr. Durant will continue President of the motors companies so ably developed and operated under his management and in which he is still the largest stockholder. E.I du Pont de Demours & Co are now represented on the Board of Directors of General Motors Corporation by J. A. Haskell, J. J. Raskob, P. S. Du Pont, Irenee du Pont and Henry F. Du Pont, the two last named having been elected yesterday... The new Finance Committee consists of J. J. Raskob, Chairman, P. S. Du Pont, H. F. Du Pont, Irenee du Pont, W. C. Durant, J. A. Haskell, and J. H. McClement.*

The article concluded with the following sentence:

> *It was explained yesterday that the Chevrolet Company, having succeeded in restoring Mr. Durant to control of his old company, was no longer needed as a separate organization,*

---

184   *New York Times* February 22, 1918.

and would accordingly be done away with as soon as the necessary intervening steps can be taken.

A few months later, Edwin journeyed home to Port Perry to visit his mother and then went to see Sam McLaughlin at his grand, new stately home Parkwood. Here after touring the palatial residence he sat with Sam in order to initiate the arrangements for the General Motors Corporation to buy out the McLaughlin interests in Canada and create General Motors of Canada.

G.M. Canada

In late 1914 even though he was still using Buick engines and Buick designed chassis, Sam McLaughlin dropped the name Buick from his vehicles, advertising and selling them as McLaughlins. Since he had been removed from the board of directors of General Motors in 1910, he supported Billy and Edwin in their plans for Chevrolet and, once the new company was underway, became one of its early investors. He bought his first shares, 200 for a price of $19,000 in January 1912.[185] In addition Sam began buying engines for his McLaughlin cars from a number of sources including Mason.

Once Billy was back in control of GM he realized that the company's further expansion should include Canada and that the McLaughlin family should share in the profits. With du Pont and Raskob, Billy and Edwin discussed that possibility, contacted the McLaughlins, and reached an agreement to buy out the McLaughlin interests. On December 12, 1918 the proposal was formally announced. Raskob suggested to the Du Pont Company that they purchase the majority of the McLaughlin family's shares for $6.5 million. This met with immediate approval. Sam and his brother George held on to a small number of shares in order to have some say in the way the Canadian operations were managed. Sam was elected

---

185   Heather Robinson, <u>Driving Force</u>, p. 154.

as the President of General Motors of Canada, a position he held until he resigned in 1945.

Expansion Again

Once Billy was firmly in control of General Motors, he again fell back into almost over-confidence in his role, much as he had in his disastrous acquisition of the Heany Light Company just prior to losing control of the Corporation in 1910. There is no indication that Edwin discouraged this zeal; nor was there any visible opposition from the board of directors. Billy was firmly in control of an organization which appeared to share in his expansionist ambitions. Ford was clearly in their sights. One indication of this was Billy's venture into tractors to compete with the Henry Ford's Fordson tractors. In order to do this he asked Edwin to begin negotiations for the Samson Sieve Grip-Tractor Company of Stockton, California while he went to see the Janesville Machine Company of Wisconsin. Early in 1919, to accommodate this venture, a new division of GM was created: the Samson Division. Its responsibility was to design and build tractors for GM to compete with Ford. Arthur Mason was given the task of heading up the design and production for the division in Flint. Mason came up with an unconventional design for the new vehicle. Named the "Iron Horse," it was a Chevrolet powered four wheeled vehicle with the driver walking behind, much as a farmer managed a team of horses. Billy happily demonstrated the vehicle at fairs across the country, but his sales and promotion failed to generate much enthusiasm. Early in 1920, after only 128 of the contraptions had been produced, the enterprise was stopped.

The estimated loss to GM was almost $33 million. This was compensated for by the fact that by the end of 1919 overall GM production had increased almost 60% over the previous year. In the same time period net profits soared from $15 million to $60 million. In spite of the Samson disaster, Billy's expansionist policies continued to race ahead.

To enable customers to buy GM cars on credit, Billy used Raskob's help in establishing the General Motors Acceptance Corporation. It was incorporated in New York in the summer of 1918. In Flint, where Billy had started his ventures, he organized a GM sponsored construction company to build houses for GM workers. This was soon expanded to Detroit and Lansing.

Later in the year, Billy went on another buying spree. His acquisitions in 1919 included: the Dayton-Wright Airplane Company of Dayton Ohio, manufacturer of electric starters for cars; the Interstate Motor Company of Muncie Indiana, manufacturer of the Sheridan Motor Car; the T.W. Warner Company, a gear manufacturing company in Muncie and the Dayton Metal Products and the Domestic Engineering Company. But his major acquisition was the Fisher Body Company, manufacturer of auto bodies. This latter investment involved almost $6 million in cash and $22 million in shares and other options.

Frigidaire

In the midst of these strategic and time consuming manoeuvres, tireless Billy became involved in yet another project: refrigerators. In July 1915, Rueben Bechtold and Alfred Mellowes built their first successful electric refrigerator and began to look for an opportunity to produce and market their invention. The Guardian Fridgerator Company was incorporated in March 1916 and began production on Twelfth Street in Detroit. By early 1918, operating at a loss after selling less than forty Guardians, the owners began to look for investors. One of the initiators of the company, J. W. Murray, approached Billy Durant and asked his advice on production methods. Billy was captivated by the invention and encouraged Murray to personally buy out all the stock in the company. Billy then bought out Murray and placed A.B.C Hardy in charge of production. Shortly afterwards the company was renamed Frigidaire and through Billy, was sold to GM in March 1919.

Chevrolet's Model T

Another indication of Billy's determination to meet Ford head on was his venture into trucks in the Chevrolet division. Henry Ford had experimented in building trucks early in his career but it wasn't until 1917 that the first purpose built model T one ton truck appeared. Billy and Edwin decided to meet that challenge in 1918 with two models. One was simply a 490 passenger car chassis marketed as a half ton truck with an engine, a cowl and front fenders but no body. Buyers could either build their own body or arrange to have another company build it. The other was a new larger one ton chassis with the engine and transmission from Chevrolet's FA series cars and covered with a cowl and cab. The half ton chassis was marketed as the "490 Commercial." With Henry Ford clearly as a target Billy named the one ton chassis the "Model T." The one-ton trucks continued with this name plate until 1922. [186]

By year's end the company's capitalization was increased to $370 million. Buoyed by this optimism, the GM board authorized Charles Kettering to lead a delegation of GM executives, including Sloan, Mott, Champion and Chrysler, off to France to explore the possibility of buying the highly successful Citroen company. After seeing the facilities and considering the capital required, the idea was rejected. GM did, however, increase its shares in Goodyear Tire and Rubber and Dunlop Rubber and other parts suppliers. In the fall of 1919, GM issued more stock and in so doing became the second corporation in US history to become a billion dollar corporation. The first was United States Steel. GM closed the year with a production total of more than 397,000 units with net sales of over half a billion dollars!

Raymere

As a result of his stock market dealings in 1916 Billy was able to declare a gross income of three and a half million dollars and a net income of nearly three million! [187] With this wealth he decided to give Catherine what she had always wanted: a home of her own. The couple had lived

---

186   Tom Brownell and M. Mueller, <u>Chevrolet Pickup Color History</u>, p. 11.

187   Figures obtained by Weisberger from Durant's secretary Aristo Scrobogna. Bernard Weisberger, <u>The Dream Maker</u>, p. 216.

with Edwin and Margery when in Detroit and New York and in hotels elsewhere. To satisfy Catherine's desire, in November they took possession of a palatial, stately home on the New Jersey coast in the town of Deal. The thirty-seven roomed white stone villa had been built by multi millionaire Jacob Rothschild a decade earlier. Rothschild died shortly after the house was completed and on the death of his widow, Billy bought the property from the Rothschilds' estate in November 1917 for $115,000. In addition Billy bought several acres surrounding the property so that he and Catherine could stroll across the lawns and down to the shoreline. Catherine took over the responsibility of the furnishings and decorations, sparing no expense to create an eclectic environment of rare paintings, European tapestries, Persian carpets, Louis XVI furniture, Chinese porcelain and Remington statues. An extensive library contained all the usual classics, current writers and numerous rare books. The gardens were adorned with fountains, fishponds, ornate statues and extensive flower beds. Catherine took great pride in gathering flowers from the garden to fill the dozens of urns and vases within the house, supplying colour and scents to drift gently through the house.

Illustration #24: Raymere, Billy and Catherine's Deal, New Jersey, 32 roomed summer home. (Photo: Courtesy Scharchburg Archives, Kettering University)

To ease his hectic schedule, earlier in the year Billy had also taken possession of a luxurious apartment on the corner of Fifth Avenue and Seventy-second Streets overlooking Central Park. The address at 907 Fifth Avenue enabled him to get quickly to business at GM's New York office at 1764 Broadway.

> "It was Mr. Durant's custom then to go to his summer home at Deal, New Jersey, each Tuesday evening carrying portfolios packed with work. He would return to town Thursday morning to remain until Friday night." [188]

When Forbes created his first list of wealthiest Americans in 1918, Billy was included in that list as being among the 30 wealthiest people in the United States.

Casualties

The euphoria which resulted from the success of GM in 1919 was tempered by some casualties. One was Walter P. Chrysler. In April 1919 Billy named Chrysler as his assistant and vice-president in charge of GM operations. Chrysler was deeply concerned about the state of the affairs at the top of General Motors. When he had struck his financially rewarding deal with Billy in 1916, as head of Buick, one condition was that he would be allowed to run the division on his own. However, Billy wanted to keep a firm control on what was happening on the production line. He frequently contacted and dealt directly with Chrysler's managers at Buick. In so doing he had clearly violated his agreement with Chrysler. Finally, in late 1919 Chrysler had reached the end of his patience; he handed in his resignation effective March 25, 1920. Billy struggled to keep Chrysler but finally gave in and let him go, but not before he had bought out all of Chrysler's shares in General Motors. Shares that had been a part of Chrysler's annual

---

[188] Alfred P. Sloan, Jr. *Adventures of a White Collar Man*, (New York, Doubleday, Doran & Company, 1941), p. 124.

salary now amounted to over $10 million. Walter P. Chrysler walked out of Billy's office and, as if to say to Billy, "this is how it should be done," using his vast financial payout, bought the bankrupt Maxwell Motor Car Company and changed its name to the Chrysler Corporation.

A second casualty was Henry Leland and his son Wilfred. Leland had become president of Cadillac in 1904, five years before Billy had purchased the company. Leland was retained as president of the Cadillac division, but as David Buick and Walter Chrysler and others had found out, Billy was the benevolent dictator. Leland disagreed with Billy on polices relating to Cadillac. This led to confrontation and eventually, Billy sent a letter to Leland on March 10, 1917, terminating his employment in July. Resentful of this dismissal, a few months later the Lelands conspired against Billy questioning Billy's loyalty in front of a U.S. Senate aircraft committee. The *Detroit Free Press* ran a headline;

> **Head of GMC Opposed War: Durant Unwilling to Take Any Part.**

The article continued with the claim:

> William C. Durant, president of the General Motors Company... was not in sympathy with the war at the time it was declared, Wilfred C. Leland of Detroit told the Senate Aircraft Committee when it visited Detroit some months ago. Mr. Leland and his father, Henry M. Leland, as a result of this attitude on the part of Durant, withdrew from the Cadillac Motor Car company, a part of the General Motors Company.[189]

Billy responded almost reluctantly:

> Under these circumstances, I regret that I am no longer able, out of consideration for the Lelands, to withhold the facts of

---

189 *Detroit Free Press* 'August 27, 1918.

> *their compulsory retirement. They did not resign voluntarily but were discharged from the management of the Cadillac Company. Their discharge had nothing to do with patriotism or the war. It was brought about by prudential business reasons; they were notified by me before the war was declared.* [190]

Billy Durant's response to Leland's trumped up accusations was somewhat superfluous as the production figures at GM showed that in spite of decreased car sales, 1918 had been a banner year for GM through its government contracts for trucks, ambulances, aircraft engines and a number of smaller manufactured parts such as mortar shells. The income for these contracts alone amounted to almost $35 million, a significant part of the company's almost $270 million in gross sales. [191]

Problems again

A further casualty was the confidence of du Pont, Sloan, Raskob and others in Billy Durant's ability to manage the huge company. The expansions that led to the crisis in 1910 paled in comparison with the wide range of factories, their 49,000 work force, and the financial institutions involved in their acquisitions in 1919. Again Billy and Edwin were the only ones who fully understood the complex arrangements of financial details. Billy moved so fast that the only directors able to keep up with him were his son-in-law and Raskob, although the latter was more likely going along for the exciting ride rather than understanding its complexities. In November 1918, Billy promoted Alfred Sloan to the position of vice- president of GM. Sloan maintained;

---

190   WCD, *Letter dated September 2, 1918*, Durant Papers, Scharchburg Collection.
191   Bernard A. Weisberger, <u>The Dream Maker</u>, p. 238.

> *Sometimes I used to feel as if he were always holding a telephone in his hand. I think there were twenty telephones in his private office, and a switchboard.*[192]

In order to try to manage the incredibly multifaceted organization, Raskob proposed to the board plans for a huge office complex, at the time the largest in the world, to be built in Detroit. Billy opposed the idea as he felt that he and Edwin knew how the Corporation was being managed and *"... he preferred to allocate funds to plant and working capital rather than in real estate."*[193] Overriding Billy's reluctance, the board approved the plan and work began in 1919 on the huge, 30 acre, 15 storey building with its 1700 offices. In an attempt to pacify Billy's reluctance in such a building, it was named in his honour: the Durant Building.

The need for such a huge office building served to underline Pierre du Pont and Alfred Sloan's increasing concern about Billy and Edwin's lack of a centralized bookkeeping and organizational record. Du Pont sent accountants from his own company to examine Billy and Edwin's accounting and they found what was at best a chaotic system with no centralized bookkeeping, no central staff, no bidding for contracts in the construction and maintenance of factories.

In late October, Raskob asked the Finance Committee, of which he was the head, for an additional $7 million to continue the construction of the Durant Building in Detroit. The building, which Billy had always opposed, had experienced severe cost overruns. Raskob asked for a further $7 million for the improvement of the New Departure roller bearing plant. Billy, as head of the Executive Committee opposed both of Raskob's requests, stating that under the growing financial strain all funds should be put into working capital and not expansion expenditures. Behind Billy's back Raskob lobbied his committee for support for his requests and five days later, the Finance Committee approved his expenditures

---

192 Alfred P. Sloan, Jr. *Adventures of a White-Collar Man*. Page 119.

193 Alfred P. Sloan, Jr. *My Years with General Motors*, (New York, Macfadden Books, 1965), p. 28.

and to pacify Billy, they also approved his request for money for his ailing tractor production. In order to finance these expenditures the Raskob controlled Finance Committee authorized the issue of a minimum of $50 million in debentures.

In an attempt to raise an expected $85 million, primarily for the Raskob proposals, in January 1920 a ten for one split in GM shares was authorized. The issue failed abysmally and after two months only a disappointing $12 million had been raised. Billy and Edwin had learned from their 1910 experiences that the economic climate of 1920 had some parallels, but they had failed to convince the Finance Committee that the existing economic climate could not support the expenditures that Raskob was promoting.

Another venture was initiated in order to raise even more capital and to maximize Billy's opportunities to manipulate GM stock. Billy gained du Pont support in creating a series of syndicates. Each syndicate *"... was to acquire and hold GM stock temporarily, bidding up its price and making it more alluring thereby to other long-term investors."*[194] Durant managed syndicate Number Six which raised $10 million, with Billy and Du Pont as the major investors. Edwin managed Number Five with a target of raising a maximum of $5 million. Edwin was the major investor in his own syndicate.

Financial Crisis

Unfortunately Billy and Edwin were unable to see that they were fighting an economic battle that was taking place, a battle that was well beyond their ability to control. The cessation of hostilities in Europe in 1918 had enormous consequences for the economy of the Western World and particularly for the United States. In the United States at the time of the Armistice over 600,000 men who had been trained and prepared for departure to Europe were abruptly discharged. A few months later the troops already in Europe began to return to civilian life in the U.S. In 1919 alone over 4 million servicemen were discharged and thrust onto an already

---

194 Bernard Weisberger, <u>The Dream Maker</u>, p. 255.

over-burdened labour market. The result was a national unemployment rate of 11.7 per cent by the end of 1920.[195]

As war-torn European nations struggled to get their own economies back to normal they were unable to afford American goods. Further complicating the European economy was the War Reparations Act through which President Woodrow Wilson demanded that Germany and her allies compensate the victorious allies for casualties and property damage. This placed increased burdens on already stressed economies. In U.S. factories, unsold goods began to gather dust and banks began to recall loans as they had done following the 1907 financial crisis. The Federal Reserve Board raised the down payment required to buy automobiles from 25% to 50%. G.M.'s huge successes of 1919 were in contrast to the crisis which faced the company in late 1920 when the country entered another depression.

Huge inventories of unsold vehicles began to fill the factory storage areas. A number of companies such as Ford, Willys-Overland, Dodge and Packard drastically reduced production. Studebaker had to completely shut down its production lines and lay off workers as winter approached. All GM divisions began to cut back production. Sloan observed another problem which was having an effect on GM's effectiveness: *"Even with reduced production schedules, however, the division managers failed to stay within their authorized limits in inventory or capital expenditures, and nothing was done effectively to control them."*[196] All GM divisions except Buick and Cadillac had to shut down production in November. It is estimated that in Detroit, by year's end, the automobile workforce had dropped from 176,000 to 24,000.[197]

Billy made every effort to prop up the value of GM's share prices.

> *I think that Mr. Durant's personal stock market operations were motivated essentially by his great pride in General Motors and everything related to it and by his unbounded confidence*

---

195   Jeremy Atack and Peter Russell, <u>A New Economic view of American History</u>, p. 565.

196   Alfred P. Sloan, Jr., <u>My Years With General Motors</u>, p. 30.

197   James J. Flink, <u>The Automobile Age</u>, p. 84.

in its future, a judgement that has been well vindicated over the years. [198]

In October he created the Durant Corporation, an organization which encouraged the ordinary man-on-the-street to become a small time investor. As an encouragement he sold these small stockholders GM shares at a dollar or so below the market value. At the same time he encouraged all his friends and associates to buy GM shares in order to keep the prices high and therefore, a good investment. As GM's share prices began to fall from $25 in early September to $14.00 in November, smaller shareholders, feeling the difficulties of hard times, were compelled to sell their shares. Here Billy's conscientious nature came to the fore and he bought their shares at the October rate of $17.00 in November. In some cases he paid them the September rate in December. In addition he was spending vast amounts of money in buying up other GM shares in order to keep the shares from falling even further. Billy was slowly emptying his personal bank account and borrowing, with GM shares as security, in order to continue to support the falling share price.

Billy, Edwin and Raskob met to discuss the falling share prices and the need for further outside investment to pick up the unsold January shares. Raskob proposed that they contact the largest banker in the world, the J.P. Morgan. Billy was forced to go against his inherent mistrust of bankers, but there seemed to be no alternative. The Morgan interests snapped at the opportunity and filled the gap by buying up the unsold shares. But, as in 1910, the price for their investment was a number of seats on the board of directors of General Motors. Six Morgan appointees, led by Edward R. Stettinius, were added to the GM board. As in 1910, all new board members had expertise in finance but none had any understanding of automobile production.

In spite of the massive infusion of investment, the value of GM shares still continued to fall, so Billy began to use his personal money to buy up large numbers of shares in order to keep their prices from falling further.

---

198 Alfred P. Sloan, Jr., <u>My Years With General Motors</u>, p. 38.

When he discovered that Stettinius, the J. P. Morgan representative on the GM board, had been manipulating GM stock in Morgan's favour by selling large numbers of shares (short selling) so that they could be bought later at a lower price, he confronted Stettinius who didn't deny the accusation and asserted his right to buy and sell on his own. Stettinius also claimed that the Morgan interests believed that the current economic climate would lead to further declines in stock prices and that they would continue to sell until the prices bottomed; then they would buy back again.

Billy's ownership of over two and a half million GM shares had now become public knowledge and Pierre du Pont became concerned about the obvious amount of money that Billy had invested, some of it his own but much of it borrowed. Raskob and du Pont confronted Billy with their concerns and found out that he had debts in excess of $34 million. Further, Billy confessed that he was having trouble keeping up the payments on his debt. And GM shares had fallen to $13.00. Du Pont and Raskob realized that Billy would have to dispose of large numbers of his shares in order to pay his bills. A sudden arrival of large numbers of shares on the market would have a negative impact on Wall Street. This had to be prevented.

A meeting was held six o'clock on Friday November 19. Billy, with Edwin beside him and other advisors on their side of the table, faced the du Pont interests represented by Raskob and du Pont and the Morgan interests on the other side, Billy gave a detailed account of the shares that he held and the amount of his indebtedness. The principals then adjourned to consider their options. At nine o'clock a second meeting took place:

> *Sitting at his* [Durant's] *side are the doctor, John Thomas, and Briggs, three of the Chevrolet crowd. Confronting him are the three plenipotentiaries from the kingdoms of high finance* [the Morgan interests]. *And the two brothers from the distinguished eastern family* [du Pont], *with their assistant* [Raskob] *who is much like Durant, and yet now cast as one of*

his rescuers and judges. Ten men, three groups. Durant at the centre, the cause of this convergence and its victim.[199]

After hours of negotiations an arrangement was agreed upon. A syndicate, The Du Pont Securities Company, would be created and supported financially by Du Pont and Morgan. The syndicate would take control of 60% of Billy's shares in GM, paying him well below the going rate, and pay off all his indebtedness.

But the most painful condition was déjà vue:

> "...my resignation as president of General Motors Corporation was desired and would be accepted, the reason given that I was not in sympathy with the policies of the controlling interests and would not cooperate. I must and do plead guilty to the charge." [200]

The papers were signed and Billy reluctantly resigned on the first day of December. Alfred Sloan commented:

> In this way 2,500,000 shares of General Motors stock passed from the ownership of W.C. Durant to the du Ponts. In this episode W.C. Durant, a man of genius, of courage, of vision and great wealth, is seen sacrificing all he had in a fruitless effort to protect, according to his way of thinking, his creation, General Motors — loyal to the very end. [201]

Edwin watched the proceedings but was powerless to offer anything but condolences. As the dust began to settle, Pierre du Pont became president of General Motors and chairman of the board. Raskob continued

---

199   Bernard Weisberger <u>The Dream Maker</u>, p. 270.

200   Personal letter of Billy Durant to Irenee du Pont March 21, 1921. Durant Papers, Scharchburg Archives.

201   Alfred P. Sloan, Jr., <u>Adventures of a White-Collar Man</u>, p. 125.

as chairman of the Finance Committee. Alfred P. Sloan was elected as the executive vice-president.

As an emphatic and ironic footnote, some thirty years later, an antitrust suit was launched against the Du Pont Company. In a pre-trial statement it was revealed that it was obvious that *"... the Du Pont group was planning on ousting Durant when the opportunity was ripe and of taking over sole and complete control of General Motors."* [202] By the time that this fact came to light, Billy had been dead for five years and away from GM for 32 years!

On the first day of December Billy Durant walked out of his office at 1764 Broadway for the last time and made his way home to Raymere. Edwin made his way to the Plaza and the next day boarded a train for California, alone.

---

202 Pre trial brief by U.S. government attorneys; United States of America vs E.I. du Pont et al., October 15, 1952 page 29. Quoted in Lawrence Gustin, <u>Billy Durant</u>. p. 220.

Chapter Nine

DIVORCE

Influenza

Margery, youthful, spirited, beautiful and impulsive, and Edwin, older, pensive, at times loud and bombastic, the strain between them increased. In Flint she had been Edwin's helpmeet and her father's close companion. In New York, there were many other alluring activities, a heavy social calendar and much more excitement. They decided that it would be in the best interest of the children if they were kept away from their confrontations as much as possible. In the fall of 1917, when he was ten years old, William was sent away to the Fay school, a prestigious residential school for boys near Boston.[203] After a few months he rebelled, ran away and made his way back to Park Avenue in New York and to Edwina, his inseparable companion. He was then placed in St Bernard's School on East 60th Street so that he could return home each evening where the two could find consolation in each other.

In June 1918 as the events of World War I began to bring the conflict to an end, an even worse catastrophe struck: the influenza pandemic. The *Journal of the American Medical Association* said:

---

203   *Handbook of the Best Private Schools of the US*. 1915, page 33.

> *The year 1918 has gone; a year momentous as the termination of the most cruel war in the annals of the human race... Medical Science... must turn with its whole might to combating the greatest enemy of all- infectious disease.* [204]

The silent killer began its perilous journey as influenza but in many cases it evolved into pneumonia and in those cases it invariably meant death. The fall of 1918 was a time of horror. In previous attacks of influenza the most vulnerable had been the youngest and the oldest in society, this time it attacked those in their prime, the healthy and robust in society and mainly in their twenties. While the country focused on winning the War, people gathered together for parades, bond drives, recruitment drives, and on September 11, Babe Ruth led the Boston Red Sox to victory in the World Series. As a result of these gatherings, the disease spread rapidly and evolved into an epidemic, and the epidemic became a national crisis. It reached its peak in mid October when 851 died in one day in New York City. Eleven thousand died in Philadelphia that month. Hollywood celebrities such as 25 year old Lillian Gish and 26 year old Mary Pickford made the headlines when they came down with the infection. President Woodrow Wilson fell victim to the flu while participating in negotiations for the Treaty of Versailles which ended the war. He was forced to spend many days in isolation. Gish, Pickford and the President were among the fortunate: they recovered. Rose Cleveland, sister of the former president Grover Cleveland was not so fortunate. She died on the day after Armistice: November 12, 1918. It is estimated that more than 675,000 Americans died, four times the number that had been killed in the war. The estimates of global deaths from the disease range from 25 to 50 million people.

Edwin and William had relatively mild attacks but Margery's attack was so severe that the children feared for her life: *It was touch and go for days, and we children were terribly frightened that she would die.*[205]

---

[204] *Journal of the American Medical Association*. December 28, 1918.

[205] Edwina Campbell Sanger, *My First 90 Years*, p. 15.

Edwin called on his best friends and acquaintances in the medical profession to help in her care, including his school friend Llewellys Barker. Barker had served as head of the Federal Plague Commission appointed by President McKinley in 1901. A few years later he moved to Baltimore to become the physician-in-chief at the prestigious Johns Hopkins Hospital. Barker took control of her care at Johns Hopkins and personally administered a number of tests. The results proved conclusively that the influenza had become pneumonia. Lying in an oxygen tent for days she held on to life by a mere thread. To alleviate her pain large doses of morphine were prescribed. She eventually survived, but at a terrible cost: she had become addicted to the morphine. For the remainder of her life, drug addiction of some kind would be a constant, lifelong companion.

When Margery had recovered sufficiently, the family all went to their home in Pasadena, California for the winter. Here William and Edwina enrolled in the Polytechnic Elementary School. Unfortunately although Margery had recovered from pneumonia and influenza, her morphine addiction complicated her weakened state and she failed to make the expected improvement. In the early spring Margery was transported back to Baltimore and remained for several months in Johns Hopkins where her care was carefully supervised by Barker again. Slowly she regained some of her weight and strength but she remained addicted to morphine. Her physical and medical experiences no doubt had an effect on her mental and emotional state.

Divorce

Eventually Margery was released from hospital and insisted that the family return to New York. Once they were back on Park Avenue, rather than remain at their suite and allow herself to be fully restored to health, she immersed herself even more compulsively in her active social life.

> *Once back in New York the parties resumed, along with more serious flirtations. Mother had become deeply involved with a married man from Connecticut. Father hired a private*

investigator to track her movements, establishing with certainty that an affair was in progress. As the quarrelling grew worse, their marriage came to an end.[206]

Illustration #25: Portrait of Margery taken by noted American portrait photographer Arnold Genthe. This portrait was taken in New York in February 1919 shortly before her divorce from Edwin. The photograph is in the Library of Congress Prints and Photographs Division, Washington D.C. Photo ID # LC-G432-2767. (Photo: Courtesy Library of Congress)

For many of the people with whom they socialized, marriage breakdowns were common occurrences. Members of the Astor and Du Pont families and many of the Campbells' acquaintances in the entertainment world

---

206 Edwina Campbell Sanger, <u>My First 90 Years</u>, p. 16.

were noted for their marital instability and frequent remarriages. Marjorie Merriweather Post, Margery's roommate at Mount Vernon College, had divorced her first husband, Edward Bennett Close earlier in the year.

When Billy and Clara divorced in Flint in 1908 they were able to convince their friend, Judge William Gage to order a press blackout for the divorce. Given the high profile of their lives in New York, Edwin and Margery would not have been able to keep their divorce from the tabloids of the day. To proceed with the divorce with as little publicity as possible they agreed that Margery would go to Paris where the divorce would not attract as much attention.

Margery, Edwina and 29-year-old maid Johanna Stonitsch (Jo), set sail for Southampton in July 1919 and then made their way to Paris where they took up residence at the Plaza Athenee. Jo acted as Edwina's governess while Margery completed the required residence in France in order to obtain the decree: *"Mother, of course, made many friends, and was wined and dined almost every night while Jo and I entertained ourselves at the hotel."* [207]

While the trio enjoyed Parisian life, Edwin and William made their way to Hotel Washington at Bretton Woods to enjoy a summer of golf and tennis. Edwin also took his son home to Port Perry to visit his mother. There they journeyed to neighbouring Blackstock to visit his cousin Dr. Archibald McArthur. Archibald had built his practice up to such an extent that he invited his brother Dr. John A. McArthur to join him. John accepted the invitation and had moved into the home in time to welcome Edwin and William.

Aftermath

Margery, Edwina and Jo returned to New York on October 9, 1920 on board the elegant *S. S. Aquitania*.[208] Edwin moved into suite 341 at the Plaza Hotel while Margery maintained their home at 635 Park Avenue. In addition to the Park Avenue residence Billy bought her a home in Westbury,

---

207   Ibid., p. 17.

208   Passenger lists

Long Island. The home was very close to Roosevelt Field, an airfield which would later play a significant role in the first Trans-Atlantic flights.

> *I spent several days looking over the estates to find one that I cared for. I was about to give up in complete discouragement when the agent drove me up to the door of what is now "Dreamwood," as I have named my home. When I looked through the open hall and out of the opposite door I saw a vista that made me exclaim: "This is where I want to live for the rest of my life!" As soon as I came back to New York I telephoned my father and asked him if he would like to go to the country with me. He did so the following morning. He went in and looked it over without saying a word. When he came out he turned to me: Is this the kind of house you would like to buy? "Just exactly," I told him. "All right," he said. And to the owner he added: "I will make you an offer for the place just as it stands, furnished. I leave my office at three tomorrow afternoon. The matter will have to be settled by then — or not at all." He made a generous offer. No discussion. No bargaining. No quibbling with me. It is a joy to see a man's mind work like that!* [209]

The amount of the divorce settlement is undisclosed, but can logically be referred to as substantial. Margery still continued her social life at the Colony Club and elsewhere as Mrs. Edwin R. Campbell. She continued to be known as Mrs. Campbell until her marriage in 1922 to Robert Daniel, her second husband. In the frequent press coverage of her social and private life she was almost always referred to as the daughter of millionaire William Durant or *"...Margery Durant, daughter of William Durant, the auto magnate."* [210]

The dynamics of the divorce changed Billy and Edwin's relationship only slightly. When Billy moved out of Edwin and Margery's home to

---

[209] Margery Durant, <u>My Father</u>, pp. 324, 325.

[210] <u>International News Services</u>: June 12, 1931.

set up an apartment in New York in 1914, their lengthy evening chats, discussions and planning sessions were substantially reduced. They still remained in contact as Margery insisted on her visits with her father when possible. When Billy and Catherine took possession of Raymere the intimate contact was further reduced. After the divorce Edwin refused to join Billy and Catherine at Raymere or at their New York apartment if Margery was also present, yet frequent telephone conversations no doubt continued, as did the almost daily correspondence when Edwin was in California. From these letters it is obvious that in spite of the physical distances between them, Billy and Edwin remained close personal friends. The camaraderie, the loyalty and mutual respect, and the exchange of information and advice continued unabated. Billy's letters to Edwin maintained their salutation of *"Dear Doctor,"* and Edwin continued to use *"Dear Pops"* as his greeting to Billy, a tradition so firmly entrenched that it continued until Edwin's death almost a decade later.

With her new found freedom Margery held lavish parties, particularly at her new home in Westbury. This resulted in a number of liaisons and much embarrassment for Edwin:

> *Back in New York City after the divorce, life continued much as before, except that father had been replaced by a succession of men who fell madly in love with my mother — with her beauty, her charm, and, in most cases, her money.*[211]

The arrangement for the children was initially heartrending:

> *We children, of course were not consulted about this arrangement, which I first heard of from my mother when we first returned to the States. I remember the scene well. We were in her bedroom, where she was having breakfast in bed, as was her custom. Suddenly she announced that as part of the divorce settlement, Bill was to go with my father and I was to stay with*

---

211   Edwina Campbell Sanger, My First 90 Years, p. 18.

> her. I sat down on the floor and burst into sobs, which I am sure could have been heard throughout the house. "You cannot take my brother away from me," I cried. "He is my playmate and my friend." ... My protests however were to no avail. Bill and I saw little of each other during the ensuing years, but much later in life we were reunited. [212]

After the divorce Edwin made every effort to help William live a normal life in New York. He enrolled him in Boy Scouts where he excelled and earned his Eagle Scout badge, the highest level in scouting, in 1922.

Over the years Edwin had encouraged his older brother to consider moving to the United States to set up his practice. Duncan joined the American Medical Association in 1910 while practicing in Cobalt, Ontario. In 1913 he made a permanent move to the United States by opening a practice in Utica, New York. Again following his brother's encouragement, Duncan re-established his medical practice in Brooklyn in 1918. He was to remain there for five years before moving to Stamford, New York.

---

[212] Ibid.

Chapter Ten

BILLY THE PHOENIX

Uncomfortable Departure

The blame for the extenuating financial circumstances at General Motors could not be laid entirely at Billy's feet. As a result of Raskob's ambitious plans for GM's Detroit Office building and his demand to refurbish some of the GM plants, he should share a substantial amount of blame. Sloan observed: *" With all I have said in appraising Mr. Durant's methods, he was no more responsible than was Mr. Raskob for the collision. "*[213]

J.P. Morgan's Edward Stettinius, in his manipulation of GM shares, also played a part in the financial dilemma.

The amount of blame which Billy carried was irrelevant. The powers had conspired against him again and he had been forced to relinquish all control of General Motors — he was out, and so was Edwin. After Billy's departure, Pierre du Pont proved to be a somewhat reluctant president of General Motors, largely due to his executive background and lack of knowledge and experience with automobiles. [214] Alfred P. Sloan was elected as the executive vice-president and the so-called Durant office

---

213 Alfred P Sloan, Jr., <u>My Years With General Motors</u>, p. 38.

214 Alfred P. Sloan, Jr., <u>Adventures of a White-Collar Man</u>, p. 130.

building complex that Raskob had so aggressively supported was renamed the GM Building.

In Billy's negotiations for his financial settlement with the Du Ponts it soon became apparent that he had few friends in that organization.

> *The position taken by Mr. Raskob was so manifestly unfair with reference to the adjustment of my claims against the company and the carrying out of the agreement (written and implied) which led to the taking over of my stock to the Du Pont Securities Co. — that it would not be in the best interests to rely upon him to continue the negotiation, and that I should employ counsel to represent me.*[215]

It took almost two years before the GM directors and the Du Pont organization closed the books on Billy. He walked away with 55,000 shares in GM and less than $400,000 in cash. With reluctance and sadness Billy Durant closed the doors on his life with his beloved General Motors. But he was not a broken man. He had risen from the ashes before, and he had an idea.

Durant Motors

In December, Edwin wired Billy from California: *"You are still young in spirit"* [216] He was, and at age 59 he was still relatively young. He still had Raymere and an adoring young wife to encourage him. Billy's despair quickly turned to enthusiasm and in early December he began planning at his usual hectic pace. Upon his return to New York he contacted Edwin and a number of friends telling them of a plan to create a new automobile company, Durant Motors Incorporated, and would be offering investment opportunities in the company. His influence and reputation in the city and among his many friends and contacts presented him with enormous support for any plan that he might devise.

---

215 *Memorandum of WCD dated Dec 31, 1920, Durant Papers, Scharchburg Archives.*

216 *Durant Papers, Scharchburg Archives.*

Documentation

It is extremely difficult to determine the exact level of involvement that Edwin or anyone else had in Durant Motors. In the late 1920s, as the prospect of the huge black hole of the Great Depression approached, it drew hundreds of thousands of people and enterprises into its vortex, many never to be heard of again. Into that vortex, the detailed records of Durant Motors — the records and names of investors, shareholders, board members, minutes of board meetings, financial records — all were pulled into the abyss. These records were either lost or destroyed as Durant Motors became yet another enterprise to be thrown on the scrapheap of history. The only viable records of the company left to us are the articles which appeared in the press. But even here, by 1923, Billy's dramatic headline grabbing exploits on the stock market began to eclipse the activities of anyone who had anything to do with Durant Motors, including Edwin. By 1924 the eclipse was almost total. Then, as we shall see, as the pending economic crash loomed on the horizon in 1928, Durant Motors began to re-emerge in the news.

Durant Grows

In 1920 when Billy made his initial offering for Durant Motors the response was overwhelming. His friends, most probably including Edwin, immediately responded and the shares were sold out within a few days and quickly became oversubscribed. It should be pointed out that Billy offered to his close friends who still owned GM shares, a stock swap of five GM shares for seven shares in the new Durant Motors. He had to turn down over $2 million in offers to invest; such was the faith of Billy's friends. On January 12, 1921 he incorporated Durant Motors with a capital stock of $5 million. When news of the share exchange offer reached the GM executives, fears of a repetition of the Chevrolet takeover of GM in 1916 began to appear.²¹⁷ But Billy was too busy to worry about GM fears. He had a new company to build.

Due to the downturn in the economy, many factories had closed their doors leaving Billy with numerous opportunities to locate factories for his new venture. He chose to start production of his four cylinder automobiles in Long Island New York in a former Goodyear Tire and Rubber Company factory. Ironically this facility had started out as a Ford assembly plant.

As in past circumstances, he hired men in whom he had complete confidence. He chose his first design engineer from his Chevrolet days: Alfred T. Sturt who had designed the Chevrolet 490. Sturt worked frenetically on a four-cylinder design for Billy and had his vehicle ready for production in two months. The Durant Four was unveiled to the public on August 4, 1921. Immediately after its first public showing Billy received orders for 30,000 cars.

The success of the Durant Four motivated another move: the creation of a new low priced car to compete with Ford's aging but still immensely popular Model T, but more importantly to compete with Chevrolet. Billy set up the Star Motor Company to produce a vehicle to challenge them head on, undercutting the retail price of the Chevrolet and meeting the model T with a retail sales price of $348.

In 1922, *The New York Times*, with a dateline of Washington, March 9, carried an article headlined:

> **DURANT RIVAL TO THE FORD. New Star Automobile to sell at $348 Shown in Washington.**
>
> *The Star automobile which in the touring car type sells at $348 and is declared to be intended as a rival to the Ford machine, was on exhibition here today.*²¹⁸

The introduction in Washington drew 30,000 curiosity seekers. Again Billy was swarmed by dealers wanting to sell his cars. Shares in the Star were sold through the Durant Corporation and were again oversold.

---

217 Pierre du Pont to WCD March 16, 1921. Durant Papers. Scarchburg Archives.
218 <u>New York Times</u> March 10, 1922.

The demand for his cars was truly overwhelming but Billy was up to the challenge. He needed a much larger facility in order to meet the demand for his cars. When the Willys Corporation went into receivership its huge factory at Elizabeth, New Jersey came on the market. Walter Chrysler placed a bid of $5 million for a facility which had cost $13.5 million. Billy outbid his rival by $200,000 and took control of the massive thirty-five acre building.

Billy again resorted to his list of outstanding and dependable former workers and hired Fred W. Hohensee to run the plant. Hohensee had worked for Billy as a foreman at the Flint Road Cart Company and then as works manager at Chevrolet. Billy strategically invited potential investors from industry and finance to a spectacular opening. By the end of the year over 63,000 Stars had emerged from the factory.

Sensing that Billy would try to make a comeback at General Motors using the Durant enterprises much as he had used Chevrolet from 1911 to 1916, many investors smiled approvingly as his empire grew and flowed along a path remarkably similar to that of Chevrolet in its early days. He even pulled off a few somewhat vindictive moves against General Motors. A second purchase for instance: a GM facility in Muncie, Indiana that was no longer needed as a result of GM's downsizing. This was the plant that Billy himself had bought for GM in 1919 in order to produce the Sheridan Car. The Muncie plant which he set up as a separate incorporation was to build an upscale six cylinder vehicle.

In order to take advantage of the rapidly growing demand for trucks, he hired Arthur C. Mason, another of his GM alumni, the designer of engines for Buick, Little and Chevrolet, to supervise the designing and building of trucks for him. Billy's failed venture into Samson Tractors while at General Motors left the Flint tractor plant empty. Billy bought it, incorporated the Mason Truck Company and put Mason in charge of design and production. Meanwhile, Edwin assisted in the creation of Durant Motors of California. Earlier, Billy's son Clifford had been placed in control of Chevrolet of California. Edwin had no trouble enticing him away from GM and placed him in charge of Durant in California.

Durant in Canada

In 1922 Edwin returned home to Port Perry and drove around Toronto looking for facilities for his father-in-law's plans for Durant Motors of Canada. He found an abandoned munitions factory in Leaside, a suburb of Toronto. Billy came to look at the plant, immediately bought it and began plans to remodel and enlarge the plant to accommodate his production plans for 175 cars a day. He later bought an adjacent 18 acres in order to expand the plant yet again. The first Canadian Durant rolled off the line on March 1, 1922.

Meanwhile Billy created a series of companies to accommodate investors and to facilitate the production of Durants, Stars and Mason Trucks. These companies were: Star Motors of Delaware, Durant Motors of Michigan, Durant Motors of Indiana, and Hayes — Hunt Body.

In an expression of his gratitude for the support he had received from the citizens of Flint, he incorporated the Flint Motor Company, bought a 100 acre property and built a huge new $15 million factory on it. Alfred Sturt was put in charge of design and Billy made it clear to Sturt that his mandate was to design a vehicle, which he named the Flint, to compete directly with the Buick. Production began in December 1922 and the Flint was introduced to the public at the traditional New York Motor show in January 1923. Unfortunately Sturt, who was only 45 years old, died later that month. In spite of this tragedy Billy now had vehicles which successfully competed with Chevrolet, Buick and Henry Ford's Model T. All he now needed was a vehicle to compete with Cadillac and meet the demands of the luxury car market. With this in mind he cast an investment eye on the floundering Locomobile Company of America, producer of the highest priced car in the U.S.

> Reports that Durant interests have become identified with the reorganization plans of the Locomobile Company of America were confirmed yesterday when it was announced that W.C.Durant had assumed the Presidency of the Locomobile Company. Mr. Durant said: "I regard the Locomobile as one

> *of the wonderful accomplishments of the present motor age..."*
> Mr. Durant emphasized that the identity of the Locomobile
> as a high class motor car product would not be disturbed. The
> Locomobile will continue to be produced at Bridgeport, Conn.* [219]

Less than a week later, it was confirmed that Billy had closed the deal.

> *The old Locomobile Company of America went out of existence
> yesterday and a newly organized Locomobile Company headed
> by W.C. Durant of Durant Motors, assumed charge.* [220]

Billy hired yet another GM alumnus: George E. Daniels who had worked his way up to the executive ranks to become a director at GM. Daniels' responsibility was design and production of the Locomobile.

Stock Market

Billy's early successes with Durant Motors, as monumental as they were, paled in comparison with his successes in the stock market. By the time that World War One came to a close in 1918 Billy had already earned a notable reputation as a successful but careful speculator on the stock market. A *New York Times* article in 1917 had the following to say about him:

> *Durant has the reputation among his friends of possessing
> imagination which could make him a leading figure in specula-
> tion if he desired to be one. But he has never appeared in the
> limelight of stock market affairs, although it is known that
> he has seen tremendous profits accrue on stocks bought at low
> figures. He buys long before the public sees the speculative merit
> of the stock involved. He is said to possess supreme confidence
> in his judgement; when he decides to accumulate stocks he gets*

---

219 *New York Times* July 23, 1922.

220 *New York Times* July 29, 1922.

> them and no changes in market conditions of a temporary sort disturb him. [221]

Over the next twelve years, he increased his power and influence on Wall Street. By 1921 he ventured beyond mere investing and began to assume a role as a critic of a variety of financial matters. In 1921 he attacked the Federal Reserve Bank for failing to stop profiteering by the banks.

> Bankers "greed" is responsible for the general business paralysis, and the Federal Reserve Bank, by its failure to stop this profiteering, by standing idly by and permitting this gouging, is mainly responsible for the present untoward situation, W.C. Durant, President of the Durant Motors, Inc., declared in a signed statement here today. As a solution, Mr Durant asks banks to put credit money back at 3%. "If this is done," he says, "the wheels of industry will again turn....There are many contributory causes, but the trouble — and we are in real trouble- is largely financial." [222]

Billy's personal response to this lack of leadership by the Federal Reserve was to create his own financial institutions. To facilitate the financial aspects of his companies and the financing of his vehicles he created the Durant Acceptance Corporation patterned closely after GMAC. He then took over the charter of the Liberty National Bank in New York, fulfilling a dream to challenge the bankers and the Federal Reserve by establishing a bank along his own principles. With Durant himself as the president, the bank established its capital through 300,000 shareholders, each limited to one share each. "No commissions, fees or bonuses in cash, goods or stock would be charged for any loans," [223] he claimed. For loans, customers would be charged interest at the current Federal rate. The bank opened its doors

---

221 *New York Times* May 13, 1917.

222 *New York Times* October 2, 1921.

223 Bernard Weisberger *The Dream Maker*, p. 299.

for business on October 8, 1923 at its first branch at 256 West 57th Street in New York and Billy placed Robert William Daniel as vice president with the responsibility of running the day-to-day operations of the bank.

Robert William Daniel

Robert William Daniel was a suave, opportunistic, southern gentleman descended from a line of Virginia land owners, including a great-grandfather who was an associate Justice of the Supreme Court and a great-great-grandfather who was the first Attorney General of the United States and Secretary of State. Daniel was a first class passenger on board the *Titanic* on its fateful 1912 maiden voyage. He managed to escape death by jumping into the water and then swam to a lifeboat and was rescued by the *Carpathia*.[224] On board the *Carpathia* he met Mrs Lucien P. Smith whose husband had drowned in the tragic event. They were married a year later.

At some point during the early summer of 1923, Billy held a private social gathering at Raymere for some of the Durant personnel including Daniel. Since Edwin was in California at the time, he invited Margery to be a part of the gathering. Here she met Daniel and the two were smitten by each other. Daniel quickly obtained a divorce from the former Mrs Smith.

Edwina, however, looked upon Daniel as one of the *"... succession of men who fell madly in love with my mother — with her beauty, her charm, and, in most cases, her money."* [225]

Margery and Daniel were married on December 1, 1923. The wedding received a flurry of publicity in contrast to his first marriage.

> Mr Daniel and Mrs Smith were married in August 1914, but the fact did not become known until several months later. The fact that they had been divorced was not generally known and the

---

[224] Logan Marshall, *The Sinking of the Titanic and Great Sea Disasters*, (Whitefish, MT, Kessinger Publishing, 2004)

[225] Edwina Campbell Sanger, *My First 90 Years*, p. 18.

family would not discuss it last night in connection with the report of the wedding yesterday.[226]

With Margery's financial backing Daniel was able to fulfill his dream of owning an historic Virginia estate: Brandon Plantation. The property was established on the James River by Captain John Martin in 1616. The main building, an elegant brick structure, may have been designed by Jefferson. When the Daniels bought it in 1926, the entire estate was quite dilapidated and needed a fortune to undergo a complete restoration. Margery provided the needed funds. The couple scoured the country searching for original American and English furniture of the 1760s. *"Mother spent vast sums of her money restoring the house and grounds, which are now an historic showplace frequented by tourists."*[227] In addition to their home on the James River in Virginia, Margery retained her apartment in New York where she was reluctantly joined in the winter time by Edwina. But Edwina was not comfortable with Daniel's southern-gentleman charms:

I disliked my new stepfather right from the start, and I knew also that he was a serious alcoholic, the kind that starts drinking before breakfast and continues to nip steadily throughout the day, so no one really knows whether he is drunk or sober. [228]

Later, in 1925, Margery gave birth to a daughter whom she also named Margery. This further increased Edwina's discomfort in the presence of her mother. In exploring alternatives to living with her mother and stepfather, the idea of a boarding school was suggested. To Edwina it offered a suitable escape from them.

---

226   *New York Times* December 2, 1923.

227   Edwina Campbell Sanger, *My First 90 Years*, p. 18.

228   Ibid.

More Market Success

Meanwhile Billy was on a roll, but not before facing what was probably the most traumatic experience he had ever to face: the death of his mother Rebecca. In February 1924, at the age of 90, Rebecca died of a stroke. Billy was devastated. After her death he kept her house in Flint as a shrine for four years, leaving it untouched except for having a housekeeper venture in to maintain it as it was when his mother was alive. When he finally sold the house in 1928 he had all the furnishings shipped to Raymere and re-established in a suite of rooms in the fashion that Rebecca would have wanted, so that he could visit and reminisce in private.

In December 1924 Bill announced to the press that he was forming his own trust company.

> William C. Durant, automobile manufacturer, whose operations in the stock market during the last year have attracted wide attention because of the large profits which have been credited to him, ranging from one to several millions of dollars, has established an investment trust and plans to sell participating bonds. These bonds will be secured by stocks of ten large railroads, industrial and public utility corporations whose share are listed on the New York Stock Exchange. The bonds will be sold through the Durant Corporation.[229]

The difference with Billy's Trust Company was that the bond holder would receive:

> ...not only his pro-rata share of the dividends paid on the respective stocks pledged under the plan, but the holders of these bonds will also participate in any profits which may accrue to the trust at the end of the ten-year term of the bonds

---

229 *New York Times* Dec 12, 1924.

> in the event that the various stocks would be liquidated for a price higher than the cost.[230]

The Liberty National Bank was named as administrator for the Trust company and custodian for the stocks, bonds and other securities held by the Trust. Billy, no doubt with some input from Edwin, chose the stocks carefully. Among them were: United States Steel, American Telephone and Telegraph, Southern Pacific Railway, American Tobacco, Westinghouse Electric, and, surprisingly, General Motors!

Less than two months later, one of Billy's greatest short term achievements on the stock market exploded onto the newspapers:

Durant's Paper Gain

A Wall Street Wonder

He Wins $2,500,000 in Two Days by Forty Point Advance in Cast Iron Pipe. $10,000,000 IN TWO YEARS

Motor Maker, Just Back From Vacation, Is Called "More Bullish Than Ever." [231]

The article went on to explain how Billy had been interested in the United States Cast Iron Pipe and Foundry Company in 1923 when its share price was $20 and rose to $169 in a twelve month period. This was due in large part to the new and improved process of manufacturing pipe so that it could be threaded, a process which Billy had watched closely.

> The comeback of William Durant from the time he was taken over by bankers and the General Motors Corporation, of which he had twice been the head, was taken away from him by

---

230 *New York Times* Dec 12, 1924.

231 *New York Times* Feb 11, 1925.

> the bankers, has been the most spectacular of recent market history. His fall occurred in the period of deflation. Since that time, through his efforts as the head of the motor company which bears his name, but mostly through his successful stock market operations, the name of Durant has become the best known in Wall Street. Most of the stock market following... has drifted slowly to Mr. Durant.[232]

Edwin in New York and California.

When Edwin was in New York, he would invariably accompany Billy to Wall Street. With Billy as his mentor, Edwin learned intricacies of the market, occasionally investing, but never on the scale of Billy's grandiose manoeuvres and never without Billy's advice. Edwin invested in many companies involved in the latest technologies. One such company was the Independent Lamp and Wire Company with its head office at 1737 Broadway. Edwin became a director, and for a short time its president. He also invested heavily in bonds in a number of cities including Boston, Buffalo, Chicago and Pittsburgh, and state bonds in Iowa, Oregon, Michigan, Missouri, New Jersey, and West Virginia. Thus with Billy's help, Edwin was on a roll himself.

Edwin also continued his affiliation with The Lambs and was present at the club when Louis Calhern the Hollywood actor, was made a member in 1922 and when Charlie Chaplin was made a member in 1925.

While in California Edwin took advantage of his friendship with Percy Rockefeller and his contacts in Standard Oil and became an investor in that company and its land holdings in California. He also developed a friendship with Dr. A. H. Giannini, a prominent banker who, with his brother founded the Bank of Italy in California. The bank was established in 1904 to cater to the financial need of the large number of Italians in San Francisco. It later took control of the Bank of America and changed its

---

232   Ibid.

name to the latter bank. Dr. Giannini's extensive involvements included the building of the Hetch Hetchy reservoir to provide water for San Francisco and the creation of the Goldwyn studios. Edwin was responsible in sponsoring Giannini's membership in to the Lambs in New York. With Edwin as his sponsor Dr. Giannini, was inducted into the Lambs in 1925.

The Society columns of California newspapers frequently made mention of Edwin's social life. One such reference headed the Virginia Woods Society Column of the *Los Angeles Times* in March, 1922.

> *Edwin R. Campbell of Orange Grove Avenue, Pasadena, was a grand host at a smart dinner-dance at the Midwick Country Club. It marked one of the most handsomely appointed functions of the winter. There were 100 guests from Los Angeles and Pasadena.*[233]

The Economy

A phenomenon of the 1920s was a significant increase in the speculative nature of Americans. A combination of factors including the increase of industrialization and an accompanying increase in wages led to a considerable growth of purchasing power. With credit, improved production methods and improved roads, the automobile exerted an ever increasing influence on lifestyle and the economy. In 1919 more than 95 percent of buyers paid in full for their vehicles. By 1925 over 68 percent were financing the purchase of their cars even though interest rates sometimes exceeded 30 percent. In spite of this striking rise in the affluence of the lower and middle classes, slight cracks were beginning to appear in the economy.

An early sign of the problems in the economy was a personal one for Edwin. In 1925 his sister Nellie (Donalda) and her husband Samuel Wilson began to experience financial problems. Later, Samuel was to declare:

---

233 *Los Angeles Times*, March 29, 1922.

> *During the year 1925 I was engaged in business as manager of the Bankers Discount Corporation. The Corporation dealt largely in live stock and agricultural paper. The corporation took out a loan from a bank in Portland and as collateral for said loan I pledged my personal property. The bank failed and was liquidated and my pledge collateral was sold.*[234]

Edwin, on hearing of their plight, immediately sent $10,000 to help them in their distress.

Billy's Train Wreck

By the end of 1925 Billy was one of the most respected and successful businessmen in the United States. He was immensely wealthy. He owned one of the most successful "new" businesses in the country. He also had all the trappings of a successful life: a huge 32 roomed rambling summer home in New Jersey, a luxurious apartment in New York and, following Edwin's example he enjoyed frequent first class travels to Europe. He lavished money on Catherine for clothes and jewels and, befitting such a successful businessman, he had his own railroad car, named "Patriot," in which he and Catherine travelled and vacationed in the United States. In January 1926 Billy and Catherine had their railroad car attached to a train on the Florida East Coast Railroad. The train to which their car was attached was heading north from Palm Beach in Florida and paused near Titusville. Another train slammed into the parked train. The impact was concentrated on Billy's car, killing two of his servants who were preparing a meal in the galley, as well as a fireman on board the train that hit them. Thirty others suffered a variety of injuries. Catherine was thrown across the car but suffered only a few minor bruises. Billy was ejected from his bed and suffered a severe blow as his head hit the wash stand. News of the

---

234 *Letter from S.F. Wilson, contained in Edwin's will,*

Wall Street emperor became immediate headline material. The press said, *"...he narrowly escaped death."* [235]

Billy was given immediate first aid; a long gash on his forehead was stitched and bandaged. He and Catherine were then placed in the first available fast train to New York in order to have his injuries more closely examined. When he arrived at Pennsylvania Station in New York, with the entire top of his head covered in bandages he was swarmed by reporters. They were surprised to find him walking and chatting confidently. Nevertheless the doctors examined him and determined that in addition to his cuts and bruises he had suffered a concussion.

In California, Edwin boarded the first available train to New York to be with Billy and Catherine. By the time he had arrived, Billy had been released from hospital and declared that he was well on the road to recovery. Unfortunately such was not the case. After a few days the wound became infected, apparently from the initial hasty application of stitches. Again Billy was hospitalized, and eventually recovered but not without some personal concern over his energy level. Edwin's advice to Billy was unequivocal: reduce the stress load by reducing business dealings. Due to his amazing successes on the stock market, the decision was made to hand over the running of Durant Motors to others. This decision again, immediately made the headlines.

W.C. Durant Quits Business Control.

Motor Man Turns the Direction of His Companies Over to Other Executives.

Action Partly Due to Advice of Doctor. [236]

Edwin, of course, was the unnamed doctor. The article made it clear that Billy still maintained a controlling stock interest in the various Durant

---

235 *New York Times* Jan 12, 1926.

236 *New York Times* February 19, 1926.

companies involved in Durant Motors. However his involvement in the daily activities of the company gradually diminished while he focussed his energies on other investments and particularly on Wall Street itself. He did take on the role as director of a number of companies in which he had invested, including Industrial Rayon Corporation.

Recuperation

Once Billy had recovered adequately, Edwin suggested that Billy and Catherine take time to take a relaxed tour of Europe. Following Edwin's advice they sailed from New York in September. Nevertheless, always the businessman, Billy turned the tour into a business venture. Details of his travels were covered by the press, anxious to find any Wall Street connections to his daily life and eager to hear his predictions. In September the *New York Times* reported:

> **Durant Predicts Big Bull Market.**
> *Tells American Journalist in London He Bought Stocks on Eve of Sailing...*
> *W.C. Durant, whose reported operations in the stock market have attracted attention lately, expects one of the greatest bull markets the country has ever known.... He has just arrived there and expects to spend several weeks touring Europe.*

In the interview Billy recommended shares in such companies as: "*United States Steel, General Motors, American Smelting, General Electric and corporations of similar calibre and management as outstanding in every respect.*" [237]

In Europe, he made contact with a number of businessmen and even met British Prime Minister Stanley Baldwin. Arrangements were probably made through Edwin's connections with Greenwood and Amery.

Upon his return, Billy was again hounded by the press;

---

237   *New York Times*, September 8, 1926.

> **MAJESTIC ARRIVES AFTER DELAY BY FOG**
> **W.C. Durant, Back From Europe, Predicts Higher Prices For Good Stocks**
>
> *Returning Americans who had met with British Premier Stanley Baldwin in London before sailing... W.C Durant ... said that in his opinion the slump in the price of cotton would have no serious effect upon the general business situation or the stock market. He was optimistic and asserted that the good stocks would see higher prices before termination of the present bull market.* [238]

At the same time that Billy and Catherine were travelling in Europe, Edwin bought a summer cottage in Stamford New York in order to visit his brother without imposing on him for accommodation. Duncan was practicing medicine in the town at the time.

After spending a few days with his brother he made his way to Port Perry and then to Oshawa to visit Sam McLaughlin who had a proposition for Edwin. Sam had visited an excellent fishing camp in Quebec and asked Edwin if he would be interested in sharing the costs of buying and maintaining the camp. Edwin immediately agreed. Sam made all the arrangements and purchased, on their behalf, Camp Cap Chat in the Gaspe. He and Edwin were to spend many pleasant hours fishing there together.

1927

On January 13, Edwin received a telephone call from his mother to tell him that his 57 year old sister Bertie (Tryphena) had died earlier in the day. Bertie had been living with her widowed mother. Edwin again made his way home to Port Perry to console his mother and to make arrangements for a housekeeper to live with his mother in the Crandell Street home.

Two months later, a few miles from Dreamwood, Margery and Robert Daniel's country home, in Westbury Long Island, a series of

---

238 *New York Times*, October 6, 1926.

historic events began to unfold. In April, the Daniels were hosting explorer Richard Byrd as he prepared for his attempt to be the first to fly across the Atlantic from the United States to Europe. The first Trans-Atlantic flight had been achieved by British aviators John Alcock and Arthur Brown in June 1919. Their flight from St. John's, Newfoundland to Clifden, Ireland covered a distance of 1,890 miles. No further successful Atlantic crossings were made until 1927. In an attempt to be the first to cross the Atlantic from the United States, Byrd was in competition with several others including Charles Lindbergh and Clarence Chamberlain. All three were to begin their flights from Roosevelt Field, only a few miles from the Daniels' home.

Byrd, with crew member Floyd Bennett, had been the first to fly over the North Pole in May 1926, although there was some question about the accuracy of the navigation of their flight path. Byrd, again with Bennett, planned his attempt at the Trans-Atlantic flight in April, 1927. Unfortunately the plane they were to use crashed during a practice takeoff, and while waiting for their plane to be repaired, they were beaten in their quest by Charles Lindbergh who also set out from Roosevelt Field and completed the Trans-Atlantic flight alone, landing near Paris on May 21, a distance of 3400 miles. Chamberlain set out on June 4 and set a long distance non-stop flight of over 3900 miles landing in Germany. After Byrd's plane had been repaired he and Bennett set out again and successfully completed the third trans-Atlantic flight landing at in Ver-sur-Mer in France on July 1, 1927.

Reception for Richard Byrd

The Daniels held a much publicized reception for Commander Byrd on his return to the United States. Daniel and Byrd, both Virginians, had been long time friends.

> *The grounds of the estate, which comprised many acres of woodland, were illuminated at night with hundreds of Japanese lanterns, and colored lights played on the numerous pools in the gardens. A feature of the outdoor decorations were*

the signs in coloured electrics showing the way to Ver-sur-mer, the North Pole, South Pole and to Lovers' Leap. The orchestra of Meyer Davis played for the reception and dancing.[239]

The elaborate welcome was somewhat reminiscent of Edwin and Margery's introduction to New York society at Jim Brady's in May 1914. Among the more than 200 guests were two sons of former president Teddy Roosevelt: Kermit Roosevelt and his wife Belle,[240] and Archibald Roosevelt and his wife Grace. Also attending was their cousin Eleanor Roosevelt, recently secretly temporarily estranged from her husband Franklin. Other guests included: Mr. and Mrs Walbridge Taft, nephew of the former president William Howard Taft; Elbert Gary, head of United States Steel; Commander Byrd's brother Governor Harry Byrd of Virginia; Grover Whalen, brother of Joseph Whalen, New York`s Chief of Police and himself chief of Police in the following year; auto magnates Walter P. Chrysler and his wife and daughter; and Chrysler's former boss John N. Willys, head of the Willys Overland Company, and his wife Isabel. They joined Billy and Catherine Durant in attendance.

This reception would have particular consequences for Margery shortly afterwards. Her spending time with Byrd generated an interest in flying, just as, a quarter century earlier she had developed an avid enthusiasm for the automobile. Within a few months this interest would develop into an obsession and with that obsession, a desire to break away, yet again, from a marriage which she considered to be too boring and restraining.

George Putnam

One of the many people to have an influence on Margery's life during this time was publisher George P. Putnam. His publishing company had been founded by his grandfather George H. Putnam in 1840. The company

---

239 *New York Times*, July 21, 1927,

240 *Kermit Roosevelt was also an explorer, having explored and mapped sections of the Amazon River jungle in Brazil in a 1913-1914 expedition.*

became G.P. Putnam's sons in 1868 and continued under that name throughout the twentieth century. In 1926 George Putnam had begun to recognize the publishing potential for books about true life adventure. With that in mind he set out on an expedition to explore Greenland and simultaneously to act as a support for Byrd's polar flight. Immediately after his return from the polar flight, Putnam pressured Byrd into completing his account of the expedition. Completed a few months later, *Skyward* became an instant best seller.

Even before Charles Lindbergh had completed his Trans Atlantic flight, Putnam succeeded in gaining the exclusive rights to a book on his adventures. Immediately after Lindbergh landed in Europe, Putnam began to pressure him into completing an autobiography as soon as possible. When Lindbergh began to procrastinate, Putnam gave Fitzhugh Green, an Arctic explorer himself and now working for Putnam's, the job of working with Lindbergh to get the book written and published during the initial flurry of publicity. This was accomplished and the result was *We,* published in July 1927. A few months after that, a biography of Byrd titled *Dick Byrd, Air Explorer*, was also released by Putnam's. It was also written by Fitzhugh Green.

Amelia Earhart

Another occasional visitor to Dreamwood was a Kansas born female flying ace who had acquired an interest in flying while working as a nurses' aide at a military convalescence hospital in Toronto. At the encouragement of some of her airmen patients she had visited a local airfield to watch Canadian airmen in training. After falling victim to the 1918 flu epidemic, she spent two month in recuperation and then returned home to the United States. Here she eventually joined her parents who had moved to California, became engaged to an engineer, Sam Chapman, and began taking flying lessons. In 1921 she bought her own plane and by the mid 1920s she was earning a reputation as a successful flyer, winning a number of races for female flyers. Her name was Amelia Earhart.

Illustration #26: Amelia Earhart as a nurses' assistant in Toronto, 1918.

In October 1927 Ruth Elder made her attempt to be the first female involved in a Trans-Atlantic flight. Her plane developed engine trouble and had to be ditched in the Atlantic. The crew had steered the plane close to a ship before ditching the plane in the sea. They were safely rescued, but not the plane: it exploded before it could be hauled on board. The episode discouraged Elder from further adventurous flying.

The following April, Putnam assigned Captain Hilton Railey, another of his employees, the task of approaching Amelia Earhart to see if she would be interested in being the first female to cross the Atlantic. Putnam arranged for two men to join her in the attempt: Bill Stultz and Lou Gordon. They had extensive experience in piloting and navigating and agreed to spell each other out in their roles as pilot, navigator and mechanic as part of a crew under her command.

She agreed to the proposal with one major condition: that she would be permitted to take the controls if weather permitted. Putnam made a counter proposal: he would agree to Earhart's conditions if the entire plan would be kept secret until the take off. She agreed. As the preparation got underway in early May, Putnam finally met Earhart for the first time. and was immediately intrigued by her. In spite of what had been an ideal marriage with his wife Dorothy Binney whom he had married in 1911, and the fact that Amelia was engaged, Putnam spent increasing amounts of time with Earhart alone and a clandestine romance began.

While waiting for the promise of better weather, Amelia stayed with George Putnam at Richard Byrd's home in Boston. On Sunday June 3, Amelia flew from Boston to Trepassy in Newfoudland. But it wasn't until the early morning of June 17 that ideal weather conditions emerged. Amelia and her crew of Stultz and Gordon then left Newfoundland and landed over twenty hours later in Burry Point, South Wales. She was the first female to cross the Atlantic. Margery sent her a congratulatory telegram. After a tumultuous welcome back in the United States, Putnam gave a large, by invitation only, reception at the Biltmore Hotel in Rye, New York. Margery and Robert were among the invited guests. In the round of publicity and endorsements that followed, Putnam encouraged Earhart, who was a non-smoker to endorse Lucky Strike cigarettes. Earhart donated the Lucky Strike endorsement money to Byrd for his Antarctic exploration. Later that year she made the first female solo U.S. cross country flight. Her book on the Trans-Atlantic crossing, *20 Hrs. 40 Min,* published by Putnam became an immediate best seller.

Shortly afterwards, Amelia broke off her engagement to Chapman, and Putnam began divorce proceedings with Dorothy. Amelia Earhart and George Putnam were quietly married on Saturday, February 7, 1931. In May 1932, Amelia flew from Harbour Grace in Newfoundland to Culmore near Londonderry in Ireland to become the first woman and only the second person in history to cross the Atlantic solo.

In July 1937 Earhart made her final and fateful journey, an attempt to circumnavigate the globe. Having completed the major section of the journey eastward from Miami, Amelia and her co-pilot Fred Noonan flew across the Atlantic to Africa, then India, landing in Lae in New Guinea on June 29. After leaving Lae on July 1, Amelia, Fred Noonan and the twin engine Lockheed Electra disappeared somewhere in that vast ocean near Howland Island in the mid Pacific.

Shortly after the reception that Margery and her husband had given for Richard Byrd in July 1927, George Putnam suggested to Margery that she write a biography of her father. Within that context Amelia Earhart introduced Margery to Fitzhugh Green who had been Lindbergh's ghost writer in the publication of *We*. This introduction later proved to be a fateful one.

Meanwhile Edwin was dividing his time between his suite at the Plaza in New York and his home on South Orange Grove Avenue in Pasadena, along with his annual journey to Europe and frequent visits to Raymere. The trips to Europe, mainly England, were usually taken with either Edwina or William. Occasionally he travelled alone. In the spring of 1927 father and son celebrated William's graduation from High School and acceptance into Princeton, by spending a month in England, travelling first class from New York to Southampton on board the White Star Line's *Majestic* [241] and arriving back in New York on June 14 on board the *Olympic*. [242]

---

[241] Board of Trade: Commercial and Statistical Department: Inwards Passenger Lists. Kew Surrey, England: The National Archives of the UK. Series BT26.

[242] Passenger and Crew Lists of Vessels Arriving at New York, New York, 1897-1957. (National Archives Microfilm Publication T715, 8892 rolls);Records of the Immigration and Naturalization Service; National Archives, Washington D.C.

Illustration #27: Amelia Earhart after her Solo flight across the Atlantic, in May 1932.

Illustration #28: Publisher George Putnam and his wife Amelia Earhart.

Chapter Eleven

THE LOOMING CRISIS

Billy and Edwin

1928 started out well for Billy. On January 4, he received accolades and extensive press coverage over a tribute to *"His 25ᵗʰ Year in Motor Industry."*[243] To celebrate the occasion, a number of dignitaries gave Billy a testimonial banquet at the Hotel Roosevelt in New York. Edwin and the President of Durant Motors in California, Norman De Vaux, journeyed all the way from California to join in the celebration.

The items of correspondence between Edwin and Billy in the 1920s suffered the same fate as the records of the Durant Motors: almost all have vanished. Of the correspondence between them during that period only one letter has so far been located. On May 9, 1928 Edwin wrote to Billy from Pasadena. He began with the usual greeting of *"Dear Pops."* After a first paragraph containing a tirade over Margery's life style, Edwin acknowledged a cable from Billy encouraging Edwin to buy shares in a company which he refers to as *"Combustion."*

---

243 <u>New York Times</u> Jan 5, 1928.

> Your cable about Combustion I received and secured some of it. I called up Miss Weiller and she had Cusick buy it for me. She thought I was in New York as she could hear me so plainly. I am leaving tonight (9th) for New York and will arrive there on the 13th. I will go down to Princeton and see the children. Edwina will be there with Billy for three weeks, getting ready for her examinations... The market seems to be boiling. Call money back at 6% today. How high is Combustion going? Should I hold it for a long pull? I wish I were over there with you — My love to you both and I hope you both keep well. ERC. [244]

Edwin's rant over Margery and her marital affairs resulted from the news that Margery was having another affair and was planning her divorce from Daniel and it would only be a matter of weeks before her divorce would be a news event across the country. The references to the children alluded to William, who was in his first year at Princeton and that Edwina was staying with her brother while she studied for the examinations which would lead to her admission to Vassar in the fall.

The stock "Combustion" which Billy had encouraged Edwin to buy was in the International Combustion Engineering Company. It had started out in Derby, England as the Combustion Engineering Corporation in 1900 and was involved in the manufacture of boilers, automatic stokers and a variety of fuel systems for heavy industry. It expanded to France, Germany, Belgium and Holland and was then incorporated in the United States in 1920. Edwin bought an unknown number of shares in the company through "Pat" Cusick, one of Billy's numerous brokers. It later became obvious that Edwin did not keep the shares for too long as he had sold them within twelve months, again probably following Billy's advice.

---

244   ERC to WCD. May 8, 1928. In the collection of Alex Sanger.

Christina

On June 17 Edwin was shaken by a telephone call from his brother Duncan in Stamford, New York. He broke the tragic news that their mother had passed away earlier in the day in Port Perry. Duncan made his way to Port Perry and began to make the funeral arrangements, appointing Willam Heard Hams a local barrister to administer the humble will.

The following day Edwin arrived to join his brother in their sad task. The *Observer* in Port Perry announced:

> Mrs D. Campbell entered into rest on Sunday June 17 at the family residence in Port Perry. Christina McArthur, widow of the late Donald Campbell in her 94th year. She is survived by two sons Dr. D. Campbell of Stamford New York and Dr. E.R. Campbell of New York City and Mrs S.F. Wilson of Portland Oregon. [245]

Christina and her brother had always been involved in friendly rivalry. After Christina had produced two sons who had become doctors, her brother Neil and his wife Mary Anne (Watson) countered by having three sons whom they also encouraged to take an interest in medicine. The three boys in turn stayed with Christina in Port Perry so that they could walk across the road to attend Port Perry High School in order to take advantage of Dugald McBride's eminence as a teacher. They then followed their cousins to Toronto to become trained and qualified as physicians. By 1928, each had his own medical practice; Dr. A. McArthur, Dr. E.C. McArthur, Dr. J. McArthur, and all returned to Port Perry to act as pall bearers for their aunt. They were joined in the heart-rending duty by their brother Donald, another cousin Howard Campbell, and Alex Ulanson. Edwin and his brother Donald and other members of the family followed the cortege to the Prince Albert cemetery. She was laid to rest beside her husband and daughter below the monument which Edwin had purchased.

---

245 *Ontario Observer*, (Port Perry), June 21, 1928.

Edwin's sister Donella was given the title to the Campbell's home at the corner of Queen and Crandell streets. The will stated that the house was left to her by her mother *"for love and affection."* She stayed in the home briefly but within a year sold the residence and moved to Toronto. The purchaser of the former Campbell home was Cecil Beare, the local Chrysler agent who had his dealership just a few yards away on adjacent Queen Street.

Edwina at School

The idea of Edwina being at boarding school was quickly accepted by Margery. In order to determine the best school for Edwina, she and her mother visited several schools before settling on Miss Porter's School in Farmington, Connecticut, a school similar to Miss Mason's Castle School that Margery had attended. At that time the school was being run by Miss Porter's nephew Robert Porter Keep and his wife. It provided a structured and cultured environment for the girls enrolled with an emphasis on languages and the arts. Edwina graduated from Farmington in the spring of 1928 with numerous academic honours as well as the tennis championship. When Margery arrived at the school for Edwina's graduation ceremonies she relapsed into a morphine induced stupor and *"collapsed on the bed in my room, and missed the entire ceremony."* [246] Edwina managed to get her mother back to her apartment in New York. Two days later, on Edwina's last day of school, Margery tried to jump out of her hotel window but fortunately was restrained by one of her servants. Edwina immediately went to New York to see her mother only to find her again in a morphine stupor and watched helplessly as doctors and nurses carried her off to a sanatorium in Reno, Nevada.

Edwin constantly berated Edwina for continuing to see her mother as he despaired of the influence she might have on the teenager. Edwina however had an abiding love for her mother, even though the trust and much of her respect was being eroded by her mother's frailties. The

---

246   Edwina Campbell Sanger, <u>My First 90 Years</u>, page 20.

prospects of living in New York with either her mother or her father brought Edwina to the realization that after graduation she would be better off avoiding both options and began to think of going to University. Several of her friends had spoken glowingly about Vassar. Her training at Farmington was *"weak in math, history and science"* [247] so, with William's encouragement she enrolled at the Hun School of Princeton, a private university preparatory school, in order to upgrade her qualifications so that she could apply to Vassar. Hun was a professor of Mathematics at Princeton where William was in his first year. She passed with glowing colours and, defying her father, journeyed to Reno to spend time with her mother who had just emerged from the sanatorium and was involved in obtaining her second divorce. Shortly after her arrival she found out that her mother was pregnant:

> *...and not by her soon-to-be-divorced husband. A gentleman of considerable renown in the art world, but of dubious morals, had arrived on the scene just before we left New York. When he reappeared in Reno, a cooperative doctor was found, the living room in the hotel was transformed into an operating suite, and mother had an abortion. Luckily all went well. The gentleman departed, leaving behind three beautiful Georgia O"Keefe paintings as a gift.*[248]

The "man of dubious morals" was Mitchell Kennerley and the O'Keefe paintings were not really a gift.

Mitchell Kennerley

Born in England, Mitchell Kennerley, encouraged by his friend author Arnold Bennett, took an early interest in book collecting. As a messenger for the Civil Service Commission in London he frequented the antiquarian

---

247 Ibid., p. 19.

248 Ibid P.22.

bookshops of the City and was offered a job as a clerk with a publisher, John Lane. Here he struck up friendships with such authors as Oscar Wilde, Aubrey Beardsley, Kenneth Grahame and George Bernard Shaw. His quick mind and knowledge of the publishing business earned him an invitation to be placed in charge of Lane's New York branch in 1896. Shortly after his arrival he struck up a friendship with the Canadian poet Bliss Carman. They became roommates and later rented a three roomed apartment on East Sixteenth Street.

At that time Carman was having a relationship with Mary Perry King, the wife of a New York physician. This affair encouraged Kennerly to follow his own pursuit of women. A number of Kennerley's letters to his friend Thomas B. Mosher attest to a number of passionate relationships, one with a prostitute and another with Aimee Lenal, a correspondent for the New York Mirror.[249] In the last of these letters he stated; *"Marriage is a mistake at the best of times and is generally committed at the worst of times."* With this frame of mind he became a *"compulsive womanizer."* [250] Exploiting his friend Bliss Carman's relationship with Mrs King, he frequently borrowed money from her and was heavily indebted to her when he left New York in January 1899 to return to England. With a lifestyle beyond his financial status he even began borrowing on the strength of a mortgage held by his father's estate.

On his return to New York in the fall of 1899 he became the business manager of a magazine *The Smart Set*. Through the magazine he became acquainted with Helen Rockwell Morley, daughter of Jesse Healy Morley, president of the Cleveland Light and Coke Company, a multimillionaire with interests in mining and manufacturing. They were married in Cleveland December 10, 1901. Her father, wary of Kennerley's money problems, set up his will to prevent Kennerley from inheriting his fortune. He did this by leaving his estate in trust for fifteen years after his death and

---

249   MK to Mosher April 1897 21 April 1897, 17 May 1897, 4 June 1897, 6 June 1897. Houghton Library, Harvard University.

250   Matthew J. Bruccolli, *The Fortunes of Mitchell Kennerley, Bookman*, (New York, Harcourt Brace 1986), p. 14.

specifying portions to his other children while leaving 22% in a further lifetime trust to Helen. He died two years after their marriage and Helen, obviously at Kennerley's request, began to draw from the interest. They bought a large country home just outside New York and travelled extensively. He also used her money to finance the publishing of his own magazine, *The Reader*.

Helen's wealth also enabled Kennerly to indulge in passions to which he had long aspired: developing an extensive collection of antiquarian books, and the establishment of his own publishing house. His publishing company launched in 1906 quickly rose to the forefront of the American trade. In 1910 he took control of the magazine *The Forum* in order to promote his publications and to provide an audience for writers. In his first year in control of the forum he published essays, poems and stories by H.G. Wells, Leo Tolstoy, Ezra Pound, W.B. Yeats, Robert Frost, Walter Lippmann , D.H. Lawrence, Bliss Carman, H.L. Mencken, and Edna St. Vincent Millay. However, always in financial difficulty, he frequently failed to pay his authors the promised fees.

> ...since from one year to the next I receive from him not one penny of royalties on any of the three books of mine which he has published.[251]

In 1913 he took on a fifteen year lease of a six story building at 32 West Fifty-Eighth Street. Alfred Knopf, later to set up his own publishing house, worked here for Kennerley. The basement and ground floor were used for his publishing business; the upper floors were rented out as office space but he did maintain one of the rooms as a place to pursue his female conquests. On Sundays Kennerley provided his client authors an opportunity to give public readings of their works and to meet the press. Among Kennerley's lovers during this period were Edna Vincent St. Millay, Isadora Duncan, and Bella da Costa Greene, director of the Pierpont Morgan

---

251   Edna St. Vincent Millay, <u>Letters of Edna St. Vincent Millay</u>, ed Allan Ross Macdougall, (New York, Harper, 1952), p. 160

Library. Kennerley made a sincere effort to be discreet about his affairs but today, through collections of correspondence and other records, it is possible to develop a detailed list of these intimate relationships. [252]

By 1914 Kennerley was involved in buying and selling rare books. The following year he took control of Anderson Galleries, a prominent auction house with a prestigious reputation for art and rare books. Because of his expertise as a publisher, his auction catalogues quickly became the standard for the industry containing facsimiles, full descriptions, and information on condition and provenance. By late in 1917, Kennerley was ready to move again, to bigger premises at 489 Park Avenue, close to the Campbells. The main floor was devoted to a 300-seat auction room along with smaller offices for customers. More offices and showrooms occupied the second and third floors. On the fourth floor a glass roofed gallery housed an exhibition room. Kennerley no longer had a need for a love nest in the building as he had a suite in the Plaza Hotel directly across the road. Kennerly frequented the Lambs and, with their mutual interests in art, probably came in contact with Edwin.

In 1925 as a result of his liaison with actress Diana Norman, he became a father of a third child, a son. There are questions about his relationship with Norman as there are no records of Kennerley's marriage to her but she listed herself as Mrs. M. Kennerley during the 1940s and a divorce certificate has been found. The son was named and raised as Richard Kennerley.

By the mid twenties the Anderson had become one of the foremost art and book auction houses in the world selling major collections from the United States and Europe. Kennerley's closest rival in the art auction business in the United States was the American Art Association. Kennerley wanted to buy out his rival but had no money. He needed $1.5 million dollars to accomplish his goal. He and Helen had legally separated in 1926 depriving him of an opportunity to obtain funding. Kennerley was again living well beyond his means and spending well over the profit margin of the operation at Anderson. Nevertheless he devised a strategy

---

252   *An extensive collection of his personal correspondence is held at Vassar College.*

to acquire control. He sold Anderson to Cortlandt Field Bishop, owner of the American Art Association, netting Kennerley a little over $400,000, but Bishop agreed to retain Kennerley as the director of the Anderson. Kennerley now had to find over a million dollars to fulfill his dream.

Kennerley and Margery

Kennerley and Margery had been friends for several years, having met at various art related events, and she had bought some paintings at the Anderson. The reception which Margery and Robert Daniel had given to explorer Richard Byrd had stirred a renewed restlessness in her. At the age of forty, she had grown beyond mere attractiveness into a mature and elegant beauty as seen in her photographic portrait by Arnold Genthe, (see page 216) a close friend of Kennerley's. She was attractive, intelligent, talented and with a broad range of interests, full of enthusiasm for life and, of prime interest to the lecherous and opportunistic womanizer Mitchell Kennerley; she was extremely wealthy. The breakdown of Margery's second marriage had left her emotionally fragile, and along with her morphine addiction, particularly vulnerable. Her enthusiasm for art was an added bonus to Kennerley. Having set his eyes on Margery, or more accurately, on her money, he pursued her with a vengeance. In late 1928 they announced their engagement even though neither had obtained a divorce.

After spending the early summer of 1928 staying with artist Augustus John at his home in France, Kennerley had joined Margery in Reno, Nevada, where she was in the process of obtaining her divorce from Daniel and then underwent the abortion. All the while Kennerley was manoeuvring to purchase both the Anderson and the American Art using the potential of Margery's money as a bargaining lever. At the same time he was negotiating with Helen to obtain a divorce from her. Edwina had stated that the Georgia O'Keefe paintings were a gift from Kennerley, but Margery had actually bought the paintings from him; however, he failed to pass the money on to O'Keefe. Kennerley kept the paintings at his New York apartment and secretly used them as collateral for a loan, part of which he used to pay off O'Keefe and the remainder he kept for his personal use. He later used the paintings a second time as security for yet another loan. [253]

MRS. DANIEL SEEKS DIVORCE

... Mrs Marjorie [sic] Durant Daniel, daughter of William C. Durant, automobile manufacturer, has been in Reno, Nev., for three weeks arranging proceedings for a divorce from Robert Daniel, President of Liberty National Bank, 50 Broadway, it became known yesterday. Beyond admitting he knew of the contemplated divorce proceedings, Mr. Daniel refused to discuss the matter.

Mr. Durant who organized the Liberty National Bank in 1923, and was chairman of the board until May 1927, said yesterday at Deal, N.J., where he is spending a short vacation, "This is just one of these unfortunate matters that cannot be helped. I am friendly to both." [254]

Margery obtained her divorce in Reno on September 28, 1928. This was announced, again with a flurry of publicity in the press:

Margery Durant Daniel... obtained a divorce here today from Robert W. Daniel...

Mrs. Daniel charged extreme cruelty, but the complaint listing the details of her charge was withdrawn by court order. The custody of Margery Randolph Daniel, 4, was divided by an agreement which also settled property rights.[255]

---

253 Matthew J. Broccoli, <u>The Fortunes of Mitchell Kennerley</u>, pp. 198-199.

254 <u>New York Times</u>, July 17, 1928.

255 <u>New York Times</u>, September 27, 1928.

Billy and Edwin in Europe

That fall Edwin briefly visited Edwina who had just begun her first year at Vassar. He then joined Billy and Catherine on a trip to Europe along with a group of automotive executives including Sam McLaughlin of General Motors of Canada and John Willys of Willys Overland, and their wives. By now Billy was one of the most influential men on Wall Street and his every move on the stock market was scrutinized in the press, even while on board the ship:

> **DURANT IN EUROPE, PHONES DEALS HERE;**
> *Holds Conversations With His Brokers Daily From Berlin, Paris or London.*
>
> **COST OF PHONE PHONE CALL $2,000**
> *Hour and Quarter on Wire and Air — His Bills Last Week Estimated at $25,000*
> William Durant is travelling in Europe and playing the stock market in New York personally. He is doing it by long-distant telephone...[256]

On October 8, the *New York Times* revealed that Billy had closed a deal with the Amilcar Company of Paris allowing him to sell Durants in France and manufacture the sporty little Amilcar in the United States. Unfortunately the deal eventually collapsed.

Billy and the other auto executives and their wives arrived back in New York on October 26 while Edwin stayed in London for a few more days and returned on board the *Olympic* docking at New York on November 20.[257] As soon as he had reached the bottom of the gangway of the *Berengaria*, Billy was besieged by reporters looking for some financial

---

256   *New York Times*, September 9, 1928.

257   *Passenger and Crew Lists of Vessels Arriving at New York, 1897-1957; (National Archives Microfilm Publication T715, 8892 Rolls); Records of the Immigration and Naturalization Service; National Archives, Washington. D.C.*

words of wisdom. Billy never failed them. He commented on the prosperity he had witnessed in Europe and then made the statement that the New York Stock Exchange would soon be handling *"from eight to ten million shares per day."*[258] The following day the *New York Times* ran three articles which used Billy as their focus. One article ran under the "TOPICS IN WALL STREET" feature.

> **Mr. Durant Returns**.
>
> *Although it has been well known that Mr. William Durant kept closely in touch with the stock market during his extended stay in Europe, his return Friday night undoubtedly had a stimulating effect, brokers said yesterday. The stocks which Mr. Durant is said to be most interested advanced sharply, and in Wall Street gossip he was credited with heavy buying of such issues. The speculative portion of Wall Street always enthuses easily over Mr. Durant's market operations, because he is consistently regarded as the most consistent "bull" operating on a large scale.*

The second article echoed the above article's statement of Billy's significance on the stock market and specifically gave credit to Billy's return as a key factor in the day's increase in volume on the market.

> **EXCHANGE IS MAKING RECORD IN TURNOVER**
> Transactions This Month to be Near 100,000,000 Shares — Now 88,193,875
> DURANT's RETURN A FACTOR
> Wall Street Stimulated by His Statement That Securities Are Not Selling Too High
> *The return of William C. Durant from a long holiday in Europe and his resumption of trading "on the scene" was said yesterday on Wall Street to be responsible in large measure*

---

258   *New York Times* October 27, 1928.

for the market's upturn after Friday's precipitate decline. Mr. Durant, upon his return on Friday night, gave an interview which had a stimulating effect upon the speculative fraternity.

His prediction of 8,000,000 share days and his statement that stocks were not trading too high were seized upon with considerable enthusiasm by traders committed to the advance. Mr. Durant was in close touch with the market while he was in Europe and on shipboard, but his operations never have the significance or reach the volume when he is away that they do when he is here.[259]

Kennerley Again

In January 1929, Kennerley had his most successful sale at the Anderson, selling off the literary collection of composer/songwriter Jerome Kern. This sale included manuscripts and rare first and second editions of works by such authors as James Boswell, Robert Browning, Robert Burns, Joseph Conrad, Charles Dickens, Lord Byron, Robert Louis Stevenson, Walt Whitman and Jane Austen. The sale grossed $1.7 million. It is interesting to note that several paintings owned by Margery were on display in the Anderson during the Kern sale. They included Gari Melchers' portrait of Theodore Roosevelt. Kennerley quickly spent his 10% commission to engage Melchers to paint his portrait and to pay off some earlier debts.[260]

Immediately following the Kern sale, Kennerley discovered that his divorce with Helen was not going as smoothly as he had hoped and his relationship with Margery had deteriorated leaving Kennerley with the full knowledge that her finances were not available to him. He resigned from the Anderson and left for England. Since Billy Durant was in London

---

259 *Ibid.*

260 *This portrait now hangs in the Gari Melchers Memorial Gallery, Mary Washington College, Fredericksburg, Va.*

with Catherine he arranged to meet Billy, possibly hoping to regain some favour with Margery through her father.

Billy is quoted as saying:

> *Kennerley is an intimate friend of mine and a charming fellow. It is true that he consulted me after my daughter reached her decision not to marry him. I was unable to be of aid in the matter.*[261]

Later that month, Kennerley agreed to his wife's conditions that he set up their two sons in the publishing business. After he agreed, Helen Kennerly sailed to Paris and obtained a divorce. It became obvious to Kennerley that he had failed to make progress with Billy in England as the news broke that on May 3 1929 Margery had suddenly married John Hampton Cooper, a New York broker. The *New York Daily Mirror* immediately responded with an article entitled *"Kennerly Jilted by Rich Patron."*[262] But this was not the last that Margery or Billy would see of Kennerley.

By January 1929 Billy could sense that all was not well on Wall Street, and he was determined to rectify the problems. Realizing that he had to focus all his energies on Wall Street he decided to give up his directorship of Durant Motors. Following Edwin's advice he had given up the presidency of the company after his accident but had maintained a position as a director. On January 11, the press announced his move:

> **W.C. DURANT DROPS MOTORS DIRECTION.**
>
> ... *William C. Durant, financier and president of Durant Motors, Inc., announced yesterday his retirement from active management of the company. The announcement was contained in a pamphlet addressed as "a message to my many dealers, to my many friends and to my loyal associates," which*

---

261   Matthew J. Bruccoli,. <u>The Fortunes of Mitchell Kennerly, Bookman,</u> p. 218.

262   <u>New York Daily Mirror,</u> July 16, 1929.

was distributed at the annual dealers' luncheon of the company held at the Hotel Roosevelt yesterday.

Mr Durant said that this step was made necessary by other demands "which must be heeded" and which would occupy his entire attention.... To these new interests, he said, he must devote all his energy. He declared that in eleven months to November of last year he had invested for banks, trust companies and individuals the sum of $1,015,000,000. Management of these enterprises, "thirty five times greater than Durant Motors with all its plants," was an enormous task, he said, requiring his entire time.[263]

By April Billy's strategy was becoming obvious and a clear target of his concern was the Federal Reserve Board and its policies. An article published on April 15 revealed that Billy had been contacting the leaders of American industry. The article stated:

He told of having asked 500 prominent industrialists in twenty cities to declare themselves for or against the board's policy. [Federal Reserve Board policy] Replies from 463 had been received, he said, and only twelve upheld the board.[264]

Billy had gone public the night before by speaking on radio.

William C. Durant made an outspoken attack last night on the Federal Reserve Board for its efforts to curb speculation through restriction of brokers' loans. He spoke for fifteen minutes from Station WABC over the coast-to-coast network of the Columbia Broadcasting System... He portrayed the Federal Agency as arrayed in "battle" on the business interests of the country. The eight members of the board were characterized by Mr.

---

263 *New York Times* Jan 11, 1929.

264 *New York Times*, April 15, 1929.

> Durant, long a big operator in the market, as an "autocratic group." Their power, he said, was greater than the President himself, a force, as he phrased it "beyond that of any constituted authority of the United States."[265]

The radio broadcast went out across the nation and its details carried the next day in local presses. Typical of the coverage across the nation was that in the *Tipton Daily Tribune* of Tipton, Indiana. They reported:

> William C. Durant is on the warpath against the Federal Reserve board...Over the radio, this big stock market operator made three suggestions to the Federal Reserve Board to meet the credit stringency:
> 1. Reduce the rediscount rate to 3 per cent.
> 2. Put back into the money market 700 million dollars which the board has withdrawn.
> 3. Halt stock issuance of any securities which the Federal Reserve is endeavouring to have member banks accept as collateral . The "Little Napoleon's" final shot was this: "Let the Federal Reserve Board keep its hands off business."[266]

When the Federal Reserve Board stepped in to quell speculation using credit, it caused an unexpected rise in interest rates. Billy reacted with an attack on the Board and even demanded an interview with President Herbert Hoover. It wasn't until December that the press reported that Billy had met with the President in April in a clandestine meeting at the White House.[267]

At the meeting with Hoover, Billy made it quite clear that if the President didn't get the Federal Reserve Board to withdraw its restrictive policy on security credit, there would be an economic collapse.

---

265   Ibid.

266   *Tipton Daily Tribune*, Tipton Indiana, April 23, 1929.

267   *New York Times*, December 14, 1929.

> Asked if he had told Mr. Hoover that a financial disaster of unprecedented proportions was threatened Mr. Durant said, "I intimated as much to him." He added that he had told the president that he considered the situation to be most serious.[268]

When the President failed to respond to his suggestion, Billy warned his friends of an impending market collapse. Among the first to be contacted was Edwin. Edwin began to divest himself of some stocks. Edwina erroneously stated that: *"Perceiving that the stock market would soon crash, father sold out his stocks before we left for Europe, [July1929] so at least we were lucky financially."*[269] In Edwin's will are declarations that he sold his shares in United States Steel in May. It is also obvious that he had sold all his shares in Durant Motors and International Combustion Engineering. Ironically he held on to several millions in shares in GM, Chrysler, various land investments in California as well as almost $3 million in bonds.[270] According to speculation in the press, Billy in contrast, had disposed of shares in Chrysler, International Combustion, United Cast Iron Pipe, Warner Brothers and General Motors.[271] His losses in the sale of these shares were staggering. Edwin's losses cannot be determined:

> W.C. Durant whose spectacular operations in the stock market on the bull side have eclipsed his activities as an automobile manufacturer is reported in Wall Street gossip to have liquidated a large portion of his holdings at substantial losses in the last few weeks. Credited with being the mainstay of the bull market, Mr Durant has been a sharp critic of the Federal Reserve Board and rumours have spread on many occasions

---

268 Ibid

269 Edwina Campbell Sanger, My First 90 Years, p. 25.

270 New York Surrogate Court documents.

271 New York Times June 2, 1929

that he has been hard hit. His present losses are said to reach many millions. [272]

By the time that this information had become public knowledge through the press, Billy and Catherine were again on holiday in Europe. The press contacted him in Paris but he quickly dismissed them with *"You've heard these rumors before."* [273] However the press did cover his address to the American Club in Paris where he continued his attack on the Federal Reserve Board.

"For the past few months," Mr. Durant said, *"the Federal Reserve has been experimenting at a frightening cost to our investing public. At the present moment the market is governed by what the Federal Reserve is going to do today. Until the situation changes and the board ceases to interfere the market will be entirely in the hands of gamblers and bargain hunters, and by gamblers I mean people who sell what they do not own, hoping that something unfavourable, real or imaginary will enable them to replace or buy back these stocks at a lower price."* [274]

Billy and Catherine returned from Europe on board the *SS Majestic* on June 12. As they disembarked they somehow eluded the press as they sped to the relative security in their Fifth Avenue apartment and then made their way to Raymere. Within a few days they were to face another traumatic event.

---

272   Ibid

273   Ibid

274   <u>New York Times</u> June 1, 1929

Chapter Twelve

EDWIN'S FINAL JOURNEY

Father and Daughter

As Edwina's first year at Vassar was coming to a close in April 1929, she telephoned her father in an attempt to improve the strained relationship with him. She suggested that an ideal way to improve their relationship would be to spend time spend time together, and an ideal way to do that would be to go to Europe, just the two of them. She persuaded him to book a sailing following her year-end exams. William was attending the Princeton ROTC program at Watertown New York. At the weekends, he and Edwin spent the time together at Bretton Woods where William was becoming a skilful golfer and tennis player. After her term-ending exams were over Edwina headed for New York and stayed with her father at the Plaza before boarding *S.S. Majestic*. She described the details of the evening before their departure:

> "That evening [July 11, 1929] we dined together on sea bass in his suite at the Plaza Hotel. Afterward we drove to the pier, settled into our adjoining rooms, and went for a stroll on the

> *top deck to watch the receding lights of Manhattan. After saying goodnight, I returned to my room and went to sleep.* [275]

Edwina had no way of knowing that this would be the last time that she would see her father alive.

> *About an hour later, there was a knock on my door. Outside was standing the ship's nurse. She said my father had taken ill and that the doctor wished to speak to me. The doctor came in and informed me that father had suffered a heart attack and was gravely ill. He went back to my father, and about ten minutes later returned to deliver the news that my father was dead. Stunned, I said nothing at all. The nurse in true English fashion offered me a cup of tea.* [276]

Edwina immediately telegrammed William to inform him of the tragic event. He responded by letting her know that he would book the next available boat to Cherbourg. While she waited for William's arrival she stayed with friends in Paris. Once united, the two made the return journey to New York. Ironically the vessel on which Edwina and William returned to New York with their father's remains was the same vessel on which Edwina and Margery had returned after obtaining her divorce from Edwin in 1920. The *Aquitania* docked in New York at 10:20 in the morning of July 20. Once it had completed its formal docking procedure, the passengers sauntered down the gangway.

---

[275] Edwina Campbell Sanger, *My First 90 Years,* p. 24.

[276] Ibid.

Illustration #29: Edwin 1929, with a great catch at Camp Cap Chat, the fishing camp in Quebec, which he shared with Sam McLaughlin. This is probably the last photograph taken of Edwin. (Photo: Courtesy Parkwood Estate Archives, Oshawa, Ontario)

At the foot of the gangway, there to comfort William and Edwina in their tragic and emotional arrival, were Edwin's brother Duncan, Dr. H.A. Bruce from Toronto, Sam McLaughlin from Oshawa and a school friend of Edwina. With the later arrival of Billy and Catherine and Llewellys Barker from Baltimore, the small gathering completed the circle of Edwin's life.

As soon as the news of Edwin's death reached the press it immediately became a feature of newspapers across the nation, not in recognition of Edwin's work and accomplishments with Billy in the automotive world but as an acknowledgement of his immense wealth. For the days and weeks following his death the press scurried frantically to find out the details of his fortune and then who would be the recipients.

CAMPBELL ESTATE PUT AT $10,000,000
Retired Physician, Son-in-Law of W.C. Durant, Willed Bulk of Fortune to Son [277]

Meanwhile, quietly, and without ceremony William looked over the available sites at Woodlawn Cemetery in the Bronx and chose a peaceful ten plot site about 200 yards from the Durant mausoleum that contained the remains of Billy's mother. William paid $7,700 for the burial site and $3,000 for a "maintenance fund for perpetual care." The massive granite headstone cost $2,850. [278]

The funeral services were held at the Presbyterian Church on Fifth Avenue on July 27.

The funeral was brief and attended by only about a dozen people, since it was July and everyone we knew was out of town. [279] The small party made its way to Woodlawn Cemetery where they bade their final farewell to Edwin.

After the funeral, Edwina and William made their way to the hotel at Bretton Woods where William had spent a few weekends during the earlier part of the summer with his father. The atmosphere there would have been extremely supportive for the young duo. Yet, for Edwina, *There were horrible nightmares, however, and I slept with the lights on all night for a long while.*[280]

---

277 New York Times, July 26, 1929.

278 New York Surrogate Court appraisal of the estate of Edwin R. Campbell, 12 December 1930.

279 Ibid.

280 Edwina Campbell Durant, <u>My First 90 Years</u>, p. 25.

Illustration #30: The headstone of Edwin Campbell, Woodlawn Cemetery New York.

They later returned to the Plaza, no doubt with some trepidation, and began the process of sorting through some of Edwin's possessions, and to discuss his estate and the execution of the will with White and Case, the attorneys handling the legalities. The resolution of Edwin's estate would obviously take many months. As it turned out, the final submission for settlement was not presented to the Hall of Records in New York until March 1931.

The Will

In the press, the estimations of the value of Edwin's estate ranged from 10 to 15 million dollars. While the estate was being evaluated, the stock market continued its downward spiral. By the time the appraisal was submitted to the Surrogate Court in New York on December 2, 1930, the estate was evaluated at $10,123,856.60. In early twenty-first century terms this would be just over a billion dollars! The appraisal was stamped as being received on December 16, 1930.

The details of the will reveal much about Edwin and his tastes. His interests in art were revealed in the numerous oil paintings and tapestries in his collection. He left oil paintings by prominent American artists: seascape artist Paul Dougherty, landscape specialist Richard Pauli, Leon Kroll, and four paintings by Kenneth Hayes-Miller, known for his portraits of middle class New York women, all in stark contrast to the Kandinski murals that he had left to Margery in their Park Avenue apartment. Also in his Plaza suite were three antique tapestries, one Flemish and two Beauvais, each valued at $8,000.

He had kept an extensive wine cellar at the Plaza holding over 500 bottles of rare wines and liquors, including 76 bottles of Haut Sauterne Bordeaux, 43 bottles of Chateaux d' Yquan Sauterne, 190 bottles of Crown R.E.I Port, 72 bottles of Gordon Dry Gin and, Edwin's favourite, 27 bottles of American Bourbon Whisky.

Going against Billy's recommendations, Edwin held on to his shares in General Motors and Chrysler Corporation. At the time of his death he had 7,000 shares of Chrysler shares valued at $514,000 and 81,000 shares in General Motors Corporation valued at nearly $6 million!

Edwin had purchased a number of bonds for various cities in the United States and several states including Iowa, Oregon, New Jersey, $146,000 in the State of Missouri bonds, $100,000 in the State of West Virginia and $287,000 in the State of Illinois Highway Bonds and $852,000 in the State of Michigan. The cities in which he held bonds were: $33,000 in the City of Pittsburgh, $50,000 in the City of Buffalo, $230,000 in the City of Chicago, $48,000 in the City of Boston and over $75,000 in the City of New York. In addition he owned shares in several land companies including the Bolsa Land Company of California valued at $150,000. He also had two Rolls Royces which he kept at the Traylor Garage on 8 West 62nd Street.

The bank accounts were substantial. Included in the accounts was an account at the Bank of Commerce in Port Perry. This was an account which Edwin had opened shortly after his father's death enabling him to provide a comfortable allowance for his widowed mother. In the summary of his estate the account was noted as holding a balance of $2,024.24.

When the will was finally resolved and all the taxes, duties and funeral expenses had been paid, William received an estate valued at just over $7 million, Edwina received an estate worth $755,000 and Edwin's brother Duncan received $76,000. In addition, Edwin left $128,000 to his sister Donella (Mrs. Samuel Wilson), and the recorded loan of $10,000 which Edwin had made to her and her husband in 1925 was written off. Unfortunately Duncan had but a few months to enjoy the inheritance. He died, as his brother had done, of a massive coronary while in St Petersburg, Florida less than a year later.

After the Funeral

In the fall Edwina returned to her studies at Vassar and William to his studies at Princeton, but not before making some decisions about their future paths. Realizing that their father's suite at the Plaza was too big and ostentatious for their needs while in New York, they stayed at the Plaza until the fall term started, while making arrangement to occupy a smaller yet comfortable and fashionable three bedroom 17th floor apartment on Park Avenue, retaining their *"father's valet, a cook and a maid."*[281] According to the will, the rent at the Plaza was paid up to September 15. Edwin had provided thoughtfully for his children by creating a joint checking account with them which at the time of his death had $28,000 in it, and a separate joint account with William for over $2,500.[282]

In December 1928 Edwin and William had spent a day together at the New York Auto Salon and where they had marveled at the star of that show: the huge, powerful new Model J Duesenberg. William, after the funeral, probably with a sense of nostalgia, before heading back to Princeton for his final year, walked down Park Avenue to the Duesenberg showroom and ordered a brand new black and chrome Model J two-seater

---

281   Ibid., p. 25.

282   Surrogate Court appraisal of the estate of Edwin R. Campbell. Submitted Dec. 12, 1930.

sports convertible with 19 inch chrome spoke wheels. It had a chassis number 2213 and engine number J194. He took delivery of the vehicle later that month and drove it to the Plaza hotel, and later to school at Princeton

His enthusiasm for the vehicle soon waned and he sold it in May of the following year to a friend, Edmund C. Converse Jr., son of E.C. Converse, one of the founders of United States Steel, President of the Bankers' Trust of New York and an early president of the Liberty National Bank. Converse senior had been a neighbour of Edwin while in Pasadena. Converse Jr. had the car repainted in a sage green with a red undercarriage. The vehicle has since remained in the hands of a series of Duesenberg enthusiasts and was sold at auction in 2010 at the RM's auction of collector cars at Meadow Brook. The hammer came down at $825,000. [283] Once he had parted with the "Doozy" William still had access to his father's two Rolls Royce cars as it would be many months before Edwin's estate was settled.

William and Edwina

After graduating from Princeton in 1930 William went to work at the Banker's Trust in New York. Eventually he succumbed to the boredom of the daily grind. Seeking a more exciting life, and following his mother's obsession, he decided that he too would like to learn to fly. Waiting until Edwina had graduated from Vassar in the spring of 1932, the two then travelled to England where William enrolled at the R.A.F flying school at Hamble Cliff, Netley Abbey, just east of Southampton.

> *We found a lovely old stone house right on the coast where the ocean liners came in, and settled down for almost two years while he commuted to school and obtained his private and commercial flying licenses.*[284]

---

283   *RM Auctions.*

284   Edwina Campbell Sanger *My First 90 Years*, p. 27.

While William was at Flying School, Edwina turned to her favourite hobby; music. She found an excellent piano teacher in London. *I practiced six hours a day, driving up to London once a week for a lesson.*[285]

Once William had obtained his flying licences he and Edwina returned to New York where he was hired by the American Museum of Natural History (AMNH) to lead expeditions to Africa. He led six major expeditions for the AMNH in the 1930s. Edwina visited her brother while he was on two of these expeditions. She then decided to follow the footsteps of her father and uncle and study medicine. Since her degree from Vassar was in the arts, she enrolled at Columbia University night school to upgrade her qualifications in the sciences in order to enter medical school. Encouraged by her father's friends Dr. Bruce in Canada and Llewellys Barker at John's Hopkins she gained admission to the College of Physicians and Surgeons, and along with 100 men and only 10 women she began classes in medicine at Columbia.

---

285   Ibid. p. 28.

Chapter Thirteen

BILLY'S DEMISE

The Stock Market Crash

The death of Edwin was the first of a series of events which would bring about the end of Billy Durant's world. Like a slow motion movie of the controlled implosion of a massive building, Billy's world came slowly crashing down after Edwin's funeral. The premature and unexpected death of such a close and personal friend would initially have had a profound effect on Billy, which in turn would certainly have affected some of his business dealings. He and Edwin had sought each other's counsel on so many issues and he had certainly depended on Edwin for advice on some of his business strategy. Edwin's death was not the major cause of Billy's financial collapse but it did have some effect and it certainly did come to symbolize that demise.

Billy's warnings to President Hoover and to the moguls of Wall Street fell on deaf ears. Three months after Edwin's death, on October 14, Black Thursday, the high and mighty of the financial world, Billy among them, were brought to their knees. Throughout the month, the market continued its plunge. Black Tuesday occurred on October 29 and the stock market eventually bottomed out, but it didn't reach its lowest point until July 1932. Billy led an attempt to stabilize the slide and to create some confidence in the market by buying up large volumes of stock. Billy invested over $210 millions in buying stock to prop up the market. He was joined in this effort by the Rockefellers who spent even more. Their efforts were in vain and they lost millions. Billy was buying shares at over $60 per share and was then forced into selling them at less than $45. The only way he managed to stay ahead was by selling far more shares than he was buying.[286] As a result, his holdings became quickly reduced. He even persuaded Catherine to let him have her remaining stock in GM so that he could sell it. In 1930 she handed him almost two hundred thousand shares in GM, shares that she had been saving to pass on to their grandchildren. Billy hadn't followed his own advice to Edwin and had kept shares in International Combustion. The Company declared bankruptcy leaving him with 30,000 worthless shares.

With diminishing demands for cars, Billy took control of the Durant Motor Company again, in a vain attempt to stem its losses. Over a period of weeks he was forced to close the doors on a succession of his factories. Most distressing to him was the human cost; his friends and other employees were put out of work. True to his word Billy compensated many investors in the Durant Motor Company. He accomplished this by selling his own shares in even more companies, always at a loss. Even his Liberty National Bank had to close its doors and sell off its assets.

---

286   *1929 Brokers Analysis and 1930 Ledger, Durant Papers, Scharchburg Archives.*

Illustration #31: Billy in his early seventies. (Photo: Courtesy Scharchburg Archives, Kettering University)

In October 1932, while again in Paris with Catherine, and again at the American Club in that city, Billy lashed out at President Hoover for failing to follow the demands he had made during their private meeting in April 1929.

> **Wants Hoover to Retire to Private Life.**
> *W.C. Durant... in a cablegram made public yesterday by the Democratic National Headquarters, declared that although he is a Republican and voted for Mr. Hoover in 1928, he is interested now in Mr. Hoover's retirement to private life. Mr, Durant, who is in Paris at present, said: "I shall not vote for Hoover next November, nor will hundreds of thousands of Republicans who, like myself, are interested in his retirement to private life. Hoover has been a great disappointment to his*

friends and the people generally. His administration has no parallel for inefficiency since the establishment of our government... His failure was largely of his own making due to his unwillingness to take advice and his inability to act promptly when prompt action is necessary. His excuses for his many failures are not accepted by thoughtful people conversant with the facts. With our country in its present deplorable condition and no improvement in sight, plain speaking is in order.

Mr. Durant criticized Mr. Hoover for having failed to control the Federal Reserve Board, for not having insisted on revision of the baking laws, for the failure of his farm relief policy... "Franklin D. Roosevelt, a man of integrity and ability, will in my opinion be elected by an overwhelming majority," Mr. Durant added.[287]

Billy was correct in his prediction. But there was no joy in the vindication. Billy was finally forced into liquidating the company that had so proudly carried his name. Probably most embarrassing to Billy was that several of his Durant factories were taken over by General Motors.

But the biggest blow of all happened on February 8, 1936: William C. Durant was forced to file for personal bankruptcy. A few months later, the press announced that Billy had opened a food market in Asbury, New Jersey and had plans to establish a chain of such stores.[288] But these plans also fell victim to the times.

Clifford Durant

A year later he was informed that his son Clifford had died in Beverly Hills, of a heart attack at the age of 46. His death on October 31, 1937 drew comments in the press on the achievements of his father and linked his successes directly to Billy's and then added: *In recent years he had dropped*

---

287   *New York Times*, October 8, 1932.

288   *New York Times*, September 15, 1936.

out of society and sports life. [289] Clifford drove in the Indianapolis race three times. He finished each time, with his best performance a creditable seventh place in 1923. On all three occasions he drove modified versions of his father's Durant cars.

He bought several planes which he flew with gusto and even made plans in 1926 to establish an airline to fly passengers and goods from New York to Havana in Cuba. This plan failed to materialize. He also bought a 26,000 acre property in Roscommon, Michigan, to be used as hunting and fishing retreat. Under his father's guidance he played the stock market with some success. But as the press commented, he slowly stepped out of the limelight. In reality he was sinking into a life of indulgence, liquor, fast women and fast cars, having a number of relationships, but had no children. As his sister had done, he married four times. His last marriage, to Charlotte T. Phillips, took place on January 5, 1935, less than three years before his death. He was laid to rest in Forest Lawn Cemetery in Los Angeles, California.

Illustration #32: Clifford Durant. (Photo: Courtesy Scharchburg Archives, Kettering University)

---

289 <u>New York Times</u>, November 1, 1937.

Farewell to Raymere

Billy and Catherine, meanwhile, struggled to survive financially and soon came to the realization that even the day-to-day running of their beloved Raymere was well beyond their financial capabilities. It was sold and the contents auctioned off in 1938. The sale of the property and the auction realized a little over $110,000, but this amount was barely enough to pay off the various brokers and agents involved in the sale and auction. He and Catherine moved into a small hotel suite, room 544, in the Durant Hotel in Flint while maintaining their humble apartment at 45 Gramercy Park in New York.

As with Catherine's GM stock which he had been forced to sell, he had also put some other small issues of stock and real estate in her name. Fortunately they were able to hold on to a few of them. With meagre income from these they were able to eke out an existence. In addition, one of Billy's former employees, an energetic European immigrant named Aristo Scrobogna, provided the aging Billy Durant with the physical help that he occasionally needed, looked after the care and maintenance of his few remaining properties, and acted as his secretary. Scrobogna's wife Mathilde became a companion for Catherine.

In 1940 at the age of 79, Billy opened a bowling alley in Flint. The opening was given considerable publicity by the newspapers which had so frequently devoted huge spreads to his opening of monstrous factories to provide employment for thousands of Flint residents. Later he opened a restaurant beside it and eventually, the first drive-in restaurant in Flint. The former Wall Street powerhouse and founder of General Motors posed for the press as a dishwasher!

On January 11, 1940 the 25 millionth car rolled off the GM assembly line in Detroit. President of General Motors, Alfred P. Sloan, invited Billy to a 5,000 guest banquet to celebrate the occasion the following day. Here he brought Billy on the platform and introduced a dapper but aging Billy Durant to the crowd and paid him honour.

While alone in his hotel room in Flint on October 2, 1942 Billy suffered a stroke. His personal secretary Aristo Scrobogna picked up Catherine in New York and brought her to the hospital where Billy languished for several weeks. Later, Catherine, assisted by Scrobogna, took Billy by train back to their New York apartment. When Sloan heard of Billy's declining health and his need for constant care, he wrote to Sam McLaughlin and others to suggest that they all share in contributing to an annual $10,000 fund to take care of the man who ...*certainly was the pioneer who started the business as a result of which we have profited handsomely.*[290] They each supported the idea and Catherine received a quarterly cheque of $2,500 from the fund.

Sometime later, Billy, with Scrobogna's assistance and encouragement, began making notes on a proposed autobiography. Many sections of the work reached a final draft stage. He began the work: *Dedicated to Walter P Chrysler, the best friend I ever had and to Arthur G. Bishop, R. Sam McLaughlin, Charles Mott, DeWitt Page, S. Sidney Stewart Jr., Nathan Hofheimer.*[291]

Those to whom he had dedicated the work were all alive at the time of writing. The omission of Edwin was due no doubt to his death a decade earlier. In the foreword he made no mention of his daughter's biography **My Father** which had been quietly released a decade earlier. There are numerous key players absent from his narrative of General Motors and there is no reference to any aspect of his private life and his family. But it should be remembered that his notes were only a draft and that he had written them after he had suffered a stroke and during the declining months of his life.

On May 1, 1946 the Automobile Manufacturers Association elected a number of pioneers in the automobile industry to the Automotive Hall of Fame. They included Frank Duryea, Henry Ford, Charles Nash, Barney Oldfield, Ransom Olds, Alfred P Sloan, but foremost among them was Billy Durant. Billy was unable to attend the ceremony.

---

290 Letter from Sloan, quoted in Bernard Weisberger. *The Dream Maker,* p. 361.
291 William C. Durant, *In His Own Words,* Page 7

Billy's End

Billy's stroke limited his ability to talk and restricted his activities to a wheelchair. In spite of the infusion of financial support from the Sloan fund, Catherine slowly disposed of her jewellery and other valuables in order to provide care for her beloved Billy. By early 1947 she was dependent on friends and family for financial support. Late in the night of March 17, with his devoted Catherine by his side, Billy breathed his last.

Within hours, the press of the nation began its tributes to the legendary William C. Durant. The *New York Times* ran a major half page article on Billy and his accomplishments:

WILLIAM C. DURANT, AUTO PIONEER DIES

Founder of the General Motors Corp.,

Spectacular Trader In Stock Market Here

Victim of 1929 Crash

Estimated $120 Million Wealth Shrank to $250 by 1936

Began as Grocery Boy

William Crapo Durant, pioneer automobile manufacturer and stock market speculator, who founded General Motors Corporation and other concerns, died early yesterday morning in his apartment at 45 Gramercy Park North, after an illness of over four years. ...In recent years he had written his memoires, which have not yet been published. At his death he had no business connections. Mr Durant leaves a widow, Catherine Lederer Durant whom he married in 1908, and a daughter, Mrs Fitzhugh Green of New Canaan, Conn

A funeral service will be held at 11 a.m. tomorrow in Calvary Episcopal Church, Fourth Avenue and Twenty-First

> Street, by the Rev. Dr. Samuel M. Shoemaker, the rector. Burial will take place at Woodlawn Cemetery.
>
> **Many Shifts in Fortune**
> At one time Mr. Durant's wealth was placed at $120,000,000. When he filed a petition for bankruptcy in 1936 he listed his assets as $250 in clothing. At the height of his activity on Wall Street his broker's annual commission was $8,000,000. Someone with a flair for figures once estimated that in the year of his most turbulent speculations he traded in securities at the rate of 5,000 shares every hour the exchange was open.[292]

The article then continued for two full length columns summarizing Billy's rise, from his humble days in Flint, to his glory days on Wall Street in the 1920s.

Two days later, Billy's funeral was also given an extensive coverage. The headline stated:

> **AUTO EXECUTIVES AT DURANT RITES**
> **Former Associates and Others in Field Among 200 Mourning General Motors Founder.**[293]

This article named many of the individuals present at the funeral including K.T. Keller, president of the Chrysler Corporation, and Billy's personal secretaries Winfred Murphy and Aristo Scrobogan. No representatives from General Motors were listed as being present. Neither was any mention made of Margery. A further brief obituary was carried two days later.[294]

As stated in the press, Billy's funeral was held at the Calvary Protestant Episcopal Church in New York on March 20 and attended by over 200 mourners. After his funeral he was buried beside his mother Rebecca in

---

292 <u>New York Times</u>, March 19, 1947

293 <u>New York Times</u>, March 21, 1947

294 <u>New York Times</u>, March 23, 1947

the family mausoleum in Woodlawn Cemetery, a mausoleum which Billy had paid for during his halcyon days. Margery's remains were placed in the mausoleum after her death in 1959 and finally, in 1974, his beloved and faithful wife Catherine joined him.

Illustration #33: The Durant Mausoleum in Woodlawn Cemetery, New York.

A month later, his old rival Henry Ford passed away. His death on April 7 commanded an even larger commemoration. Ford's company still bore his name and Ford, and his children still ran the company. His casket lay in state at Greenfield Village while mourners, stretching out over a mile, passed by his casket to pay their respects. His funeral at St. Paul's Episcopal Cathedral drew a crowd of over 30,000, most of whom stood in silence outside the Cathedral.

To celebrate the fiftieth anniversary of the founding of General Motors in 1958, a monument in the form of a ten foot square, two foot high platform made of marble was placed opposite the Alfred P. Sloan Museum in the Flint Cultural Centre. Carved on one side is the epitaph:

> **William Crapo Durant, 1861-1947, Founder of General Motors, 1908: In the golden milestone year of the corporation its proud birthplace dedicates this plaza in lasting appreciation of what his vision, genius, and courage contributed to his home city and to the renown of American industry.**

Alfred Sloan was unable to attend the dedication. He died eight years later.

Edwina and William

After completing her medical studies at Columbia in February 1939 Edwina began her internship in internal medicine at Presbyterian Hospital in New York. Here she met Grant Sanger, a Cornell Medical School graduate who was undergoing surgical training at Presbyterian. The two began dating and soon announced their engagement. They were married on September 30, 1939. Grant was the son of Margaret Sanger, founder and pioneer of the birth control and family planning movement.

Illustration #34: Edwina and Grant Sanger (Photo: Courtesy Alex Sanger)

William meanwhile continued his work as a field associate in Africa for the American Museum of Natural History. Prior to the outbreak of World War Two, he met Beatrice Hawn, a Canadian working at as a nurse at the Presbyterian Hospital in New York where Edwina and Grant were also working. The two were married quietly in Hartford, Connecticut in 1940. Their only child, Margot was born in 1943. When W.W.2 broke out William volunteered for the military and eventually became a major. After hostilities he continued his humanitarian efforts through his involvement as a leader in the Boy Scout movement and was frequently joined by Beatrice in his work. William served on the World Scout Committee beginning in 1961 and was instrumental in establishing the World Scout Foundation, serving as its chairman from 1969 to 1977. He received numerous awards from the scouting fraternity. In adulthood their daughter Margot continued her father's work in scouting and similarly became a leader of the World Scout Committee. She also served as Chairman of the Board of Sarah Lawrence College and then followed her grandfather's footsteps with his interest in art. She is currently Chairman of the Board of the Frick Collection in New York, one of the foremost galleries in the United States.

Chapter Fourteen

MARGERY

Challenges

Throughout her life Margery experienced an ever increasing amount of emotional and mental turmoil. In adulthood she engaged in several relationships and four marriages, but her marital instability was only one of the manifestations of her demons. It could be convincingly argued that Margery was a victim of time and circumstance.

The first four decades of the twentieth century were confusing and contradictory for women. In the first two decades, women struggled for their right to vote, finally gaining that right in 1920, but that was followed by the struggle for identity as women sought to define their roles in a rapidly changing society.

For Margery this struggle was further complicated by her childhood and youth. When she entered private school as a teenager her emotional relationship with her mother, Clara, became increasingly distant. She was neglected by her father until her early teenage years and then became a centre of his attention. As his daughter approached her teens Billy spent more frequent and increasingly longer periods of time in New York, complicating his growing estrangement with Clara, but at the same time increasing his attention to Margery. As Billy had been the centre of attention for his grandfather and then his mother, he turned his devotion to his daughter. Every aspect of her father's life, his successes and failures in business and private life had a profound effect on Margery.

Immediately after her marriage to Edwin, Billy moved in with them. When Margery was not at home reading her husband's books and journals she would be driving around with him, sitting in his car while he administered his patients, but promptly at six o'clock she would then drive over to the factory to pick up her father. When Billy moved to Detroit, Margery insisted that she and Edwin also take up residence there. When Durant moved to New York and took an apartment at 907 Fifth Avenue, Edwin and Margery soon followed him and after their three month stay in the Plaza they took an apartment at 635 Park Avenue on the corner of 66th Street. Margery chose this address to be near her father. Billy then moved his mother into an apartment on Park Avenue so that he could be close to her.

When Margery was 21, Durant divorced Clara and the next day married one of Margery's close friends, a girl 28 years younger than himself: 19 year-old Catherine Lederer. It is worth noting that in her biography of her father, Margery never mentioned her father's divorce and second marriage, nor did she ever mention Catherine by name. Durant's first wife Clara then moved to California, remarried and was rarely seen by Margery again. Edwin and Margery quickly immersed themselves in a busy New York lifestyle of work and social activities. This absence of a close maternal role model may have played some part in Margery's difficulty in facing the challenges in marriage and parenting.

Shortly after arriving in New York, Margery began to experience difficulties in her relationship with Edwin. Edwin and Margery's social environment was not entirely conducive to a stable marriage. A further mitigating factor for Margery was her addiction to morphine developed while undergoing treatment for pneumonia in the fall of 1918. The psychological and biological implications of drug addiction and the effects that they have on human behavior are, even today, far from definitive. The understanding of them in the 1920s was even less. Margery spent extended periods of time in various sanatoriums across the country as she struggled to deal with her addiction and fluctuated from relatively normal behavior to erratic and frequently suicidal behaviour for the remainder of her life. In spite of these problems, she was able to take pleasure in many enjoyable experiences.

The year 1929 was an unusually challenging one for Margery. Her divorce from Robert Daniel in September 1928 enabled her to become engaged to Kennerley. That engagement lasted only a few weeks before she hurriedly married John Hampton Cooper in April 1929. A few months later Edwin died, but the impact of his death on her emotional state is difficult to determine. While this was happening, with the assistance of Fitzhugh Green, Putnam's ghost writer, Margery was putting the final touches to her biography of her father.

Kennerley and Margery Again

In 1930, in spite of the financial crisis which was now having horrendous repercussions, Kennerley had persuaded friends in London to finance his desire to open another publishing company. This he did in London with his sons Morley and Mitchell, Jr. as partners. Leaving them in charge, Kennerley returned to New York and took up a more humble apartment in the Sherry-Netherland Hotel. Even though he was almost penniless he was able to hold onto the lease on the Anderson building.

Bishop had combined the Anderson Galleries with the American Art Association and then moved out of the Anderson and located the combined operation on Madison Avenue, leaving Kennerley holding the lease on an empty building.

With his ear to the social network, Kennerley learned that Margery's marriage with Cooper had started to fall apart within weeks of asserting their vows. Kennerley quickly moved in to offer Margery a sympathetic ear. Cooper and Margery were officially granted a divorce on December 12, 1930. *John Hampton Cooper, said to be a New York physician [sic]...was granted a divorce here today from his wife on grounds of desertion.*[295]

---

295   <u>Reno Evening Gazette</u>, Friday, December 12, 1930.

The speed of Margery's marriage breakdown and divorce elicited an equally rapid response from opportunist Kennerley. He was broke and Margery was vulnerable. In March he and Margery announced their engagement again, much to the amusement of the press.

Durant Heiress, Thrice Freed, Will Wed Mitchell Kennerley.[296]

The Mirror announced him as a *"wealthy art connoisseur,"* but the truth was completely the opposite. A month after his announced engagement, desperate for funds he discreetly had his private collection of rare books and other literary items auctioned off at the amalgamated AAA/AG. The auction grossed just over $35,000. In spite of this infusion of cash, he was evicted from his apartment a few months later for non-payment of rent.

The rare book collection that Kennerley had disposed of is not to be confused with another Kennerley collection; his collection of the books that he had published. In September 1930, in what appears to be an attempt to appease Margery's growing doubt about his sincerity, Kennerley donated to Vassar College the more than four hundred books that he had personally published. He also included in his donation many books by others who had dedicated their works to him along with his extensive correspondence with hundreds of authors. It was no coincidence that Margery's daughter Edwina was in her second year at Vassar.

In spite of Kennerley's generosity to her daughter's school Margery again became leery of his financial status and thus his motive for marriage. The relationship lost momentum and simultaneously the press gave extensive publicity to Margery's plans for an airplane journey in Europe and the Middle East. The elusive Margery abandoned Kennerley again, slipping out of his sites as a potential target for the last time.

---

296 <u>New York Daily Mirror</u>, *March 26, 1930.*

Charles La Jotte

In the fall of 1929 the 340-page volume, **My Father**, was published. In December 1929, shortly after Margery's divorce from her third husband John Cooper, George Putnam obtained a divorce from his first wife Dorothy Binney. On February 7, 1931 Amelia Earhart, with some apprehension, even reluctance, married George Putnam in a private ceremony at Putnam's mother's home with only four guests witnessing the ceremony.

On April 23, 1931, Margery set out on a well publicized journey to Europe and then Africa. Margery boarded the *S.S. Hamburg* along with pilot and adventurer Charles La Jotte, mechanic Everett Smith and with her plane, a Lockheed Vega named "Ariel" lashed to the deck. La Jotte was an American WW I pilot and had served as one of the first Air Mail flyers. In August 1927 he became an instructor at the American Aircraft Flying School in Santa Monica where Margery was taking flying lessons. La Jotte's first student was Howard Hughes.

After the *Hamburg* docked at Southampton they flew the plane to Hamble where William would begin his flying instruction a few months later. Here the plane was thoroughly tested before the trio set out on their epic journey.

Illustration #35: Margery standing for a publicity shot beside her plane, a single engine Lockheed Vega. With a top speed of 185 m.p.h., it had a range of 720 miles. This was the same kind of plane that her friend Amelia Earhart was to use in her epic solo Trans-Atlantic flight in May 1932. (Photo: Courtesy Alex Sanger)

Illustration #36: *Margery and La Jotte standing in the cockpit of Margery's plane at Newark Airport in 1931.(Photo: Courtesy Alex Sanger)*

On May 4, the Vega took off from Croydon, south of London, and landed in Paris. From there they flew to Rome, Tunis and then across North Africa to Cairo. They explored Egypt by plane and then headed for central Europe. During July and August they flew to numerous cities across Europe arriving back in Hamble on August 23. Two days later they loaded the plane on the deck of the *S.S. Hamburg* at Southampton for the return journey to New York.[297]

The press had covered her entire journey. The *Chicago Daily Tribune* ran a front page photograph of Margery and her crew with the caption:

> **AUTO PIONEER, AIR PIONEER.**
>
> *Margery Durant, daughter of W.C. Durant, automobile magnate, among the first women to drive a gas buggy, now the first woman to bring her own plane to Europe with an aerial chauffeur and mechanic. She will make a leisurely tour anywhere she feels like it, to show that flying is the fastest, cleanest and most comfortable mode of traveling.*[298]

---

297 Alexander Sanger <u>Margery Durant Goes to Africa, 1931-32</u>, (New York, Blurb Inc, 2009).

298 <u>Chicago Daily Tribune</u>, May 6, 1931

Time Magazine, in a more cynical fashion reported, on Monday September 14, 1931:

> It is sometimes suggested that pleasure flying is a better sport for women than men, since women have more spare time to learn and to stay in practice. Especially to daughters of rich men might this apply. One such, Margery Durant, daughter of Motor Tycoon William Crapo Durant, had time this summer to tour Europe for three months.
>
> She did it all dressed up in her black and white Lockheed Vega Ariel accompanied by a French [sic] pilot.
>
> Tourist Durant last week returned from her trip, announced that she had flown 12,000 miles over 19 countries at a cost of 7cents a mile. "All I can say," said she, "is that flying over North Africa, Western Asia and the Balkans is no Sunday School Picnic." [299]

In December Margery took possession of a more substantial craft: a twin engine Sikorsky amphibian. She had the name "Silver Wings" painted on the nose of the plane. Before the end of the year, Margery and the crew had accompanied the craft by boat to Southampton and flown it to Paris. In mid-January they headed for Monte Carlo and the Riviera before flying to Rome and Athens. The major emphasis of this expedition was a journey following the Nile south into Central Africa and then on to the Eastern Mediterranean. On May 18, they loaded the plane on board the *S.S. Olympic* and arrived back in New York six days later.

---

299 *Time Magazine*, September 14, 1931.

Illustration #38: Margery's plane for her 1932 flight. This photo was taken in Egypt. Her head can be just seen above the cockpit. The plane was a Sikorsky S-38 Flying Boat. The plane had two Pratt and Whitney Wasp engines giving a top speed of 110 m.p.h. The craft had a wingspan of 72 feet, almost twice that of the Lockheed Vega.(Photo: Courtesy Alex Sanger)

In October the crew again made the journey across the Atlantic for another flying tour of Europe, visiting William and Edwina at Hamble before arriving back in New York on board the *Majestic* on November 2. The following day William was awarded with his pilot's license at the Hamble Cliff aerodrome at Nettley Abbey near Southampton.[300] William stayed on in England until the following year. Margery's time spent with La Jotte on this last journey appears to have been critical in her relationship with him, for that was the last voyage they made together.

Fitzhugh Green

On her return from Southampton she began a courtship with the man to whom she had been introduced by Amelia Earhart, George Putnam's ghost writer Fitzhugh Green. Green brought with him an air of adventure, an exciting breath of hope and the promise of fulfillment to her

---

300 Pilot's licence issued 3 November 1932 at Air Service Training Ltd, Southampton.

restless nature. This was the era of polar explorations and there wasn't a single explorer that Green could not refer to as a personal friend; Peary, Byrd, Rasmussen and others. Green had also a number of books to his credit, many on polar explorations and he had co-authored with aviator Charles Lindberg, the Lindberg autobiography; **We**.[301]

But Green also brought an eerily dark and unnerving aspect of his personality into the relationship. On Peary's 1906 exploration of the Arctic, while in the northern regions of Axel Heiberg Island, Peary claimed that he had seen a range of high mountains to the northwest. He stated that these mountains were on an unexplored land which he named Crocker Land after one of his wealthy benefactors George Crocker.

When Peary reached the North Pole in April 1909 he was accompanied by Donald Baxter MacMillan. Peary had discussed Crocker Land many times with MacMillan. With his polar exploration days behind him, Peary encouraged MacMillan to explore and map Crocker Land. With that in mind MacMillan set out in 1913 to follow his mentor's lead. Sponsored by the American Museum of Natural History, The American Geographic Society and the University of Illinois he set out on his quest. Among the leaders in his expedition was 25-year-old Fitzhugh Green, a graduate of the Naval Academy who had just obtained his Master of Science degree from Washington University.

On March 10, 1914 MacMillan, Green and six Inuit made their way across Ellesmere Island to the spot where Peary had claimed to have seen Crocker Land. Green was the first to see the land and excitedly pointed it out to MacMillan. MacMillan later recorded; "… a tremendous land extending through 150 degrees on the horizon." The Inuit guide quietly explained to the ecstatic MacMillan that it wasn't land at all, just an Arctic mirage generated by the sea ice. Unconvinced, Macmillan led the party further north to the spot where there should have been land. Here MacMillan was forced to concede "My dreams of the last four years were merely dreams, my hopes had ended in bitter disappointment."

---

301   Charles Lindberg, <u>We</u> (New York, G.P.Puntam's Sons, 1927)

Rather than abandon the expedition he sent Green and an Inuit named Puigaattoq (MacMillan called him Pee-a-wah-to), each with a sled and a team of dogs to explore more of the western shore of Axel Heiberg Island. Puigaattoq had been an experienced and trusted guide and companion for Peary, Rasmussen and MacMillan in their earlier polar explorations.

When a storm engulfed the two, Puigaattoq built a shelter to protect them. After the storm had abated Green discovered that his own team of dogs had been buried in the storm and had died. Puigaattoq suggested that they return to the base where MacMillan was located, but Green insisted on continuing.

After another storm, Puigaattoq announced that he was returning to the base. Green reluctantly agreed and they set off with Puigaattoq manning his sled and dog team while Green walked beside him. At some point, as Green was lagging behind, he shouted to the Inuit and ordered him to wait. Once Green had caught up, he took a 22 calibre rifle from the sled and ordered Puigaattoq to stay behind him. Shortly afterwards as Green gained a slight lead, he turned around to see Puigaattoq heading off in another direction. What followed was reported dispassionately in Green's journal; *"I shot once in the air. He did not stop. I then killed him with a shot through the shoulder and another through the head."* [302]

On Green's return to the base, he reported the incident to MacMillan who in turn recorded Green's description of the event, but this time, with more gruesome detail;

> ... *looking back a few minutes later I noticed that he had left the trail again. I shot over his head. He did not stop so I shot him through the body. He fell back against the upstanders. As the dogs did not stop I thought that possibly he might be*

---

[302] FitzhughGreen, Sr. papers: Box 2 Fold 8 . *Crocker Land Expedition; Journal Extract April 30 to May 4, 1914.* Georgetown University.

> *still alive so I shot again splitting his head open so that the brains fell out...*[303]

MacMillan also added *"... Green, inexperienced in the handling of Eskimos, and failing to understand their motives and temperament had felt it necessary to shoot his companion."*

MacMillan had been deeply disturbed by the murder, as Puigaattoq had been a trusted and reliable guide to him in his earlier travels to the region. MacMillan and Green conspired to hide the circumstances from the other Inuit, by claiming that Puigaattoq had been suffocated in a snowslide.

MacMillan stayed in the Arctic for another two years, giving him adequate time to cover up the crime. On their return to the United States the murder was never investigated even though the tragedy was mentioned in their reports to their sponsors. Apparently Green avoided even a reprimand for his action.

When interviewed a quarter century later, the Inuit had another version. They claimed that Green had lusted after Puigaattoq's wife, a beautiful Inuit woman who had previously born two children to Peary while he was in the Arctic.

Now that all the principals in this incident passed away long ago, it is impossible to know whether Margery was aware of the affair. It is also not clear how much this event contributed to Green's eventual demise into a life plagued by alcohol and drug abuse, dragging Margery with him. Nevertheless, the tragedy is profoundly disturbing.

In April 1933, in spite of the fact that Green was still married, Margery set out on a flying holiday with him.

> *She and her new paramour travelled all over Europe, openly living together on the French Riviera and other choice spots frequented by the likes of the Kennedys, Fitzgeralds, Picasso and Hemingway. Fortunately or unfortunately I never met*

---

303 Fitzhugh Green Sr. papers; Box 2 Fold 7 Crocker Land Expedition; Donald MacMillan Journal Extract May 4, 1914. Georgetown University.

any of them on my occasional visits. Mother was heavily addicted to morphine at the time, and he to alcohol. Before long he too became addicted to morphine. After divorcing his wife, he married mother and they built a lovely house in New Canaan, Connecticut. [304]

The two flew to Cairo and then Mombassa before exploring the Riff Valley. For Margery, this experience and the relationship she enjoyed with Green proved to be more rewarding and satisfying than with La Jotte. In November 1933, Margery married Fitzhugh Green for her fourth and final marriage. By coincidence, her marriage to Green was reported in *Time* magazine in the same issue as Lammot Dupont, who was at the time the chairman of General Motors, was recorded as marrying his fourth wife, Margaret Flett[305].

For Margery, her life at their New Canaan, Connecticut home must have seemed almost idyllic. The home was frequented by explorers, flyers, writers and numerous adventure seeking individuals, including George Putnam and his wife Amelia Earhart, all profoundly exhilarating for Margery.

Meanwhile her father was in serious financial trouble, far worse than his previous dilemmas. In February 1938 he wrote to Margery to ask for money, $1200 a month, until he could *"get on [his] feet."* [306] She complied. He even suggested to her that she contact her son, his grandson William Campbell, for some financial aid. There is no record as to whether or not Margery approached William and there is no record of a response from him. In the summer of 1937 Margery and Fitzhugh made a trip to New Zealand and had a comfortable lodge built near Taupo.

World War Two came along and Fitzhugh returned to the navy to resume his career, but alcohol abuse was becoming a serious issue for him. In the aftermath of the conflict he returned to New Canaan to settle into

---

304   Edwina Campbell Sanger, <u>My First 90 Years</u>, p. 26.

305   <u>Time Magazine</u>, Monday Dec. 4, 1933.

306   Bernard Weisberger, <u>The Dream Maker</u>, p. 355.

a more sedate existence in their comfortable country estate but here his alcohol problems escalated dramatically and became further aggravated by drug abuse. Margery was no help. She joined him in his source of solace and the extent of it was compounded when her father died on March 18, 1947. This event was devastating for Margery.

Six months later, on September 27, 1947, the *New York Times* featured a sensational story. It was headlined:

> **Narcotics Charge Laid to Durant Kin.**
> *Daughter of Automobile Maker and Writer Husband*
> *Are Indicted With Detective.*
> *New Haven. Conn., Sept 26 (A.P.) The daughter of a pioneer automobile manufacturer, her husband, a retired naval commander who served in two wars, and a private detective have been indicted here on charges, respectively of buying, and selling narcotic drugs.*

The event was followed closely through subsequent issues of the *Times* and newspapers in every city in the nation from the *Chillicothe Constitution* of Chillicothe, Missouri to the *Union Bulletin* of Walla Walla, Washington, to the *San Antonio Light*. In most newspapers it was a front page item.

The *New York Times* article presented the skeleton of the story; other newspapers filled in the flesh. The *New York Daily News* added:

> *The Greens, both named as drug addicts, had paid more than $100,000 for narcotics in the last two years, the indictments charged.*
> *... Federal officials said that existence of an organized dope ring was indicated in records found in Deisler's hotel room in New York. Among those involved, according to agents, are a prominent South American diplomat stationed in New York, a Manhattan attorney and two New York doctors. They ere not identified.*

> ...Mrs. Green has been an addict since 1928 and her husband has used drugs "for many years,"... The South American diplomat entered the picture, federal agents said, when he received $13,000 from the Greens on his promise that he obtain drugs for them.[307]

The sale of drugs involved in the indictment had taken place three months earlier. The private detective, Clemens Deisler, was arrested on July 10 in New York. It appears that he was a drug dealer, selling to the Greens. The Greens were not indicted until September 25. In the meantime, Margery had been committed to the Institute for Living at Hartford, a mental hospital.

In the trial, September 26, it was revealed that the Greens *"...had been buying drugs for several years."* [308] U.S. Attorney Adrian W. Maher told the court that he had been informed by narcotics agents that a large quantity of the drug had been seized in Mr. Green's New Canaan home.

Deisler pleaded guilty to *"transportation, sale and exchange of narcotics."* He received six months in jail and was fined $2,000.

Dignified and unsmiling Green told the court: 'On the advice of my counsel I am pleading guilty although it is not true.'[309]

Fitzhugh Green was placed on probation for five years but didn't live to complete his probation. On the evening of December 1, his family, concerned about his over indulgence in alcohol, had taken him to Easy Acres, a private sanitarium run by Alcoholics Anonymous. A few hours later he was transferred to the Danbury Hospital in Danbury, Connecticut and died shortly after his admission.

The *New York Times*, in its reports of Green's death, led the article with accounts of his recent crime, giving emphasis to his weaknesses, thus reducing his notable record as a Naval Commander and explorer to

---

307 *New York Daily News*, September 16, 1947.

308 *New York Times*, September 27, 1947.

309 *Chillicothe Constitution-Tribune*, Monday October. 6, 1947.

secondary significance. Other newspapers followed suit. Green's death brought an end to the F.B.I.'s "dope ring" investigations.

Nevertheless, Margery was told by the judge that she had to undergo treatment for her addiction at the Institute for Living at Hartford. She remained there for eight years!

> *The withdrawal was very, very slow and towards the end of it she plunged into a deep depression, unable to get out of bed or even speak. Her lawyer and I visited her once a month, and it was a disheartening sight.*[310]

Her restless and tumultuous life came to a quiet end at the age of 87 in the Good Samaritan Hospital, West Palm Beach, Florida, on 3 Feb, 1969. She was cremated and, following a memorial service held at the Chapel of St. James Church on Madison Avenue in New York City, her ashes were appropriately and symbolically laid to rest with her father in the in family vault at Woodlawn Cemetery.

Illustration #39: Margery Durant Campbell. (Photo: Courtesy Scharchburg Archives, Kettering University)

---

310 Edwina Campbell Sanger, <u>My First 90 Years,</u> p. 46.

Chapter Fifteen

AFTERMATH

Dr. H.A.Bruce

Dr. Bruce's practice was so successful in Toronto that in 1911 he bought a huge home on Wellesley Street in Toronto. He remodeled and expanded it and opened it as the Wellesley Hospital. During World War 1, Dr. Bruce became the Inspector General of the Canadian Medical Forces and was appointed the Consulting Surgeon to the British Armies in France. In 1913, he played a critical role in the creation of the American College of Surgeons and served on its first Board of Regents. During World War 1, Dr. Bruce became the Inspector General of the Canadian Medical Forces and was appointed the Consulting Surgeon to the British Armies in France.

Immediately after the war, while still in England, Dr. Bruce married Angela Hall, a British nurse. Dr. Bruce returned to Toronto bringing his bride with him and immediately resumed his duties as head of Wellesley Hospital. He was called upon by the United States government for advice in Medical affairs for the US armed forces. In response to these requests he frequently traveled to Washington and New York. During these visits he usually stayed with Edwin and Margery in their apartment in New York. In October 1932, Dr. Bruce was appointed Lieutenant Governor of the Province of Ontario, a position he held until 1937. He maintained controlling interest in the Wellesley Hospital until 1948 when it was taken over by the Toronto General Hospital.

In 1940 when he was 70 years old he was elected as the Member of Parliament for the riding of Parkdale in Toronto. Dr. Bruce made his mark on Ottawa in his first speech, by calling for the resignation of the Prime Minister, Mackenzie King. Bruce resigned his own seat in 1946. He died in 1963 at the grand old age of 94.

In his memoirs, Dr Bruce recalled fond memories of Port Perry and his school days there. He noted with admiration, his teachers, particularly the math teacher George Stone, and Principal Dugald McBride. He also made a detailed reference to his school friends including Dr. Edwin Campbell.

Edwin's grandson, Alex Sanger recalled, *"Every year when a new official portrait of the Queen was released we would receive one from Dr. Bruce."*[311] After Edwin's death, the Bruce family maintained their contact with the Campbell family and even after Dr. Bruce's death in 1964, Angela continued that friendship and attended weddings of some of the Campbell grandchildren.

Illustration #40: Colonel the Honourable Dr.Herbert A. Bruce, in his regalia as Lieutenant Governor of Ontario. The portrait was painted in 1938.(Photo: Courtesy Ontario Legislature, Toronto.)

---

311 *Interview with Alex Sanger, Edwin's grandson. 15/08/2010*

Hamar Greenwood

In England Hamar Greenwood ran for Parliament winning the seat as a Liberal candidate for the City of York in the 1906 election. From 1910 to 1922 he was the member for Sunderland. He became Parliamentary Secretary for Winston Churchill who was also a Liberal at that time. Both later changed to become Conservatives with Greenwood as the Treasurer of the Conservative Party.

When Greenwood married Margery Spencer at Westminster Abbey in 1911, wedding guests included the British Prime Minister Herbert Asquith, the future Prime Minister Lloyd George and the Canadian Prime Minister Sir Wilfrid Laurier. Greenwood was appointed as Under Secretary for Foreign Affairs in Lloyd George's cabinet, and in 1920, he was given the most difficult cabinet post, that of Secretary of State for Ireland. In that position he played a key role in bringing about the treaty which created the Irish Free State in 1922.

In 1929 he was named a baronet and took his seat in the British House of Lords and was elevated to a Viscount in 1937. After leaving his seat in the House of Commons he became involved in many aspects of British industry, serving as the president of the British Iron and Steel Federation in 1938.

Sir Hamar Greenwood frequently returned to Canada and was honoured many times by the city of Whitby and is regarded as their most famous son. On Edwin's annual visits to England, he usually visited the Greenwoods.

Illustration #41: Hamar Greenwood (left) and Sam McLaughlin (right) at Sam's stately home, Parkwood, in Oshawa, Ontario, 1938. (Photo: Courtesy Parkwood Estate Archives, Oshawa, Ontario)

Sam McLaughlin.

The McLaughlin name re-appeared on the Buick as the McLaughlin Buick in 1923 and the Canadian made Buick continued under the McLaughlin Buick nameplate until 1947.

In 1935 the McLaughlin Buicks gained worldwide acclaim as they were chosen by England's Prince of Wales as his personal vehicle. He also selected another for his companion, Mrs. Wallace Simpson. When he became King Edward VIII the following year, the Oshawa based company boasted that this was the first time that a king of England had purchased a non-British vehicle. As a result, Buick sales in England went from 1,000 in 1935 to 2,000 the following year. Several other members of the Royal family purchased McLaughlin Buicks. Edward continued to buy McLaughlin Buicks each year until the outbreak of World War II. When George VI, Edward's brother, became king and toured Canada in 1939, he insisted that McLaughlin Buicks should be used during the royal tour.

When the McLaughlin family shares in GM were sold to the du Ponts in 1918, Sam continued to hold position as President of General Motors of Canada. He maintained this position until 1945 when he resigned as President but remained on the board and continued his position as Chairman. He was seventy-five at the time. He remained as Chairman until his death on January 6, 1972. He had celebrated his 100th birthday the previous September.

Leopold Amery

Hamar Greenwood's sister Florence married Leopold Amery. Amery had attended Harrow school with Winston Churchill and maintained a friendship with him throughout his life. He went on to achieve popularity and fame as a leading politician in the 1930s and during WW2. Amery is well remembered for his confrontation with British Prime Minister Neville Chamberlain in a debate in November 1940. Chamberlain appeased Adolf Hitler on several occasions and, after the Nazis had invaded Poland and were inflicting heavy casualties on the Polish people as well as in Scandinavia, Chamberlain refused to declare war on Germany. During the so-called "Norway Debate," Amery stood up in the House and repeated the famous quotation from Cromwell; *"You have sat too long here for any good you have been doing. Depart, I say, and let us have done with you. In the name of God, go."*

The ensuing debate led to the downfall of Chamberlain two days later and the formation of a new national government under Winston Churchill. Amery was Secretary of State for India and Burma throughout Churchill's time as Prime Minister. The Amerys frequently travelled to Canada particularly after Amery's appointment as Secretary of State for the Colonies in 1924, a position he held until 1929. During this time, on one of his visits to Canada, he explored the Canadian Rockies, and in 1927 a mountain near Banff was named after him.[312]

Ironically, Amery's son John had become a Nazi sympathizer while in Germany during the war and made broadcasts as a supporter of the Nazis. He tried to encourage captured British soldiers to fight alongside the Nazis. At the end of the war he was arrested and tried for treason. He was convicted and executed. Florence never recovered from the tragedy of these events. Doctors Edwin Campbell and Herbert Bruce frequently visited the Amerys and the Greenwoods when in London.

Llewellys Barker

Under the direction of Sir William Osler, another Canadian, Barker became resident pathologist at Johns Hopkins in 1894. Sir Edmund Osler, William's brother, later helped finance Dr. H. A. Bruce's Wellesley hospital in Toronto. In 1900 Barker accepted an appointment as Chair of Anatomy at the University of Chicago.

When William Osler was appointed to Oxford University in 1918, Barker was recalled to Baltimore to be his successor as Professor of Medicine and Physician-in-Chief of the Johns Hopkins Hospital. Edwin called on Barker's expertise when Margery became critically ill in 1918. Barker made significant contributions to the medical profession while at Johns Hopkins. His books on anatomy and internal medicine remained standard reference works for many years. He also reorganized the Medical clinic there, establishing three distinct and basic laboratories: physiology, chemistry and bacteriology.

---

[312] *Ibid.* p. 22.

Illustration #42 Dr. Llewellys Barker, Director of Medicine and Physician-in-chief, Johns Hopkins Medical School.

"Diamond Jim" Brady.

In the 1800s "Diamond Jim Brady had a close relationship with the leading singer and actress of the time, Lillian Russell. One of her closest friends was Edna McCauley who was simultaneously Brady's mistress and constant companion. In 1898 Russell divorced her third husband and rumours spread that she would marry Brady. He showered her with valuable jewelry including a gold plated bicycle with diamonds and rubies set into the spokes and handlebars. When the weather was suitable, on Sundays Miss Russell would appear in a white cycling suit and pose with the bicycle for photographers. Brady and Lillian developed a reputation for their enormous and legendary appetites. In the early summer of 1912 Brady developed a serious stomach pain and was hospitalized at Johns Hopkins Hospital in Baltimore. He underwent surgery and after his recovery he expressed his gratitude: *"...by summoning all the children in the neighborhood of the hospital and scattering broadcast a bountiful supply of pennies nickels, dimes and quarters."* [313]

He also donated $220,000 to *"the ward of the hospital of the Johns Hopkins Hospital in which kidney and stomach troubles are treated."* [314]

While Brady was in hospital Russell abandoned him and married her fourth husband, newspaper magnate Alexander Pollock Moore, leaving Brady to lavish his full attention on Edna McCauley. In a twist of irony, Russell departed for a singing tour of Europe, leaving behind her lover Jess Lewisohn. Lewisohn developed an illness and Brady sent him to his (Brady's) farm in New Jersey to recuperate and sent McCauley to nurse him in his recovery. On one of Brady's visits to his farm to see how Lewisohn was progressing, Lewisohn and McCauley informed Brady that they were in love and were making plans to marry. Infuriated, Brady returned to New York to continue his lavish lifestyle which included other chorus girls, but never a constant companion as McCauley had been.

After their first invitation to the Brady gathering at Greenbrier in May 1914, Edwin and Margery continued to be invited to his annual extravaganzas until his death at the age of 61 in April 1917. The announcement of his death in the *New York Times* stated that his fortune was worth between $10 and $20 millions. [315] Since he had no offspring, his fortune was distributed among various institutions, the major recipients being several hospitals including Johns Hopkins. Multi millionaire John Lewisohn died in 1918, a victim of the influenza epidemic. Lillian Russell died in 1922.

---

313   *New York Times* August 13, 1912

314   Ibid.

315   *New York Times* April 17, 1917.

David Dunbar Buick

David Buick handed over his position as manager of the Buick Motor Company to Durant in 1906. He continued to hold stocks in the company until 1908 when Billy took over full control of the Buick Motor Company. Durant gave an undisclosed amount to Buick. Gustin speculated, *"Reportedly Durant gave Buick $100,000 to invest as he chose."*[316] David's son Thomas operated a brass foundry which supplied radiators to the Buick Company. David's first wife Caroline died in 1912.

After leaving Buick, David moved between a variety of ventures including land speculation in Florida. He and Tom took out a patent for a carburetor design and David became president of Lorraine Motors in Grand Rapids Michigan in 1921. Two years later he tried building cars again and introduced his car named the Dunbar, but this one off failed to attract any investors and he began teaching at the Detroit School of Trades in 1928. By now his physical condition had declined, probably as a result of the cancer which killed him a few months later. In relative obscurity and with little to his name he died in the Harper Hospital in Detroit on March 5, 1929. Whatever money he had received from Durant had long since disappeared. He was buried in the Woodmere Cemetery in Detroit. Among those who attended the funeral were his wife Margaret, his sons Thomas and Winton and his daughters Mabel and Francis. His son Thomas had named his son, David Dunbar Buick on honour of his own father. Ironically David Buick II worked for many years as a clerk at the Chrysler Company.

In 1937 David Dunbar Buick was formally remembered in modern Buicks when the Buick car used a simplified heraldic crest as its symbol. The crest incorporated the Buick family's Scottish ancestral arms. The crest was used in a variety of forms and today this is continued in the three shield badge.

---

316   Lawrence Gustin, <u>Billy Durant</u>, p. 96.

Bob Burman

Bob Burman who chauffeured Margery around Flint and Detroit, became one of the foremost racing drivers in early U.S. automotive history. Along with Margery, Burman became Buick's test driver. He first rose to fame in the racing world in 1907 driving the Buick "Bug," a specially design racing machine used to promote Buick through racing exploits. He successfully campaigned with the Buick all over the United States. Unfortunately his car could not compete with the larger and more powerful European cars of the period. In the Grand Prix Classic at Savannah Georgia in November 1908 for instance, he remained well up in the standings of the 500 mile race until he experienced mechanical problems just having completed 300 miles. The race was won by a huge Fiat and a Benz finished second. No American cars finished in the top ten places.

His luck turned in February 1909 when he won his first major race with the Buick, a 100 mile event in New Orleans. Later that year he won a 250 mile race at Indianapolis, the Vesper Club race at Lowell Massachusetts, Fairmount Park, Pennsylvania and a 24 hour race at Brighton Beach N.Y. These successes placed him in third place in the National Championship standings for 1909. In what was probably his greatest achievement in motor racing he set a new world speed record driving a European Blitzen Benz at a speed of over 141 m.p.h.

The Indianapolis Motor Speedway ran its first race in August 1909. At that time it consisted of many races of differing classes according to distance or engine size. On August 19, Burman won a 250 mile race for unlimited engine size and in the first Memorial Day event in May 1910 he won a 5 mile race. The first Memorial Day Indianapolis 500 was held on May 30, 1910. Although he competed in every running of the race, victory always eluded him. His best performance was a sixth place finish driving a Peugot in 1915 just before his death. In 1920, Gaston Chevrolet, Louis' brother won the Indianapolis race outright driving a Monroe.

Louis Chevrolet

After parting company with Durant in 1915 he sold his Chevrolet stock back to Billy and ventured into building racing cars with Howard Blodd of Allegan, Michigan. They entered the Indianapolis 500 race that year and with Chevrolet behind the wheel placed 20th in the event. He competed in the Memorial Day Classic four more times with his best performance being a seventh place finish in the 1919 event. The following year he designed and built a car which his younger brother Gaston drove to outright victory at an average speed of 89.62 m.p.h. Louis also drove one of his cars in the same race but finished in 18th position after he developed steering problems.

Losing most of his life savings in the 1929 crash he went to work as a humble line worker in the Chevrolet factory later that year. He died in relative poverty in 1941. His life is remembered at the Indianapolis speedway with a large bust and memorial dedicated to him at the entrance to the Museum at the facility.

Robert W. Daniel

Daniel and Margery were divorced in September 1928. He continued to live at his Virginia plantation, Brandon. A year later he married another wealthy woman, a widow from Richmond Virginia, Mrs. Charlotte Bemiss Christian. This was Daniel's third and final marriage. Daniel was elected to the Virginia State Senate but died of a heart problem at the age of only 56, in Richmond on December 20, 1940. The Brandon Plantation which he and Margery restored during their marriage is today a National Historical Landmark and is owned and operated by Daniel's son Robert Daniel Junior.

Walter Chrysler

When Chrysler resigned as president of Buick, Durant paid Chrysler an estimated ten million dollars for his GM stock. He then went to work in

Toledo for John Willys at his Willys-Overland Motor Company. The following year after some disagreements with Willys, Chrysler tried to take control of the company. When that failed he left and took control of the Maxwell Motor Company. Here in 1925, he used the company to form the basis of a new company, the Chrysler Corporation. In 1928 he added the Plymouth and De Soto lines to his products and then bought out the Dodge brothers' line. The same year (1928) work began on his building on 42nd Street in New York. When opened in 1931 the Chrysler Building was the tallest building in the world. Less than a year later it was surpassed by the John Raskob and Pierre Du Point owned Empire State Building. The Chrysler family maintained ownership of their building until it was sold in 1947. It is somewhat ironic that at his death, Edwin held a considerable number of shares in Chrysler, but none in Durant.

Dallas Dort

Dallas Dort had become a close friend of Edwin's as they had both served on the first board of directors of Chevrolet in 1911. Two years later Dort left Chevrolet and created his own company in Flint and began producing cars which he named Dort. He continued his friendship with both Edwin and Billy for the remainder of his life. After his first wife's death in 1900 he married Marcia Webb in 1906, the year of Edwin's marriage. The Dort's second child, born in 1911 was named Margery, after Billy's daughter and Edwin's wife.

In 1915 a Canadian, Robert Gray made arrangements with Dort to produce Dorts in Chatham, Ontario. The company grew quickly over the Gray-Dort's reputation for quality and reliability, particularly its ability to start in the harsh Canadian winters. After Dallas Dort decided to get out of the automobile business in 1923, Gray tried to persuade Dort to continue production but failed. Gray tried to find another automobile partner, but to no avail and he was forced into selling off the assets of the Canadian Gray-Dort Company. In the lifetime of the Canadian company over 26,000 Gray-Dorts were produced. In Flint, Dort produced approximately that same number each year of its production.

On May 17, 1923, Dallas Dort ventured out onto the Flint Country Club for a round of golf with some business associates. While on the course he suffered a massive heart attack and died before his friends could get him to hospital. The company closed its doors shortly afterwards. The City of Flint commissioned two life sized statues to be built in front of the door of the original Durant-Dort factory, statues of Dallas Dort and Billy Durant.

The Kandinsky Paintings

The four Kandinsky panels which Edwin had commissioned in 1914, have become icons of modern art and are given prominence at the New York Museum of Modern Art (MOMA). As part of their divorce arrangement, Margery maintained possession of the four panels and they were auctioned off in 1940.

> *When an appraiser came to sell her furniture, he failed to recognize the value of the Kandinsky paintings, shipping them off to an auction in Ridgefield, Connecticut, where two of them were bought for $25 a piece. It so happened that Alfred Barr of the Museum of Modern Art was watching the auction on TV in New York City. Instantly recognizing the paintings he sprang into action, located the buyer, and purchased them for the MOMA for an undisclosed sum.* [317]

In the 1950s two other panels found their way into the Guggenheim Collection. It wasn't until 1983 that the MOMA acquired the Guggenheim pair to reunite the four original panels and displayed them as they had originally adorned the foyer of the Campbell's Park Avenue apartment. The MOMA frequently has special showings of the paintings as part of modern art presentations. Each is dedicated as "Panel for Edwin R. Campbell."

---

317   Edwina Campbell Sanger, My First 90 Years, .p. 46.

Mitchell Kennerley

After the failure of his second engagement to Margery, thus failing to acquire financing for his ventures, Mitchell Kennerly briefly regained dignity in October 1931 by being appointed as the managing director of The Printing House, an exclusive printing company in Vermont. He lasted a year. Kennerley and his sons' London publishing company folded in 1932. Mitchell, Jr. returned to New York and opened a bookshop. His son Morley stayed in the publishing business in England with Faber and Faber.

Following Margery's marriage to Fitzhugh Green in November 1933, Kennerley wandered through temporary jobs with little remuneration for the remainder of his life. Always in debt, he attempted to borrow from his numerous friends including Fanny Borden. He had a brief reprieve when in 1937 the combined American Art Association / Anderson Gallery was left without a rudder. The widow of former owner Cortlandt Field Bishop and a companion who were left in control called on Kennerley to assume leadership even though he had a longstanding debt of $70,000 with the company. The ladies overlooked this in order to retain him as the company president. He formally entered that office in 12 November 1937. By December he had published the first of his new memorable catalogues for the first major sale under his tenure.

Kennerley handled the auction of Bishop's own library, one of the richest collections of rare books in America at that time. The sale took place over several days in April 1938. Kennerley's sale was an immense success grossing over half a million dollars and earned the praise of the press including the prestigious *New York Times Book Review*. Unfortunately Kennerley was forced out of his position by members of Bishop's family and former employees of the gallery. The Gallery was bought by Milton Logan, Bishop's former private secretary.

The *New York Times* commented

> That he will be missed there can be no question, particularly in the light of his brilliant record at the American Art Anderson Galleries last season.[318]

Out of work and out of money again, Kennerley's next attempt to raise money was to organize an allegedly non-profit book collectors' club in 1939. It failed. He survived by browsing through second hand book shops looking for rare books which he would then resell to collectors. He also wrote the occasional article for a variety of literary magazines.

Kennerley's final notable contribution to the world of book auctions world occurred in 1948 when he was retained, at the age of seventy, to oversee the sale of Cortland Bishop's Paris book collection in New York. For this sale, he again prepared the catalogue. On this occasion however he received a meagre salary and no part of the commission.

He continued to exploit numerous women for support. His conquests included Dorothy Gordon, wife of a Yale professor; Joan Coons, a budding novelist whose only published novel, **Without Passport**, received much praise; and wealthy Minnesota widow Mrs. Vernon Wright who promised to leave him $50,000 but died before she had changed her will. Kennerley also renewed a friendship with his first wife who was still quite wealthy.

On February 22, 1950, depressed, unemployed and without a penny to his name, he hanged himself in room 1828 of the Shelton Hotel in Manhattan leaving several suicide notes. He was seventy-one years old. His death certificate noted yet another relationship: a divorce from an unidentified woman in Mexico in 1936. Kennerley had earned a reputation as a notable publisher, and auctioneer of fine arts and as one of the world's leading book collectors. His antiquarian expertise had been sought in Europe as well as America. But in the process he had squandered several fortunes and numerous relationships with women, Margery being but one.

---

318   New York Times Book Review, 9 October 1938.

Henry Leland

After Billy Durant fired him as head of Cadillac, Henry Leland organized a new company and named it after his hero Abraham Lincoln. With the war still in progress, the Lincoln Motor Company began operation in the fall of 1917 by producing Liberty aircraft engines. At the end of hostilities, the Lelands immediately started to build what they had set out to do initially: build the highest quality and most luxurious car in North America, the Lincoln. Unfortunately the public saw it as an outrageously expensive Cadillac. Sales failed to meet costs and the Lelands declared bankruptcy at the end of 1921. As soon as the assets came up for auction they were bought by Henry Ford. The Lelands were not hired by Ford, but the Lincoln brand name was continued as Ford's luxury vehicle.

Charles W. Nash

After his controversial departure from General Motors on June 1, 1916, Charles W. Nash continued his interest in the automobile through his alliance with James Storrow. Nash and Storrow initially tried to negotiate the purchase of the Packard Motor Company but when that failed they bought the Thomas B. Jeffery Company, producer of the Rambler car and four-wheel drive trucks

Illustration #43: Charles Nash

Various automotive historians disagree on the final price paid to Jeffrey but the range is between 5 and 10 million dollars. Whatever the price, Nash took control of the company in August 1916 and became its president, Storrow became chairman of the board and the company was renamed the Nash Motors Company. Charles Jeffery remained on the board of directors. Walter Chrysler was invited to join them but he remained with Durant at General Motors. Nash also persuaded several key General Motors personnel to join him at Nash Motors. They included Walter Alford, former comptroller of G.M, who became Nash's vice president and comptroller; Charles Vorhees, former sales manager at Oakland; and Nils Erik Wahlberg, former chief engineer at Oakland. Nash completely reorganized the factory and restructured the company. His efforts paid off with increased quality, production and sales, from 6,725 in 1916 to 22,344 units in 1917. The Jeffery nameplate was continued on his cars until July 1917 when the first Nash plated cars appeared and the Jeffery nameplate was discontinued.

Under Nash, production peaked at over 135,000 units in 1926 placing it in eighth position in U.S. individual makes. Truck production came to a close in 1929. Charles Nash remained as president until 1932 and then took on the role of chairman. In 1934 Nash merged his company with the Kelvinator Corporation producer of refrigerators. He finally retired at the age of 73 in 1937 and handed the reins of the Nash-Kelvinator Company to George W. Mason, former president of the Kelvinator Corporation.

Charles Warren Nash died on June 6, 1948 and six years later his name would cease to appear on automobiles. In January 1954 the Nash-Kelvinator announced a merger with the Hudson Motor Car Company and the new company formed was the American Motors Corporation. In 1986 the press announced that talks were underway between AMC and the Chrysler Corporation. The merger was approved by the AMC stockholders on the 5th of August 1987 and AMC was also relegated to the pages of history.

635 Park Avenue

This is the 13-story building in which Edwin, Margery and the children lived until their divorce and in which Margery lived until 1930. Their apartment was on the 6th floor. In 1994 Conrad Black paid $3 million for an identical apartment in the same building. When Black was incarcerated in 2005 it was sold for $10 million.

William B. Powell

William B. Powell, the best man at Edwin and Margery's wedding in 1906 continued his banking and business interests and became the manager of the R.G. Dun & Company in Boston. Unfortunately Powell found that his wife had been having an affair with their butler, Michael J. Maloney. The allegations ended in disaster:

> *Differences between Powell and his wife over alleged intimacy with Michael J. Maloney, the butler and houseman, culminated in a final quarrel last night in which Powell killed his wife after firing three shots at Maloney, servants told police today.* [319]

After shooting his wife Powell turned the shotgun on himself.

John Jakob Raskob

Pierre du Pont recognized a brilliant mind when he first hired the young John J. Raskob to be his personal secretary in 1901. Raskob rose through the du Pont ranks rapidly to become the company's treasurer in 1914 and four years later was promoted to position of vice president for the DuPont organization and General Motors. His interest in politics led him to become the chairman of the Democratic National Party in support of the presidential bid of Democrat Al Smith against Herbert Hoover in 1928. This move angered Hoover supporter Alfred Sloan who demanded that Raskob leave either GM or the DNP. Raskob chose the former and sold all his GM stock. With his vast holdings he joined with Pierre Du Pont in building the Empire State Building in New York. The building was completed in 1931 and remained not only the tallest building in New York but also the tallest building in the world until World Trade Centre was completed in 1972. When terrorists destroyed the World Trade Centre in September 2001, the Empire State building regained its status as the tallest building in New York City.

Raskob married Helena Springer Green in 1906 and the couple eventually had 13 children. He died in 1950 and is buried in Wilmington, Delaware.

Percy Rockefeller

Brothers William and John D. Rockefeller founded the financial empire of the Rockefeller family by investing in railroads, public utilities and banks.

---

319   New York Times May 4, 1922.

One of their more lucrative investments was in the creation and expansion of the Standard Oil Company. Percy Rockefeller, one of Edwin's friends in New York, was the son of William Rockefeller. It is interesting to note that Percy was a member of the legendary and controversial Skull and Bones society while attending Yale University. Fellow "Bonesmen" included banker Morgan Stanley, Percy Rockefeller's uncle John D. Rockefeller, future presidents Howard Taft (1878), George H.W. Bush and his son George W. Bush, as well as George H.W. Bush's father Prescott Bush and uncle George Herbert Walker Jr. Ironically John Kerry, political rival of George W. Bush in the 2004 presidential election was also a member, as was Richard Wagoner who became president and CEO of General Motors in 2000. He became chairman of GM in 2003. Wagoner was forced to resign in 2009 after the company lost $85 billion under his leadership.

James J. Storrow

Storrow remained in Boston as an investment banker. Immediately after his removal from the board of directors of GM, he was elected to serve the Boston City Council (1915 until 1918). The Mayor of Boston, Andrew Peters appointed Storrow to chair a committee to consider the Boston Police request to organize a union. Several city police organizations across the United States had been granted charters, including Washington D.C. and Los Angeles. However the Boston Police Commissioner Edwin U. Curtis claimed that the police were not entitled to organize a union. Storrow suggested that the police be permitted to organize a union but insisted that it be an independent union and not affiliated with the AFL. Curtis rejected Storrow's recommendation. The police reacted by striking on September 9. That evening looters took advantage of the absence of law enforcement and the entire city centre erupted in violence. The Mayor appealed to the State Governor Calvin Coolidge to call in the Massachusetts State Guards which he promptly did. The violence and rioting continued for three days until the State Guard finally prevailed.

In the aftermath, Curtis, supported by Coolidge, refused to rehire the striking police who wanted to return to work. Instead he hired unemployed servicemen returned from WW I. The event and the firmness of Coolidge on the issue of law and order was the major contributing factor to his nomination as the Republican candidate for vice president in 1920.

In 1925 Storrow was elected as the second national president of the Boy Scouts of America in 1925, a position later held by Edwin's son William Durant Campbell.

Storrow died in 1926 and was posthumously awarded the Boy Scouts' Silver Buffalo Award. Storrow Drive, a highway named in his honour, runs along the Charles River.

The Legacy of Dugald McBride

In addition to Edwin Campbell, his brother Duncan, the their three McArthur cousins and Dr. H.A. Bruce, the notable graduates of Port Perry High School who received their foundation under McBride and went on to become doctors include:

— Dr. Walter Gillespie. Graduated from PPHS in 1882, married Edwin's sister and became a long-time popular family physician in Cannington, Ontario.

— Dr. Malcolm McPhail. Graduated from PPHS in 1882. He graduated from the University of Toronto and then followed post graduate studies in New York and Edinburgh, then moved to Detroit where he became a leading practitioner.

— Dr. James McClintock. Graduated from PPHS in 1891 and later attended University College in London, England. He gained an enviable reputation as a surgeon, developing many innovative surgical practices.

— Dr. James Moore. Graduated from PPHS in 1888 and while serving as an army surgeon in WW I he developed many new battlefield military surgical procedures. His older brother John, a PPHS graduate also became a doctor. Both practiced in Brooklin, Ontario, in the 1920s and 1930s.

— Dr. Frederick Rundle. Graduated from PPHS in 1900. He had a successful practice in Whitby before becoming the Medical Officer of Health for East Whitby in 1912. He served his community by becoming president of the Oshawa hockey club and an Oshawa Alderman in 1933. His father was the Reeve of Port Perry in 1922.

— Dr. Walter C. Shier. Graduated from PPHS in 1895 and went on to become the coroner for Ontario County in 1908.

Dugald McBride retired from teaching in June 1910. He had spent 54 years in the classroom, 40 at Port Perry High School. He lived a pleasant retirement with many of his former students visiting him from time to time. One evening during the Easter Holidays in April 1926, the High School caretaker Mr. Allin paid his usual evening visit to the school to check on the huge wood-fired furnace in the school basement. On opening the front door of the school, he was greeted by a mass of flames. By the time the firefighters arrived, the entire school was engulfed in flames and there was little that they could do.

The *Port Perry Star* reported with almost a sense of celebration: *It was a wonderful spectacle. That roaring furnace of flame, situated as it was at the highest point in the town, lit up the whole countryside.*[320]

The proud and elegant building, with its graceful portal tower reaching high above the town, was lost forever. There is no doubt that the students would also have celebrated at the school's burning, but their joy was short lived as alternate accommodation for their learning was found in a variety of halls and rooms around the town. A year later a massive parade celebrated the official opening of a new building; an eleven-roomed conventional rectangular building.

Four months later, on September 24, 1927, Dugald McBride passed away at the grand old age of 88. The obituary in the *Port Perry Star* was given a surrounding black banner to mark its importance. The article gave credit to his 40 years as principal of the High School:

---

320   *Port Perry Star*, April 17, 1926.

> *Mr. Dugald McBride served the people of Port Perry... with unusual ability and fidelity. Indeed his service as Principal of Port Perry High School was of a quality that has been the inspiration and blessing to hundreds of students who have passed under his tuition, and who have filled places of eminence in the business and professional world.* [321]

A massive funeral reflected the respect that the community had for this scholarly gentleman. His faithful wife Nancy died eight months later.

Today, after several additions to the 1927 building, over a thousand cheerful and energetic students fill the halls of Port Perry High School each day. Many of the students walk past a cairn on the front lawn of the school, commemorating McBride and his famous students. With the changing approaches to education, Latin is no longer on the curriculum and gone are McBride's strict rules of behaviour and decorum.

Dugald and Nancy McBride had three children: Samuel who died aged 15, Mable who married a local businessman Charles Forman, and Sarah who became a highly respected High School teacher in Oshawa but never married. The simple and solid grey monument in the Pine Grove Cemetery brings an air of closure to their lives, but not to the legends created by Dugald McBride's ceaseless demand for academic excellence. The grey granite monument to commemorate their lives stands less than 50 metres from the south end of the Pine Grove Cemetery in Prince Albert.

---

321 <u>Port Perry Star</u>, September 27, 1927.

Conclusion

The more imposing memorial to Edwin's parents and family stands at the opposite end of the cemetery from that of the McBride family. The Campbell story and its legacy continues through the generations of their descendants. For Edwin and Margery, their two children provided the continuity. Edwina and Grant Sanger had six children. Their third son, Stephen, tragically, was killed serving his country in the far-off jungles of Viet Nam in 1967 but all the other children married and had children. William and Beatrice had one child, Margot, who married Jeremiah Bogert in 1964. They have two children. To date, a dozen grandchildren of William and Edwina carry on the family traditions.

The romance and marriage of Edwin and Margery started out with great promise but their move to New York a decade after their wedding presented enormous challenges to its sustainability. In spite of shared interests in the arts and in Billy's welfare and business affairs, the social life of the city during the "Flapper Age" pulled them apart. Edwina, who spent the last few hours of her father's life with him took time to write this comment on her parents and their relationship:

> *She certainly had her faults, but she was beautiful, charming intelligent, and generous so that she had a string of admirers a mile long. Years ahead of her time, she was adored by many,*

including my long-suffering father, who continued to love her until the day he died.[322]

On that endlessly hot and humid July day in New York, Edwin's restless urges, inherited from his grandfather, were finally laid to rest. In death he was spared from witnessing the slow and agonizing downfall of his closest friend and compatriot; from auto magnate and multi-millionaire Wall Street guru, to dishwasher, to a poor, inarticulate and paralyzed shadow of a man.

He was also spared from reading about or hearing of his former wife's own troubled searching for contentment as she fought with her demons of drug addiction and emotional instability.

Edwin lies alone in the serenity of that quiet glade in Woodlawn Cemetery in New York. Margery's remains lie a few hundred yards away with her father, her grandmother and with the step-mother whom she could not bring herself to name when writing the biography of her beloved father.

General Motors has gone through many changes since Edwin and Billy were forced off the board in 1920. At the end of World War 2 it became the world's largest corporation and by mid century over 60% of all vehicles sold in North America carried GM nameplates. However, by the end of the century, through mismanagement, particularly the failure to understand the demands of the market, that figure had dropped to less than 25%. When the economy wrestled with the recession of 2008 the company was saved from bankruptcy by an infusion of financial aid through the Governments in Washington and Ottawa. As the company struggled to maintain 15% of the market, it was restructured and the venerable lines of Pontiac and Oldsmobile were dropped from production, but Chevrolet, the line that Edwin had played such a key role in creating, was retained along with Buick and Cadillac.

It is to be hoped that under the restructuring of the company, with its renewed attention to Billy's key precepts of quality, reliability and

---

322 Edwina Campbell Sanger. *My First 90 Years*, p. 46.

customer service, that the realization of Billy and Edwin's ambitions and dreams for Chevrolet and General Motors will once more be fulfilled.

SOURCES

Briscoe, Benjamin. "The Inside Story of General Motors," *Detroit Saturday Night,* Jan. 15, 22, 29, Feb 5, 1921. Burton Historical Collection, Detroit Public Library.

Brownell, Tom and Mueller, Mike, *Chevrolet Pickup Color History*. Osceola Wisconsin: MBI Publishing, 1994.

Bruccoli, Matthew B. *The Fortunes of Mitchell Kennerley, Bookman*. Orlando, Florida: Harcourt Brace Jovanovich, Publishers. 1986.

Bruce, Herbert. *Varied Operations.* Toronto: Longmans Green and Company, 1958.

Butler, Susan. *East to the Dawn. The Life of Amelia Earhart.* New York: Da Capo Press, 1999.

Chesler, Ellen. *Woman of Valor. Margaret Sanger and the Birth Control Movement in America.* New York: Simon and Schuster Paperbacks, 2007.

Chrysler, Walter P. and Sparkes, Boyden. *Life of an American Workman.* New York: Curtis Publishing, 1938.

Cray, Edward. *Chrome Colossus: General Motors and its Times*. New York: McGraw Hill, 1980.

Dammann, George H. *Sixty Years of Chevrolet.* Glen Ellyn, Illinois: Crestline Publishing, 1972.

Dunham, Terry B. and Gustin, Lawrence R. *The Buick, A Complete History.* Kutztown, Pennsylvania: Automobile Quarterly Publications, 1987

Durant, Margery. *My Father.* New York: G.P. Putnams Sons, 1929.

Durant, William. *William C. Durant. In His Own Words. The Unedited*

Memoirs of William C. Durant. Flint, Michigan: Scharchurg Activities at Kettering University. 2008.

Flink, James J. *The Automobile Age*. Cambridge, Mass.: The MIT Press, 1992.

Godfrey, Charles. *Aikins of the UofT Medical Faculty*. Madoc, Ontario: Codam Publishers, 1998.

Bruce: Surgeon, Soldier, Statesman, Sonofa. Madoc, Ontario: Codam Publishers, 2001.

Gustin, Lawrence R. *Billy Durant, Creator of General Motors*. Grand Rapids Michigan: William B. Eerdmans Publishing Company , 1973.

Helk, Peter. "Twenty four Hours to Go. A Saga of the Dirt Track Grinds in America." *Automobile Quarterly*, Volume V Number 1, Summer 1966, Kutztown, Pennsylvania.

Hyde, Charles K. *Storied Independent Automakers*. Detroit: Wayne State University Press, 2009.

Kimes, Beverly Rae. "Wouldn't You Really Rather be a Buick?" *Automobile Quarterly*, Volume VII Number 1, Summer 1968, Kutztown, Pennsylvania.

"The Kingdom and the Buick." *Automobile Quarterly*, Volume XII Number 4, Winter 1974, Kutztown, Pennsylvania.

Kimes, Beverley Rae & Ackerson, Robert C. *Chevrolet. A History from 1911*. Kuztown, Pennsylvania: Automobile Quarterly Publications, 1986.

Kimes, Beverley Rae & Cox, James H. *Walter Marr: Buick's Amazing Engineer*, Boston, Racemaker Press, 2007.

Langworth, Richard M. and Norbye, Jan P. *The Complete History of the Chrysler Corporation 1924-1985*. Greenville, South Carolina, Crescent Publishing Company, 1985.

Lindberg, Charles. *We*. New York: G.P. Putnam's Sons, 1927.

Lovell, Mary S. *The Sound of Wings. The Life of Amelia Earhart*. New York, St. Martin's Press. 1989

Ludvigsen, Karl E. "Chevrolet, The Winner and Still the Champ." *Automobile Quarterly*, Volume 2 Number 3, Winter, 1969.

Madsen, Axel. *The Deal Maker, How William Durant Made General Motors*. New York: John Wiley and Sons, Inc., 1999.

May, George S. *R.E.Olds: Auto Industry Pioneer*. Grand Rapids, Michigan: Wm. B. Eerdmans Publishing Co., 1977.

A Most Unique Machine. The Michigan Origins of the American Automobile Industry. Grand Rapids, Michigan: William B. Eerdmans Publishing Company, 1975.

Morris, Lloyd. *Incredible New York*. New York: Random House, 1951.

Pelfry, William. *Billy, Alfred and General Motors*. New York: AMACOM, 2006.

Pound, Arthur. *The Turning Wheel. The Story of General Motors Through Twenty Five Years*. New York: Doubleday, Doran & Company, Inc., 1934.

Robertson, Heather. *Driving Force, The McLaughlin Family and the Age of the Car,* Toronto: McClelland and Stewart Inc., 1995.

Sanger, Alexander. *Margery Durant Goes to Africa 1931-32*. New York: Blurb Creative Publishing Services, 2009.

Sanger, Edwina Campbell. *My First 90 Years*. Lunenburg, Vermont: The Stinehouse Press, 1999.

Scharchburg, Richard P., ed. *The Gentlemen of General Motors*. Flint, Michigan: McVey Marketing and Advertising, Inc., 2000.

Sloan, Alfred P. *Adventures of a White Collar Man*. New York: Doubleday, Doran & Company, 1941.

My Years With General Motors. New York: Macfadden-Bartell Corporation, 1965.

Weisberger, Bernard A. *The Dream Maker, William Durant, Founder of General Motors*. Boston: Little, Brown and Company, 1979.

Yanik, Anthony. *Maxwell Motor and the Making of the Chrysler Corporation*. Detroit: Wayne State University Press, 2009.

INDEX

Abelson, Augot, 168
AC Spark Plug Division, 130
Adams, Pres. John, 11,
Aikins, Dr. William, 55 - 57
Alcock, John, 239
Alcoholics Anonymous, 300
Aldrich, Fred, 97
Aldrich-Vreeland Act, 146
Alford, Walter, 319
Alger, John, 66
Allegan, Mich., 313
Allen, Mr., 182
Allin, Mr. 323
Allison, S.E., 38, 39
Althouse, C.W., 95
Amalgamated Copper Co., 135, 145
American Aircraft Flying School, Cal., 291
American Art Association, 254, 255, 289, 316
American Club (Paris), 264, 277
American College of Surgeons, 175, 303
American Federation of Labor, (AFL), 237
American Geographic Society, 295
American Locomotive Company, 161
American Medical Association, 174, 220
American Motors Company, 194, 319
American Museum of Natural History, 273, 286
American Smelting Co., 237
American Telephone & Telegraph, 232
American Tobacco Company, 147, 232
Amery, John, 308
Amery, Leopold, 40, 41, 237, 307, 308
Amilcar Company of Paris, 257
Anderson, Elise, 168
Anderson Galleries, N.Y., 254, 259, 289, 316
Argyle, Ontario, 4
Argylshire, Scotland, 3
Asbury, N.J., 278
Asquith, Herbert, 305
Association of Licensed Automobile Manufacturers, 87
Astor family, 172, 216.
Austen, Jane, 259
Auto Crank Shaft Company, 128
Automotive Hall of Fame, 281
Automobile Manufacturers Association, 281
Axel Heiberg Island, 295, 296

Babcock, H.H., 45
Bakers Cars, 131
Baldwin, Robert, 9
Baldwin, Stanley, 237, 238
Ballenger, William, 151
Baltimore, Md.,
Bank of America, 234
Bank of Commerce, 270

Bank of Italy, *233*
Bankers Discount Corp., *235*
Bankers' Trust, *272*
Bardswell, Dr. H., *87, 89*
Barret, Dr., *56*
Barker, Dr. Llewellys, *38-40, 56, 57, 215, 267, 273, 308, 309*
Barrymore, Lionel, *171*
Bates, Madison, *124*
Bay City, Mich., *86*
Bayne, Howard, *187*
Bayne, S.G., *187*
Beardsley, Aubrey, *252*
Beare, Cecil, *250*
Beaverton, Ontario, *3*
Bechtold, Rueben, *199*
Bedford, Sarah (Jones), *48*
Bedford, Thomas, *48*
Bedford Truck Co., *134*
Begole, Charles, *98, 151*
Bell, Alexander Graham, *39*
Belmont Hotel, N.Y., *182*
Bennett, Arnold, *251*
Bennett, Floyd, *237*
Benz, Carl, *77, 78, 312*
Berlin, Germany, *81*
Berlin, Irving, *171*
Bermuda,
Beverly Hills, Cal., *278*
Bidwell, Marshall Spring, *12*
Bigelow, Joseph, *29*
Billings, C.K., *167*
Binney, Dorothy, *243, 291*
Bishop, Arthur, *105, 159, 281*

Bishop, Cortlandt Field, *255, 316, 317*
Black, Conrad, *319*
Blackstock, Ontario, *7, 9, 134, 217*
Blodd, Howard, *313*
Blossom, C.W., *187*
Blue Ribbon,
Bobcaygeon, Ontario, *59*
Bogert, Jeremiah, *325*
Bois Blanc Island, Ont., *15*
Bolsa Land Co., *270*
Bond Head, Sir Francis, *12*
Booth, John Wilkes, *19*
Bordeaux, France, *56*
Borden, Fanny, *316*
Boston, Mass., *130, 213, 214, 233, 243, 270, 320, 321*
Boswell, James, *259*
Bowmanville, Ontario, *44*
Boy Scout Movement, *220, 286, 323*
Boyd, Mossum, *59*
Boyer, Joseph, *184*
Boyne, Battle of, *8*
Brady, Anthony, *147*
Brady, "Diamond" Jim, *163-165, 240, 309, 310*
Brandon Plantation, *230, 313*
Bretton Woods, *176, 182, 265, 268*
Briscoe, Benjamin, *94, 95, 119, 121, 122, 129, 155*
Briscoe, Frank, *94.*
British Gynaecological Society, *81*
British Iron and Steel Federation, *305*
Brock Township, Ont., *6*
Brooklands, England, *133*

Brooklin, Ontario, *39, 323*
Brooklyn, New York, *63, 76, 220*
Brown, Arthur, *239*
Brown, George, *27*
Browning, Robert, *259*
Bruce, Angela (Hall), *174*
Bruce, Dr. H.A. *38-41, 53, 56, 57, 61, 76, 79, 105, 106, 174, 267, 273, 303, 304, 308, 322*
Bruce, Stewart, *38*
Bruce, Isabella (Morrow), *38*
Brush, Alanson, *130*
Buffalo, N.Y., *24, 101, 233, 270*
Buick Auto-Vim &Power Co., *93*
Buick, Margaret, *311*
Buick Motors, *94, 95, 99-102, 108, 111, 118, 119, 127, 133, 137, 140, 148, 149, 151, 161, 191, 197, 202, 203, 225, 226, 307, 311-313, 326*
Buick, Caroline, *311*
Buick, David, *92-99, 102, 110, 155, 203, 311*
Buick, Thomas, *96, 311*
Buick, Winton, *311*
Burman, Bob, *99, 137-139, 189, 312*
Burmuda, *155*
Burns, Robert, *259*
Burry Point, Wales, *243*
Bush, Pres. George H., *322*
Bush Pres. George W., *322*
Bush, Prescott, *322*
Byrd, Harry, *240*
Byrd, Richard, *239-241*
Byron, Lord, *259*

Cadillac Motor Company, *101, 130-134, 203, 226, 317, 318, 326*
Cadillac, Antoine de la Mothe, *133*
Cairo, *298*
Calhern, Louis, *233*
California (also see Pasadena), *222, 226, 236*
Calvary Episcopal Church, N.Y., *283*
Cameron, James, *4*
Camp Cap Chat, Que., *238, 267*
Campbell, Alexander, *4, 7*
Campbell Archibald, *4, 7, 27*
Campbell, Beatrice (Hawn), *286*
Campbell, Catherine, *4*
Campbell (McArthur) Christina, *4-8, 23, 32, 52, 84*
Campbell, Donald, *4-9, 19, 2, 32, 52, 84, 108,*
Campbell, Donalda or Donella, *7, 51, 108, 234, 250, 271*
Campbell, Duncan, *4, 51, 52, 108, 220, 249, 267, 271, 322*
Campbell, Edwin,
- birth, childhood, youth, *1, 8, 9, 23, 37-45, 51, 52, 62, 322*
- Buick, *99, 110, 111, 140, 146*
- business, general, *99, 114,*
- Chevrolet, *151-159, 182-190, 225*
- divorce, *176*
- death, *265-271, 275, 314, 325, 326*
- Durant, personal, *111-114, 176-178, 247, 260, 275*
- Durant Motors, *223-228*

- family, *83, 84, 134, 168, 169, 235, 238, 257, 287-289, 319, 320*
- General Motors, *117-122, 126-136, 144, 146, 172, 181-194, 211, 263, 270, 326*
- medical pactice, *63-66, 84, 86*
- medical training, *83*
- marriage, *103-106, 320*
- social life, *165, 200, 216-220, 238, 267, 303, 305, 308, 314, 315*

Campbell, Edwina, *141, 168, 170-172, 175, 176, 213, 215, 217, 218, 230, 248, 250, 251, 257, 265-269, 285, 294, 325, 326*

Campbell, Florence, *4*

Campbell, Howard, *249*

Campbell, John, *4*

Campbell, Mary, *4*

Campbell, Margery (Durant),
- children, *111, 134, 141, 168, 169, 230*
- death, *301, 325, 326*
- divorces, *215-217, 255-257, 266*
-driving, *89-92, 97-100*
-flying, *290-294*
- health, *213-215, 287-289, 298-301, 308*
-courtship, marriage, *103-106, 152, 176, 229, 230, 255, 288, 315-317*
- book My Father, *86, 118, 145, 154, 281*
- social life, *164-169, 172, 173, 200, 255, 303, 315-317, 319, 320*

Campbell, Margot (Bogert), *286*

Campbell, Mrs. Patrick, *167*

Campbell, Peter, *3*

Campbell, (Leach) Sarah, *3*

Campbell, Tryphena, *7, 51, 78.84, 108, 238*

Campbell, William, *111, 141, 168, 175, 176, 215, 220, 248, 265-273, 294, 323, 325*

Canadian Cycle and Motor Company (CCM), *109*

Canada Dry Company, *44*

Canadian Medical Forces, *303*

Cannington, Ont., *84, 322*

Carman, Bliss, *25, 252*

Carter, Byron, *131*

Cartercar Company, *131, 143*

Carton, John, *129*

Cartwright Township, Ontario, *7, 8, 38*

Cavan Township, Ontario, *41*

Chamberlain, Neville, *307, 308*

Champion, Albert, *130, 200*

Champion Ignition Company, *130*

Chamberlain, Clarence, *239*

Chaplin, Charles, *171, 233*

Chapman, Sam, *242*

Charles, Henry, *25*

Charlottetown, *27*

Chatham, Ont., *121, 314*

Chatham & Phoenix Bank, N.Y., *159*

Cheever, Dr., *19.*

Cherbourg, France, *266*

Chevrolet, Arthur, *138*

Chevrolet logo, *154, 155*

Chevrolet Motor Company, *150-155, 183-189, 200, 224, 314, 326, 327*

Chevrolet, Gaston, *138, 312, 313*

Chevrolet, Louis, *138-140, 150-156, 313*

Chicago, Ill., *124, 233, 270*

Chillicothe, Missouri, *299*

Christian, Mrs. C.B., *313*
Churchill, Winston, *305, 307*
Chrysler, Walter, *161, 190, 200, 202, 203, 225, 240, 281, 313, 314*
Chrysler Corp., *311, 314, 319*
Cincinnati, Ohio, *174*
Citizens National Bank, *67*
Citroen Car Company, *200*
Civil War, U.S. *14*
Clark, Emory, *147, 186, 187*
Clemens, Dr., *58*
Cleveland Light and Coke Co., *252*
Cleveland, Pres. Grover, *214*
Cleveland, Rose, *214*
Clyde, Ohio, *129*
Cobalt, Ontario, *220*
Coburg, Ont., *41, 55, 56*
Cohen, George M., *171*
Coldwater, Mich., *66, 67*
Collinge, G.B., *187, 188*
Colony Club, N.Y., *173, 218*
Colt Revolver Factory, *132*
Columbia Broadcasting System, (CBS), *261*
Columbia University, *273*
Confederation, *21.*
Conrad, Joseph, *259*
Converse, Edmund, *272*
Coolidge, Pres. Calvin, *322, 323*
Coons, Joan, *317*
Cooper, John Hampton, *260, 289, 291*
Coram, H.G., *61*
Corcoran Lamp Co., *152*
Cornell University, *285*

Corona, Cal., *189*
Council of National Defence, *174*
Courtleigh, William, *171*
Couzens, James, *120, 121, 134-136*
Cowan, John, *44*
Cox, Claude, *136*
Cox, James, *115*
Crandell, Caleb, *84*
Crandell, Catherine, *27*
Crandell, Reuben, *27, 28, 84*
Crapo, Mary (Slocum), *67-69*
Crapo, Henry, *67-69*
Crapo, William, *68, 99, 129*
Crawford, Duncan, *34*
Crocker, George, *295*
Cromwell, Oliver, *307*
Croydon, England, *292*
Curtis, Edwin, *321*
Cusick, Pat, *248*

Daimler, Gottleib, *75*
Danbury Hospital, Conn., *300*
Daniel, Margery, *230*
Daniel, Robert, *218, 229, 230, 239, 255, 289, 313*
Daniels, George, *127, 227*
Day, Joseph P., *159*
Dayton Electric (DELCO), *194*
Dayton Metal Products, *199*
Dayton-Wright Airplane Co., *199*
Deal, N.J., *201, 256*
De Dion-Bouton, *75, 76, 138*
Deisler, Clemens, *300*
De Kalb, Ill., *72*

Deluxe Motor Car Co., *128*
Denver, Col., *140*
Detroit, Michigan, *68, 92, 94, 103, 128, 130-134, 155, 198, 199, 205, 207, 322*
Detroit Automobile Company, *131*
Detroit Horseman's Club, *131*
Detroit School of Trades, *311*
DeVaux, Norman, *247*
Dewar Trophy, *133*
De Waters, Enos, *101*
Dickens, Charles, *259*
Dodge Motor Co., *207*
Domestic Engineering Co., *199*
Dort, Dallas, *67-74, 97, 99, 105, 144, 155, 314, 315*
Dort, Marcia (Webb), *314*
Dort Motor Co., *156*
Dougherty, Paul, *270*
Dow Rim Co., *134*
Dowling, J.L. *34*
Downey, Charles, *99*
Drake, John, *167*
Dreamwood, *239*
Dresden Hotel, Flint, *134*
Duesenberg, *271, 272*
Duke, Benjamin, *167*
Duke University, *167*
Dun, R.G. Co., *320*
Dunbar car, *311*
Duncan, Isadora, *253*
Dunlop Rubber Co., *200*
Du Pont family, *204, 216, 307*
Du Pont, Henry, *196*
Du Pont, Irenee, *196*

Du Pont, Lammott, *298*
Du Pont, Margaret (Flett), *298*
Du Pont, Pierre, *159, 182, 184, 190, 195, 204, 206, 209, 221, 320*
Du Pont de Nemours & Co., *159, 182, 184, 190, 204, 209, 221, 320*
Durant Acceptance Corp., *228*
Durant, Catherine (Lederer), *105, 111-113, 118, 140, 165, 200-202, 240, 264, 276, 277, 280-284*
Durant, Clara (Pitt), *65, 66, 70, 71, 73, 87, 97, 102, 106, 111-113, 217, 287, 288*
Durant, Clifford, *73, 113, 153, 156, 189, 225, 278, 279*
Durant Corp., *208, 231*
Durant Dort Carriage Works, *74, 97, 107, 108, 146, 155*
Durant, Margery (See Campbell)
Durant Motors, *223-228, 231, 236, 237, 260-263, 276, 314*
Durant Motors of California, *226*
Durant Motors of Canada, *226*
Durant, Rebecca, *69, 231*
Durant, W.C. (Billy),
- Buick, *110, 141, 146*
- Chevrolet, *182-190, 225, 313*
- death, *282-285*
- divorce, *102, 111-114, 217, 255, 256, 287*
- Durant Motors, *223-228, 260, 276*
- family life, *65-75, 83, 86, 87, 102, 107, 200-202, 264, 292, 293, 325*
-General Motors, *117-123, 126-137, 146, 176-178, 181-194, 284, 313, 319, 326*
- health, *235*

-Republic Motors, *154*
- social life, *165, 240, 264, 281*
-stock market, *257-259, 263, 275-276*
Durant, William Clark, *69*
Duryea Brothers, *77, 131*
Duryea, Frank, *281*

Earhart, Amelia, *242-245, 291, 294, 298*
Eastman Commercial College, N.Y., *48*
Eastport, Maine, *24*
Eaton, William, *127*
Eccles Hill, Que., *25*
Edison, Thomas, *86*
Elder, Ruth, *242*
Eldon Township, *27*
Eldorado, Ont., *47*
Ellesmere Island, *295*
Elmore Manufacturing Company, *129, 143*
Empire State Building, N.Y., *320*
Enniskillin, Ont., *41-43*
Eloise, *168*
Everitt-Metzger-Flanders Company, *128*
Ewing Automobile Company, *129, 148*

Fairbanks, Douglas, Sr., *171*
Farmer, Samuel, *37*
Farmers' Loan & Trust Co., *164*
Farmington, Conn., *250*
Faulconer, Robert, *132*
Fay School, *213*

Federal Plague Commission, *215*
Federal Reserve Board, *207, 228, 261, 264, 277, 278*
Fenians, *23-26*
Fiat Co., *138*
Fields, W.C., *171*
Firestone, Harvey, *137*
First National Bank, Detroit, *148*
First National Bank, N.Y., *129*
Fitzgerald, F. Scott, *167, 297*
Fisher Body Co., *199*
Flett, Margaret (See Du Pont)
Flink, James, *144*
Flint, Michigan, *68-74, 83, 84, 98, 101, 144, 159, 183, 198, 226, 314, 315*
Flint Automobile Co., *87*
Flint Country Club, *314*
Flint Gear and Top Company, *72, 74*
Flint Roadcart Company, *72, 225*
Flint Wagon Works, *95, 151*
Flint Varnish Works, *74*
Florida, *235, 311*
Florida East Coast Railroad, *235*
Flower, James, *92*
Forbes, *202*
Ford, Henry, *77, 92, 101, 109, 111, 114, 121, 124, 131, 132, 134, 148, 153, 157, 198, 199, 281, 284, 317*
Ford Motor Co., *120, 121, 122, 132, 134, 144, 157, 198, 207, 224*
Forest Lawn Cemetery, L.A., *279*
Forman, Charles, *325*
Fort Erie, Ontario, *24*
French, Francis Ormond, *164*

Frick Collection, N.Y., *286*
Frigidaire, *199*
Frost, Robert, *253*

Gage, William, *112, 217*
Gananoque, Ontario, *46*
Gates, John, *167*
General Electric, *237*
General Motors, *126-135, 143, 162, 172, 174, 179-188, 190-197, 222, 223, 232, 233, 237, 257, 263, 278, 281-285, 318-320, 326, 327*
General Motors Acceptance Corp., (GMAC), *198, 233*
General Motors of Canada, *197, 198*
General Motors Truck Company, *130*
Genessee County Savings Bank, *114, 129, 159*
Geneva, Ohio, *126, 129*
Genthe, Arnold, *216*
George VI, King, *307*
George, Lloyd, *40, 305*
Gerry, Robert Livingston, *164*
Gershwin, George, *171*
Giannini, Dr.A.H., *233, 234*
Gibson Girl, *80*
Gillespie, Dr. Walter, *52, 78, 84, 323*
Gish, Lillian, *214*
Glidden Tour, *102*
Good Samaritan Hospital, Fla., *301*
Goodyear Tire & Rubber Co., *200, 224*
Gordon, Dorothy, *317*
Gordon, Lou, *243*

Goss, Arnold, *146*
Gould, George J., *167,*
Grahame, Kenneth, *252*
Grand Hotel, Mackinac Island, *65, 66*
Grand Rapids, Mich., *311*
Gray-Dort Cars, *314*
Gray, Robert, *314*
Green, A.H., *147*
Green, Fitzhugh, *241, 244, 289, 294-300, 316*
Green, Helena, see Raskob.
Greenbank, Ontario, *5, 6, 52, 64*
Greenbrier Resort, W.V., *164, 310*
Greene, Bella da Costa, *253*
Greenfield Village, Mich., *209*
Greenwich Village, N.Y., *160*
Greenwood, Hamar, *40, 41, 237, 305-307*
Greenwood, Margery (Spencer), *305, 307*
Greenwood, Florence, *40, 41, 308*
Grosse Point, Mich., *96, 131*
Guardian Fridgerator Co., *199*
Gugenheim Collection, *315*
Gustin, Lawrence, *83, 110, 113-115, 193, 311*

Hall, Angela, see Bruce
Halsted, William, *56*
Hamble Cliff, Hants, England, *272, 292, 294*
Hams, William, *249*
Hammerstein, Oscar, *171*
Harbour Grace, Newf., *243*

Hardy, A.B.C., *74, 77, 87, 92, 146, 151, 183, 199*
Harper Hospital, Mich., *311*
Harriman, Florence, *172, 173*
Harriman, Mrs. Oliver, *167, 172*
Harris, Dr. Robert, *134*
Hartford, Conn., *286*
Haskell, J.A., *195*
Hastings County, Ontario, *47*
Hatheway, Curtis, *127, 147, 151*
Havana, Cuba, *279*
Hawn, Beatrice, see Campbell.
Hayes-Hunt Body, *226*
Hayes-Miller, Kenneth, *270*
Head, Sir Francis Bond, *13, 18*
Heany Electric Lamp Co., *134, 143, 144*
Hemingway, Ernest, *297*
Henry Ford Company, *135-137*
Herrick, John, *91*
Herrick, Robert, *184*
Hetch Hetchy, *234*
Heyworth, Mrs. Young, *167*
Hezzlewood, Oliver, *45, 109, 110*
Hills, Dr. Herbert, *97*
Hirkcanta, Aina, *168*
Hitler, Adolf, *307*
Hofheimer, Nathan, *157, 159, 177, 281*
Hohensee, Fred., *215*
Hook, Robert, *6*
Hoover, President Herbert, *262.263, 275, 277, 278, 320*
Housman, Fred., *164*
Hospital For Women, London, *79*
Howell, Dr. George, *63*
Hudson Motor Car Co., *319*
Hughes, Howard, *291*
Hun, Professor, *251*
Hunters' Lodges, *14-16*
Hurd, Abner, *20, 28*
Hyatt Automotive, *143*

Ilion Buckboard Car Co., *101*
Illinois, State of , *270*
Imlay City, Michigan, *48, 63*
Imperial Wheel Company, *74, 98*
Independent Lamp & Wire Co., *233*
Indianapolis Motor Race, *279, 312, 313*
Industrial Rayon Corp., *237*
Influenza epidemic of *1918, 213-215*
International Combustion Engineering Co., *248, 263, 276*
Institute for Living, Conn., *300, 301*
International Motor Company, *126*
Interstate Motor Co., *199*
Inverary, Scotland, *82*
Iowa, State of, *233, 270*
Ireland, *305*
Isaacs, James, *45*
Isaacs, Metta (Jones), *45*

Jackson, Michigan, *98, 99, 108*
Janesville Machine Co., *198*
Jaxon Steel, *194*
Jefferson, President Thomas, *10, 11, 29*
Jeffery, Charles, *77, 190*
Jeffery, Thomas B., *77, 190, 318*

Jessop, Dr. Elisha, 62
John, Augustus, 255
Johns Hopkins University Medical
   School, 39, 164, 215, 273, 308, 309, 310
Johnson, Pres. Andrew, 24, 26, 27, 32
Jolson, Al, 171
Jones, Anna, Catherine (Martin), 48
Jones, Anna (Paxton), 48, 49
Jones, Dr., Charles, 47-49, 58
Jones, Dr. George, 47-50, 58, 63
Jones, Rev. George, 47
Jones, Dr., Richard, 47-50, 58
Jones, Metta, 49
Jones, Sarah, 48
Jones, William, 48
Jussila, Alma, 160

Kandinsky, Wassily, 170, 270, 315
Kansas, 63
Kaufman, Louis-Graveret, 159, 182, 184
Keddie, J.B., 41
Keep, Robert Porter, 250
Keller, K.T., 283
Kelvinator Co., 297
Kennedy family, 297
Kennerley Helen, *see* Morley
Kennerley, Mitchell, 251-255, 259, 260, 289, 290, 315-317
Kennerley, Morley, 289
Kennerley, Richard, 252
Kenosha, Wisc., 190
Kentucky, 155
Kern, Jerome, 171, 259

Kerry, John, 322
Kettering, Charles, 194, 200
Kettering University, 117
Kimes, Beverly Rae, 115
King, Mackenzie, 304
King, Mary Perry, 252
Kingston, Ont., 17, 55
Knickerbocker Trust Company, 120, 145
Knopf, Alfred, 253
Koch, Robert, 57
Koehler, H.J., 98
Kroll, Leon, 270

La Jotte, Charles, 291-294
Lake St. Clair, Mich, 109
Lamb, Charles, 171
Lambs, Club, N.Y., 170, 171, 233, 234
Lane, John, 252
Lansing, Mich., 99, 121, 124, 198
Laurier, Wilfrid, 305
Lawrence, D.H., 253
Leaside, Ont., 226
Lederer, Catherine, see Durant
Lee, Ivy, 162
Leland, Henry, 132-134, 203
Leland, Wilfred, 133, 147, 203, 204, 317, 318
Lempster, New Hamps., 69
Lenal, Aimee, 252
Lerner, Alan J., 171
Levassor, Emile, 75
Lewisohn, Jesse, 164, 310

Liberty National Bank, 228-230, 232, 256, 272
Library of Congress, 216
Lincoln Motor Company, 317
Lincoln Pres. Abraham, 5, 317
Lincoln Trust Co., 145
Lindberg, Charles, 171, 239, 241, 295
Lindsay, Ont., 59
Lippman, Walter, 253
Lister, Joseph, 56
Little, William, 101, 151, 153, 225
Liverpool, England, 106
Lockheed Electra, 244
Lockheed Vega, 291, 292
Locomobile, 226, 227
Loewe, Frederick, 171
Loffler, Freidrich, 57
Logan, Milton, 316
London, England, 80, 81, 257, 292, 323
London, Ont., 134
Londonderry, Ireland, 243
Lorraine Motors, 311
Lount, Samuel, 13
Loyalists, 9, 11, 12
Lowell, Mass., 312
Lusitania, 190

MacDonald, Sir John, 16
Mackenzie, William Lyon, 12, 13
Mackinac Island, Mich., 65, 66
Mackinaw County, 63
MacMillan, Donald Baxter, 295-297
Madoc, Ontario, 47
Madison, Pres. James, 11, 12

Madison, Wisc., 72
Madison Square Gardens, 72
Maher, Adrian, 300
Maloney, Michael, 320
Manchester, England, 114
Manchester, Ont., 47
Manhattan Trust Co., 164
Marr, Walter, 94-98, 115, 129, 137, 140, 150
Marcuse, Benjamin, 127
Marquette Motor Company, 129, 146
Martin, Captain John, 230
Mason, Arthur, 101, 151, 188, 198, 225
Mason, C.E., 89
Mason, George, 319
Mason Truck Co., 197, 225, 226
Masonic Order, 11, 41, 65, 86
Matthews, Peter, 13
May, George, 128
Maybach, Wilhelm, 75
Mayer, Louis B., 171
Maxwell Briscoe Motor Company, 95
Maxwell Motor Co., 95, 119, 155, 314
Maxwell, Jonathan, 119
McAlpine family, 3
McArthur Albert 12
McArthur, Dr. Archibald, 52, 134, 217, 249, 322
McArthur, Christina, 249
McArthur, Dr. Edwin, 52, 249, 322
McArthur, Dr. John, 52, 217, 249, 322
McArthur, MaryAnne (Watson), 249
McArthur, Neil, 52, 249

McBride, Dugald, *33-38, 51, 249, 304,*
322-325
McBride, Nancy, *324*
McBride, Samuel, *325*
McBride, Sarah, *325*
McCauley, Edna, *165, 309, 310*
McCaw, W.H., *61*
McClement, James, *147, 148, 179, 180,*
182, 196
McClintock, Dr. James, *323*
McCorqudale family, *3*
McFayden family, *3*
McGregor, Gordon, *110*
McKenzie, James, *34*
McKinley, Pres, *158*
McIntyre family, *3*
McLaughlin, Adelaide (Mowbray),
46
McLaughlin Buick, *109-112, 306, 307*
McLaughlin Carriage Company,
44-46
McLaughlin, Eleanor (McCulloch),
46
McLaughlin, Eliza (Rusk), *41*
McLaughlin, George, *41-43, 45, 158.*
McLaughlin, James, *42-44*
McLaughlin, Jane, *41*
McLaughlin, John (Jack), *41*
McLaughlin Motor Co., *134, 197*
McLaughlin, Mary Jane, *43*
McLaughlin, Robert, *41-46*
McLaughlin, Sam, *41-46, 62, 109-111,*
118, 134, 146, 147, 157, 158, 162, 193, 238,
257, 267, 281, 306, 307

McLaughlin, Sarah Jane (Parr), *42*
McLaughlin, William, *41*
McLinton, Dr., *58*
McMeehan, Rev.J., *78*
McPhail, Dr. Malcolm, *323*
McRoberts, *135*
Meade, Gen. George, *24, 32*
Meadowbrook, *292*
Medical Surgical Association, *174*
Melchers, Gari, *259*
Mellowes, Alfred, *199*
Menken, H.L., *253*
Mercedes, *139*
Metcalf, E.D., *184*
Metro Goldwin Mayer, *171, 234*
Michigan Auto Parts Co., *134, 146*
Michigan Motor Castings Co., *134*
Michigan, State of, *32, 233, 270*
Michigan, University of, *69*
Midwick Country Club, Cal., *234*
Millay, Edna St. Vincent, *253*
Milton, Tommy, *315*
Miss Mason's School for Girls, *89,*
103, 250
Miss Porter's School for Girls, *250*
Missouri, State of, *233*
Mombassa, *296*
Monroe Body Company, *128, 312*
Monte Carlo, *293*
Montreal, Que., *131*
Moore, Alexander, *312*
Moore, Dr. James, *323*
Moore, Dr. John, *312*
Morgan, Anne, *173*

Morgan, J. Pierpont, *119*, *253*
Morgan, J.P. Co., *122*, *123*, *164*, *208*, *209*, *221*
Morley, Helen, *252*, *253*, *259*, *260*
Morley, Jesse, *252*
Mors Co.,, *75*
Morton, William Thomas, *54*
Mosher, Thomas, *252*
Mott, Charles, *101*, *186*, *200*, *281*
Murray Hill Hotel, N.Y., *141*
Mount Vernon Seminary College, *103*, *217*
Mount Washington, N.H., *101*
Mull, Isle of , *3*
Mundy, Edward, *33*, *49*
Muncie, Ind., *225*
Murphy, Edward, *130*
Murphy, Julia, *141*
Murphy, M.J., *147*, *184*
Murphy, Simon, *131*
Murphy, William, *131*, *132*
Murphy, Winfrid, *140*, *141*
Murray, J.W., *199*
Museum of Modern Art, (MOMA), N.Y., *315*

National City Bank, N.Y., *144*
National Cycle Manufacturing Co., *188*
National Monetary Commission (1908), *146*
Nash, Charles, *72*, *162*, *182*, *183*, *187*, *190-192*, *281*, *318*, *319*
Nash-Kelvinator Co., *319*

Nash Motors, *190*, *319*
Nash, Jessie (Hallock), *72*
National City Bank, N.Y., *135*
Naval Academy, U.S., *301*
Nazis, *307*, *308*
Neal, Thomas, *147*, *184*
Nelson, Dr. Robert, *13*
Neutrality Act (1838), *18*
New Bedford, Mass., *67-69*
New Canaan, Conn., *298*
New Departure Co., *194*, *205*
New Guinea, *244*
New Jersey, State of, *118*, *233*, *270*
New York Armory, *170*
New York, City, *45*, *77*, *87*, *105*, *134*, *138*, *160*, *215*, *236*, *250*, *257*, *266*, *270*, *287*, *314*, *316*, *322*, *325*
New York Motor Show, *77*, *87*, *98*, *101*, *226*
New Zealand, *298*
Newark, N.J., *101*
Newfoundland, *243*
Niagara Falls, *51*
Noonan, Fred, *244*
Norman, Diana, *254*
North Pole, *295*
Northern Motor Car Company, *128*
Northway Motor & Man. Co., *134*
Norton, Charles, *132*
Novelty Incandescent Lamp Co., *134*

Oakland, Cal., *183*
Oakland Motor Car Company, *130*, *319*

O'Brien, Thomas, 66
O'Keefe, Georgia, 170, 251, 255
Oldfield, Barney, 138, 139, 281
Olds, Metta (Woodward), 124
Olds Motor Vehicle Company, 124
Olds Motor Works, 123, 124, 131, 144
Olds, P.F. Company, 123, 124,
Olds, Pliny, 123
Olds, Sarah (Whipple), 123
Olds, Ransom, 77, 94, 95, 120, 121, 123-126, 281
Olds, Wallace, 123
Oldsmobile, 121, 141, 326
O'Neill, John, 23
Orange Order, 7-9
Oregon, State of, 270
Orillia, Ont., 158
Oshawa, Ont., 46, 110, 111, 238, 267
Otto, Nicolaus, 75
Osler, William, 308
Overland, see Willys-Overland
Owosso, Mich, 130
Oxford University, 308

Packard Motor Company, 76, 109, 120, 190, 207, 316
Page, DeWitt, 281
Panhard, Rene, 75, 76, 89
Papineau, Louis, 12
Paris, France, 76, 77, 81, 217
Parkwood, 197
Pasadena, Cal., 156, 178, 187, 215, 234, 239, 244, 272
Pasteur, Louis, 54

Paterson, William, 72, 87
Patriot Hunters, 13-18
Paxton, Mary, 48
Paxton, Thomas, 47
Peary, Robert, 295-297
Pedley, Charles, 34, 37
Peerless Thomas, 76, 120
Pelee Island, 15
Pennsylvania Military College, 113
Pennsylvania Station, N.Y., 236
Perkins, George, 122, 126
Perlman Rim Co., 194
Perry, Peter, 7, 11, 12, 28, 29
Perry, Robert, 11, 12
Peters, Andrew, 321
Peterson, Annette, 167
Peugot, 189, 312
Philadelphia, 30, 77, 94, 214
Phillips, Charlotte, 279
Picasso, Pablo, 170, 297
Pierce Arrow, 120
Pierpont Morgan Library, 253
Pickens, William, 132
Pickford, Mary, 214
Pigeon Hill, Que., 23
Pine Grove Cemetery, Prince Albert, Ont., 80, 324, 325
Pitt, Ralph, 70
Pittsburgh, Ill., 161, 233, 270
Plaza Hotel, N.Y., 166-168, 217, 244, 254, 269-272, 288
Plymouth cars, 314
Polytechnic Elementary School, Cal., 215

Pontiac car, *130*, *326*
Pontiac, Mich., *128-131*
Pope Steam Cars, *131*
Port Hope, Ont., *58*
Port Perry, Ont., *4*, *18*, *28*, *29*, *59*, *62*, *64*, *70*, *78*, *106*, *108*, *134*, *238*, *249*, *270*, *323*, *324*
Post, Marjorie Merriweather, *103*, *105*, *217*
Poughkeepsie, N.Y., *48*
Pound, Ezra, *252*
Powell, William, *105*, *320*
Presbyterian Church, *31*, *38*, *39*, *41*, *50*, *51*, *268*
Presbyterian Hospital, N.Y., *285*, *286*
Price, Theodore, *164*
Prince Albert, Ont., *25*, *28*, *29*, *33*, *249*
Prince, Col. John, *16*
Prince of Wales (Edward), *307*
Princeton, University, *248*, *251*, *272*
Prior, Samuel, *186*
Pugsley, Cornelius, *164*
Puigaattoq, *296*, *297*
Putnam Dorothy (Binney) *248*
Putnam, George H., *241*
Putnam, George P, *241-245*, *289*, *291*, *294*, *296*

Quakers, *30*

Rae, Alexander, *34*
Railey, Hilton, *242*
Rainier Motor Car Company, *129*
Rambler, *77*, *190*, *318*

Rapid Vehicle Company, *130*
Raskob, Helena (Green), *321*
Raskob, John, *159*, *184*, *195*, *197*, *198*, *204-206*, *222*, *320*, *321*
Rasmussen, Knud, *296*
Raymere, *165*, *200-202*, *211*, *219*, *222*, *244*, *280*
Reach Township, Ontario, *3*, *4*, *20*, *26*, *28*, *31*
Reach Volunteers, *26*,
Rebellion of *1837*, *12*, *13*
Reese, William, *27*
Reliance Motor Truck Company, *130*
Remy Electric, *194*
Renault, *72*, *73*
Reno, Lenore, *168*
Reno, Nev., *251*, *255*
Reo Motor Car Company, *121*, *123-126*
Republic Motor Company, *156*
Rhode Island, *20*
Richard, Eugene, *94-96*
RM Auctions, *272*
Roberts, Dr. F.A., *128*
Robinson, John Beverley, *30*
Rockefeller, John, *172*, *276*, *321*,
Rockefeller, Percy, *172*, *179*, *181*, *233*, *276*, *322*
Rockefeller, William, *172*, *276*, *322*
Rolls Royce, *270*, *272*
Rolph, Dr., *56*
Rome, Italy, *292*, *293*
Roosevelt, Archibald, *240*
Roosevelt, Belle, *240*
Roosevelt, Eleanor, *240*

Roosevelt Field, N.Y., *218, 239*
Roosevelt, Franklin, *278*
Roosevelt Hotel, N.Y., *247, 261*
Roosevelt, Kermit, *240*
Roosevelt, Pres. Theodore, *240, 259*
Roscommon, Mich., *279*
Rose, Dr. Paul, *128*
Ross, Dr. James, *57, 79*
Ross, Robert, *44*
Rossland, B.C., *51*
Rothschild, Jacob, *201*
Rouen, *92*
Russell, Lilian, *165, 309, 310*
Rundle, Dr. Frederick, *324*
Russian-Japanese War, *120*
Ruth, Babe, *214*
Rye, N.Y., *171, 243*

Sabin, Charles, *184*
Sacket's Harbour, N.Y., *16*
Saginaw, Mich., *129*
Saeger Engine Works, *129*
Saint Albans, Vermont, *21, 24*
Saint Bernard's School, N.Y., *213*
Saint Ignace, Mich., *63-65*
Saint James Church, N.Y., *301*
Saint John, New Brunswick, *46*
Saint John's Newf., *243*
Saint Paul's Episcopal Cathedral, Detroit, *284*
Saint Petersburg, Fla., *291*
Saintfield, Ontario, *4, 8, 27, 52, 64*
Samson Tractors, *198*
San Francisco, Cal., *120*

Sanger, Alex, *169, 175, 176, 304*
Sanger, Edwina (Campbell) see Campbell
Sanger, Grant, *80, 285, 325*
Sanger, Margaret, *80*
Sanger, Stephen, *285*
Santa Monica, Cal., *291*
Sarah Lawrence College, *286*
Saratoga, N.Y., *28*
Satterlee, Herbert, *121, 122, 126*
Savannah, Georgia, *312*
Schmedlen, William, *66*
Scientific American Magazine, *124*
Scotland, *21*
Scugog, Lake, *28, 59*
Scrobogna, Aristo, *280, 281, 283*
Scrobogna, Mathilde, *280*
Seaboard National Bank, *187*
Seligman, J&W., *146, 147*
Shaw, George Bernard, *167, 252*
Shelton Hotel, N.Y., *317*
Sheridan Motor Car, *199, 225*
Sherwood, William, *92*
Shier, Dr. Walter, *324*
Shoemaker, Dr. Samuel, *283*
Sikorsky S-38 Flying Boat, *293, 294*
Simcoe, John Graves, *9, 30*
Simpson, James Young, *55*
Simpson, Mrs. Wallace, *307*
Sims, Dr. Marion, *80*
Skull & Bones Society, *321*
Sleepy Hollow Country Club, *172, 179*
Sloan, Alfred P., *101, 194, 196, 200, 204, 205, 210, 221, 280, 281, 285, 320*

Smith, Al, *320*
Smith, Angus, *124*
Smith, Everet, *291*
Smith, Fred, *124, 126, 132*
Smith, Mrs. James Henry, *167*
Smith, John Thomas, *159*
Smith, Mrs. Lucien, *229*
Smith, Dr. Protheroe, *80*
Smith, Samuel, *124, 125*
South Bend, Ind., *128*
Southampton, England, *291, 292, 293*
Southern Pacific Railway, *232*
Sparrow, Edward, *124*
Springfield, Mass., *132*
Springfield Rifles, *132*
Stamford, N.Y., *238, 249*
Standard Wheel Co., *136*
Stanley, Morgan, *322*
Star Motor, *224-226*
Stearns, *137*
Sterling Motor, *153*
Stettinius, Edward, *208, 221*
Stevenson, Robert Louis, *259*
Stewart, Sidney, *281*
Stewart, W.F., *87, 129*
Stieglitz, Alfred, *170*
St. Louis, MO, *183*
Stockton, Cal., *198*
Stone, George, *38, 304*
Stonitsch, Johanna, *217*
Storrow, James, *147-149, 179-186, 190, 318, 319, 321, 322, 323*
Stoutt, Elizabeth (Organ), *31*
Stoutt, Samuel, *29, 31*

Stowe, Augusta, *57*
Strang, Lewis, *137*
Strauss, Albert, *147, 186, 192*
Studebaker Company, *128, 129, 133*
Stultz, Bill, *242*
Sturt, Alfred, *156, 224, 226*
Sunderland, Ontario, *52, 53*

Taft, Henry, *164*
Taft, Pres., Howard, *164, 240, 322*
Taft, Walbridge, *240*
Tarrytown, New York, *119, 160, 183*
Tasmania (Van Diemen's Land), *13, 17*
Taupo, New Zealand, *298*
Tecumseh, Mich., *47*
Tennessee, *55*
Temperance Movement, *5, 64*
Terre Haute, Ind., *136*
Texas, *144*
Thayer, John, *164*
Thomas Flyer, *101, 120, 136*
Thomson, Kay, *168*
Tilney, N.L., *147, 184*
Tipless Lamp Co., *134*
Tipton, Indiana, *262*
Titusville, *234*
Toledo, Ohio., *314*
Tolstoy, Leo, *253*
Toronto, (York) Ont., *13, 85, 322, 323*
Toronto General Hospital, *303*
Toronto School of Medicine, *55, 56, 79*
Toronto, University of, *40*
Traylor Garage, N.Y., *270*

Trepassy, Newf., 243
Trinity College, Durham N.C., 291
Trust Company of America, 145
Tudhope, Jim, 158
Tunis, 292
Tyler, Pres. John, 17, 26
Tyrone, Ont., 40

Ulanson, Alex, 249
Union Pacific Railway, 161
United Motors, 122, 194
United States Cast Iron Pipe Co., 232, 263
United States Motor Company, 129
United States Steel Company, 119, 200, 232, 237, 240, 263, 272
Union Trust & Savings Co., 129
Uxbridge, Ontario, 5, 6, 33, 53

Van Buren, Pres. Martin, 17, 26
Vanderbilt, Alfred, 167
Vanderbilt, Cornelius, 167
Vanderlip, Mr., 135
Vassar College, 248, 251, 265, 271, 272, 273, 290
Vermont, 8, 10, 11.
Versailles, Treaty of, 203
Ver-sur-mer, France, 239
Victoria College, 55
Victoria County, 3, 5
Victoria, Queen, 79
Victoria Vehicle Company, 53
Vienna, Austria, 60
Viet Nam, 325

Virginia, 229, 230
Virginia Woods, Cal., 234
Vorhees, Charles, 319

Wagoner, Richard, 322
Wahlberg, N.H., 319
Walker, G.H., 321
Walkerville Wagon Works, 109, 110
Walla Walla, Wash., 299
Wall Street, N.Y., 123, 275, 283
Wallace, James, 147
Waltham, Mass., 101
Ward, Heyden & Satterlee, 126, 127
Warner Brothers, 263
Warner, T.W. Co., 199
Washington, President George, 11
Watertown, N. Y., 45
Wayne Automobile Company, 128
Webb, Marcia, see Dort
Webster Vehicle Company, 72
Weisberger, Bernard, 112
Welch-Detroit Co., 134, 147
Welch Motor Car Co., 131, 146
Wellesley Hospital, Toronto, 303
Wells, H.G., 253
Wertheim, Jacob, 184
West Virginia, State of, 233
Westbury, N.Y., 217, 218, 239
Westergren, Berna, 168
Westinghouse Electric, 232
Weston Mott Co., 87, 101, 108, 134
Whalen, Grover, 240
Whalen Joseph, 240
Whitby, Ont., 33, 59, 60, 305, 323

Whiteman, Rev., 78
White Cars, 131
White Sulphur Springs, W.Va., 164
Whiting, James, 69, 72, 95-98, 111
Whitman, Walt., 259
Wiggin, Albert, 186
Wilberforce, William, 30
Wilde, Oscar, 252
Wilkes Booth, John, 17
Willett, Alice, 188
Williams, Elias, 28
Wilmington, Del., 159, 321
Willson, Dr. James, 68, 69, 99, 129
Willson, Rhoda (Crapo), 50
Willys, John, 136, 240, 257, 314
Willys-Overland Co., 136, 137, 148, 194, 207, 225, 257, 314
Wilson, Mercer, 9
Wilson, Samuel, 235
Wilson, Pres. Woodrow, 207, 214
Windmill, Battle of, 16
Windsor, Ont., 15, 16
Winton, Alexander, 131, 132
Wisner, Charles, 87
Witt, George, 138
Witten, Allace, 182
Wolverine Road Cart Company, 74
Woodlawn Cemetery, N.Y., 268, 269, 283, 284, 301, 326
Woodman, Steamship, 28
Woodmere Cemetery, Detroit, 311
Workman, Dr., 56
World Scout Committee, 286
World Scout Foundation, 286

World Trade Centre, N.Y., 321
Wright, Dr., 56
Wright, Joshua, 56
Wright, Mrs. Vernon, 317

Yasidy, Louise, 141
Yeats, W.B., 253
Yonge Street, Toronto, 7
Yorton, Dora, 141
Youmans, James, 33

Printed in Canada